English ⌗ Heritage
Book of
Maiden Castle

Niall M. Sharples

B.T. Batsford/English Heritage
London

First published 1991

Typeset by Servis Filmsetting Ltd., Manchester
and printed in Great Britain by
The Bath Press, Avon

Published by B T Batsford Ltd
4 Fitzhardinge Street, London W1H 0AH

A CIP catalogue record for this book is available
from the British Library

ISBN 0 7134 6079 2 (cased)
0 7134 6083 0 (limp)

Contents

Illustrations

Colour plates

Acknowledgements

This book would have been impossible to produce without the active co-operation of a number of individuals and it is necessary to express my gratitude for this help. Much of our knowledge of what takes place around Maiden Castle depends on the field work of Peter Woodward, who has been involved in work in and around Dorchester for over twenty years. Most of the details of the finds from Maiden Castle are derived directly from the main published excavation report. For the Neolithic, Peter Bellamy, Ros Cleal, Fiona Roe and Mark Edmonds were of great help and for the Iron Age, Lisa Brown, Kathy Laws, Peter Northover, Cynthia Poole and Chris Salter are the main sources. The environmental and economic information discussed in the text was derived from the reports of Miranda Armour-Chelu, John Evans, Rowena Gale, Martin Jones, Carol Palmer and Amanda Rouse. My involvement in the Maiden Castle Project has greatly benefited from discussions with Tim Champion, Barry Cunliffe, Andrew Lawson and Geoff Wainwright and the latter two supervised the project's progress.

Throughout the writing of this book I have been actively encouraged by Stephen Johnson (my editor at English Heritage) and Peter Kemmis Betty (at Batsford) and the following people have read and commented on the original drafts: Jo Chaplin, Jane Downes, Pam Graves and John Thurley. Throughout my involvement with Maiden Castle I have had invaluable support from many colleagues in the Central Excavation Unit, the Trust for Wessex Archaeology and English Heritage, and the drawing offices in the latter establishments have provided many of the illustrations in this book.

I would especially like to thank all the staff and excavators who worked on Maiden Castle. They were a pleasure to work with and provided not only much of the information in this book but also the intellectual stimulation which has encouraged my interpretation of the monument.

The following bodies are to be thanked for providing illustrations: The Society of Antiquaries: 1, 20, 24, 51, 54, 55, 62, 63, 71, 75, 80, 89, 92, 94, 95, 101. The Ashmolean Museum: 38, 49. Cambridge University's Commitee for Aerial Photography: 39, 40, 44, 99 and colour plate 2. English Heritage Ancient Monuments Laboratory: 74 and colour plate 9. Royal Commission on the Historical Monuments of England: 2 and colour plate 5. HMS *Osprey*: 48, 65 and colour plate 5. R.J. Mercer: 31. The Trust for Wessex Archaeology: 4, 15, 36, 50, 68, 76, 77, 82, 83, 84, 85, 87, 88. Peter Woodward: 34, 43, 45, 46. Dawn Flower at English Heritage: 7, 16, 21, 28, 29, 37, 41, 42, 56, 59, 60, 61, 64, 67, 90, 93, 96, 97, 98. Chris Hooper: 5, 35, 70, 72, 73, 78, 79, 81, 86, 91. Alan Graham: 69. John Evans: 14. Andrew McLaren: 27. Miranda Schofield produced the reconstruction drawings.

Illustrations 44 and 99 are produced with the permission of the Controller of HMSO.

——— 1 ———
An introduction to the
monument

Maiden Castle is one of the most famous ancient monuments and the largest hillfort in the British Isles; and depending on your definition it could also be claimed as the largest hillfort in western Europe. Its defences are by far the most impressive in both size and complexity, and the multiple overlapping earthworks that conceal the entrances to the fort are unsurpassed amongst British hillforts.

It is one of the few remnants of our ancient past that has retained a physical presence of such grandeur that it has influenced some of the twentieth century's greatest artists. Thomas Hardy incorporated the monument into his novels and poems and as a local resident had an intimate knowledge of the complexity and beauty of its great earthwork defences. His detailed and often quoted description is worth repetition:

> At one's every step forward it rises higher against the south sky, with an obtrusive personality that compels the senses to regard

1 *The western entrance of the final hillfort, 1935. (The Society of Antiquaries.)*

it and consider. The eyes may bend in another direction, but never without the consciousness of its heavy, high shouldered presence at its point of vantage ... The profile of the whole stupendous ruin, as seen at a distance of a mile eastward, is clearly cut as that of a marble inlay. It is varied with protuberances, which from hereabouts have the animal aspects of warts, wens, knuckles and hops. It may indeed be likened to an enormous many-limbed organism of antediluvian time . . . lying lifeless and covered with a thin green cloth, which hides its substance . . . (1).

The description appears in a short story caricaturing the activities of the local antiquarian Edward Cunnington, who spent much of the later part of the nineteenth century exploring Maiden Castle. It has to be admitted, however, that this description owes its substance more to Hardy's literary abilities than the physical appearance of the monument. I lived within a mile of the ramparts (**colour plate 2**) for four years and to me the monster conjured up by Hardy was instead a sleeping giant resting on a low, though conspicuous, ridge which only attained a significant height when I had to climb it every morning on the way to work. To some extent, however, the unprepossessing nature of the hill heightened its mystique as it led me into the great earthworks with a false sense of security. The size and symmetry, and the extent and complexity of these defences never fail to impress me even today after innumerable visits (**2**).

These remnants of past activity are, however, only one attraction of the hilltop. The defences enclose one of the largest areas of easily accessible chalk downland in southern England which provides an invaluable resource to the inhabitants of the towns and villages of south Dorset. On the hilltop it is sometimes possible to feel intimately connected to the landscape, as though all activity was focused on it. You can hear and see the traffic on the trunk roads to Weymouth and Bridport; the trains carrying tourists to the coast; the loudspeakers in the football ground; children in the school playing fields; and when they are roasting the hops you can smell the brewery. On sunny summer days the hilltop is thronged with people walking dogs, flying kites, courting; school parties charge across the earthworks re-enacting imaginary battles; farmers tend their livestock

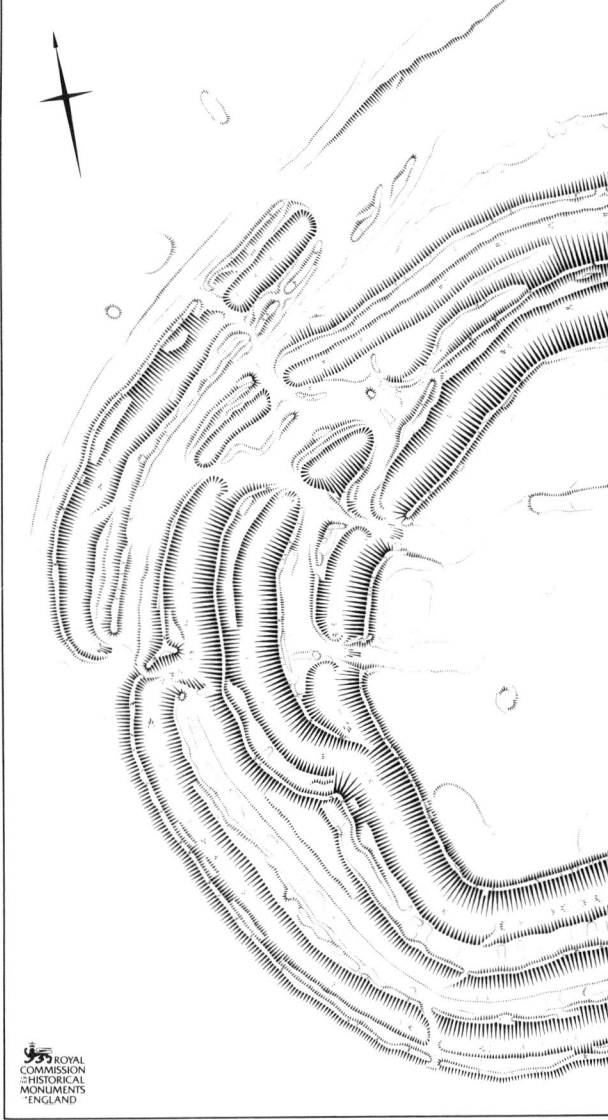

ROYAL COMMISSION ON THE HISTORICAL MONUMENTS OF ENGLAND

and harvest their crops. One day, you might, if you are lucky, come across an archaeologist digging the earth in a desperate attempt to try to reconstruct the ancient inhabitants' lives. On these days it is not difficult to imagine the bustling ancient communities that must have existed when the earthworks were created.

The atmosphere can change dramatically, however, particularly in the winter when the hilltop is often completely isolated from its twentieth-century environment. On many days a vicious south-easterly wind drives an icy horizontal rain into faces and through all but

12

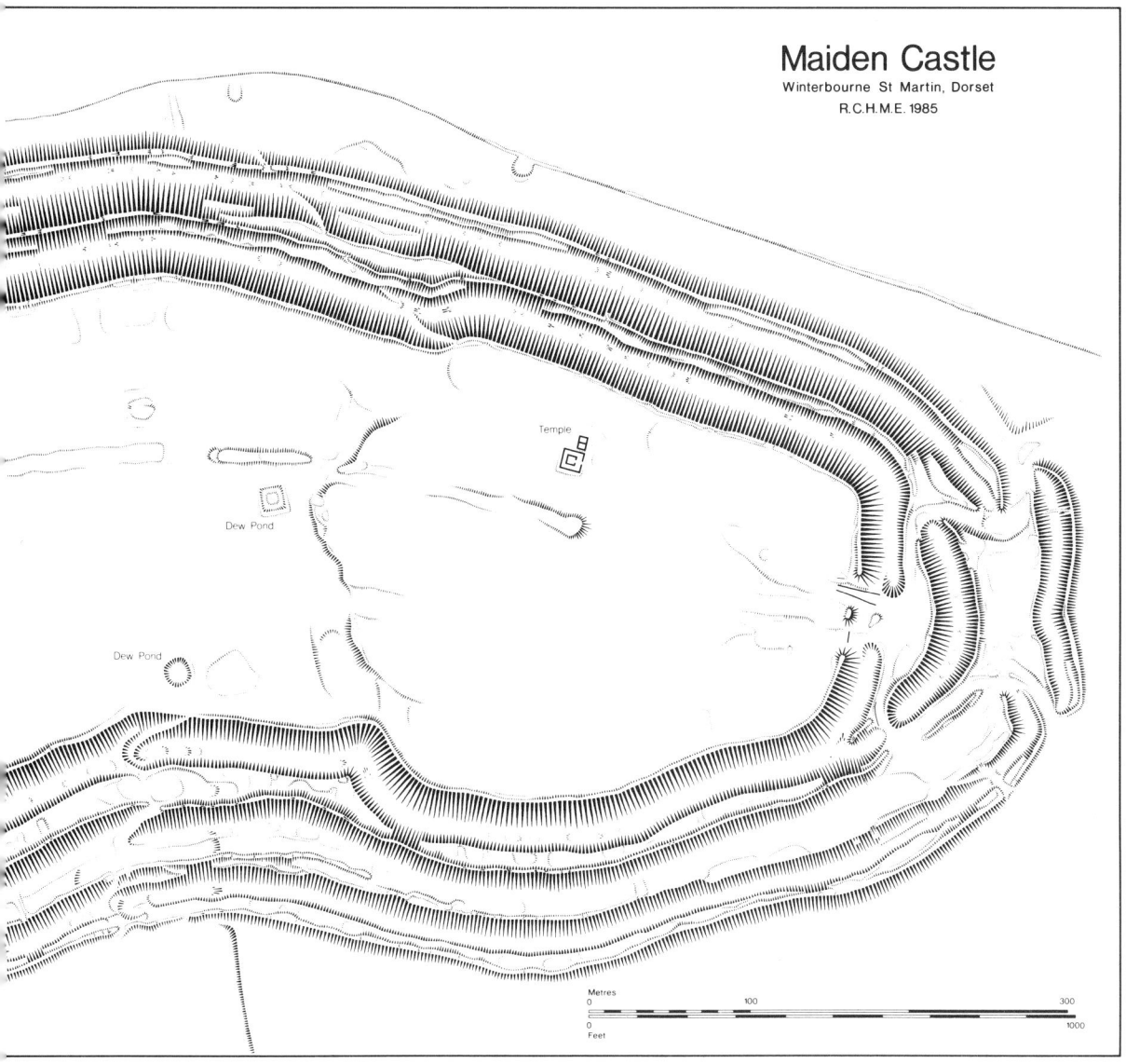

Maiden Castle
Winterbourne St Martin, Dorset
R.C.H.M.E. 1985

Temple

Dew Pond

Dew Pond

Metres
0   100   300
0   1000
Feet

the most robust protective clothing. At such times a visit becomes a personal battle with the elements. Do you have the strength to walk the crest of the ramparts or will you admit defeat and shelter in the ditches to watch the elements rage above your head? Even in the fiercest storms the ditches are deep enough to provide a sheltered haven from the elements. Then the great earthworks can be deserted and the sense of isolation amidst the awe-inspiring remains can play tricks on the imaginations of the more susceptible visitors.

2 *The earthworks of Maiden Castle as planned by the Royal Commission on the Historical Monuments of England in the winter of 1984–1985.*

The archaeological sequence
The importance of Maiden Castle, however, rests not just on its physical attributes; perhaps more important from an archaeologist's point of view is the presence of a unique sequence of occupation which is unparalleled in its length

13

Chronological table for Maiden Castle

Date	Period	Activity at Maiden Castle	Activity around Maiden Castle
BC 4250	Early Neolithic		Agricultural settlement of south Dorset. First barrows constructed.
4000		Enclosure at Maiden Castle created.	Settlement at Rowden on South Dorset Ridgeway and Flagstones Dorchester.
3750		Enclosure becomes important focus for the communities in South Dorset.	
3500		Bank Barrow constructed. Abandonment of hilltop.	Flagstones enclosure created.
3250	Late Neolithic		
3000		Sporadic activity on hilltop.	
2750			Maumbury Rings, Mount Pleasant and Greyhound Yard henges built.
2500			Large numbers of round barrows built particularly on South Dorset Ridgeway.
2250		Settlement and final clearance of hilltop	
2000			Mount Pleasant timber enclosure constructed.
1750	Middle Bronze Age		Settlements and field systems such as Rowden and Poundbury become common.
1500			
1250			
1000	Late Bronze Age		Linear earthwork systems constructed.

Chronological table for Maiden Castle (*cont'd.*)

Date	Period	Activity at Maiden Castle	Activity around Maiden Castle
BC 1000	Late Bronze Age		
900			
800			
700	Early Iron Age		Hillforts built at Chalbury and possibly Poundbury.
600		Construction of small hillfort.	
500			
	Middle Iron Age	Enlargement of hillfort.	Abandonment of other hillforts and settlement in vicinity of Maiden Castle.
400			
300			
		Reorganization of hillfort.	
200			
100	Late Iron Age		Reappearance of settlements around Maiden Castle and Poundbury.
		Gradual breakdown of occupation of hillfort.	
0			
	Roman period	Military occupation?	Invasion. Durnovaria established.
AD 100		Hilltop abandoned.	
200			
300			
		Temple constructed.	
400			End of Roman control.
	Early Medieval period		
500			
		Abandonment of hilltop.	
600			

3 *A chronological table showing the relationship between the activity at Maiden Castle and in the surrounding landscape.*

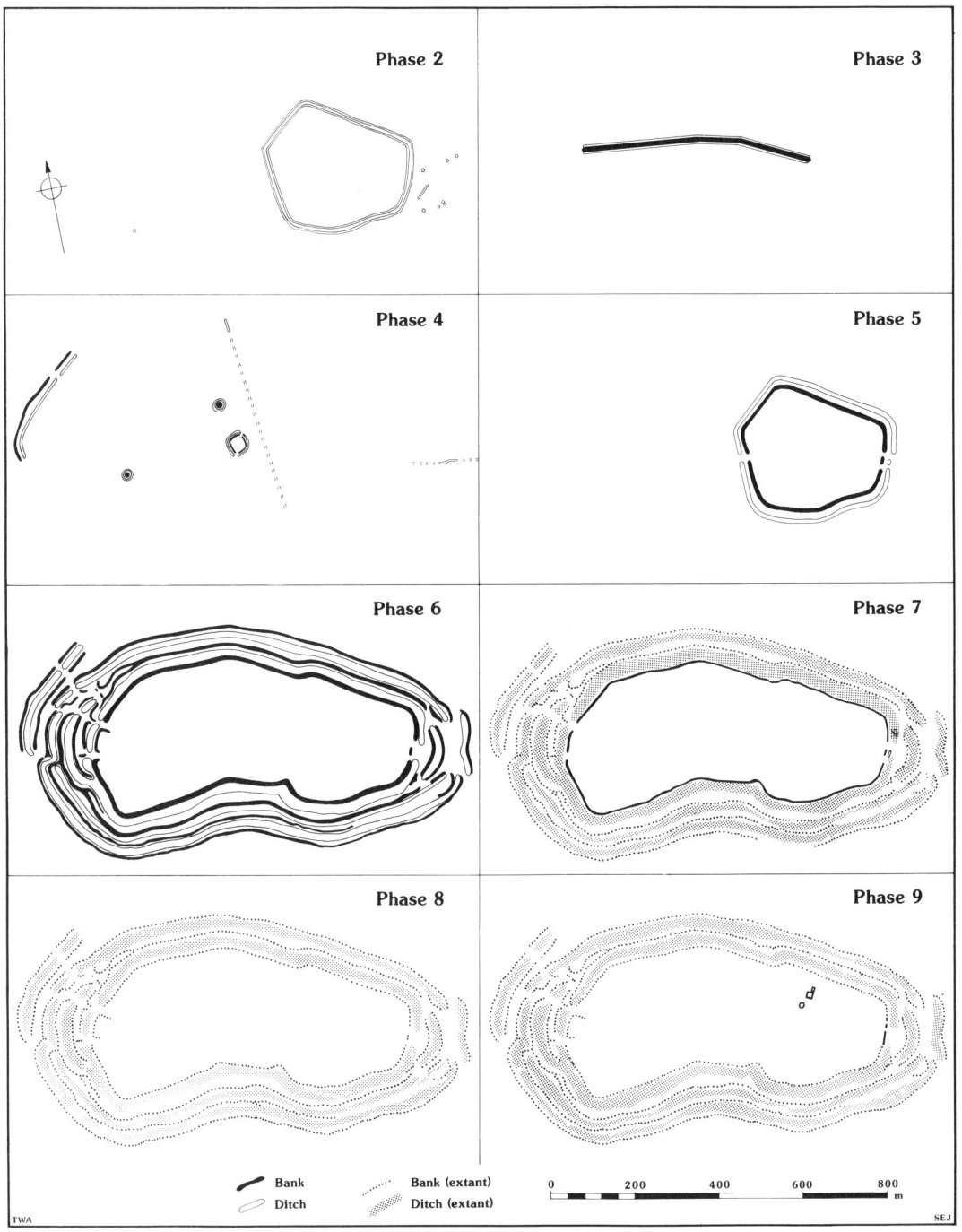

4 *The different phases of activity at Maiden Castle:*
1 *The undisturbed hilltop (not illustrated);*
2 *The Causewayed Camp;*
3 *The Bank Barrow and Late Neolithic occupation;*
4 *Bronze Age activity on the hilltop;*
5 *The Early Iron Age hillfort;*
6 *The expanded Middle Iron Age hillfort;*
7 *Late Iron Age activity;*
8 *Early Roman activity;*
9 *The Late Roman temple.*

and complexity by any other archaeological monument in the British Isles (**3, 4**).

The principal features visible today are the massive ramparts built between 400 and 200 BC in the period known as the Middle Iron Age. These ramparts enclose an area of over 19 ha (47 acres) which at that time would have been densely covered with houses, granaries, silos and other structures. It was probably home to several hundred people as well as cattle, sheep and other animals. Today, however, there is little evidence for this occupation. The hillfort was ploughed in the later Middle Ages and all apparent trace of these houses and structures was obliterated.

The only visible structure in the interior is the foundations for a Romano-Celtic temple built at the end of the third century AD. The temple appears to have been the focus for the religious needs of the local communities for several centuries and was probably still important when the Saxons occupied Dorset.

Between the occupation of the hillfort and the construction of the temple the hilltop underwent profound changes. During the later part of the Iron Age the occupation of the interior declined dramatically and the ramparts appear to have lost a great deal of their significance. The status of the occupants was, however, as important as it had been in the Middle Iron Age as the richest and largest cemetery known in this period was found in the eastern entrance of the hillfort. This rather reduced hillfort was captured by the Romans in AD 43. For the next forty years it continued to be occupied, perhaps by the invading army itself, before the hilltop was abandoned for the newly created regional capital at *Durnovaria*.

Iron Age and Roman activity has, however, obscured a long sequence of earlier monuments which have been progressively erased. The Middle Iron Age hillfort was only an addition to an existing Early Iron Age fort; this enclosed an area of 6.5 ha (16 acres) on the eastern summit of the hill and is, unlike the later fort, comparable to many other hillforts of this period in Wessex. Only the abandoned western rampart of the earlier fort is now visible while the enormous 7 m (23 ft) deep ditch which cut across the hilltop is invisible, filled in by the later Iron Age occupation. The inner rampart of the later hillfort marks the extent of this fort and its very angular shape suggests that the circuit may have originally been dictated in turn by a series

of earlier boundaries created around 1000 BC.

These Bronze Age divisions partitioned an agricultural landscape which was established on the hilltop when it was cleared of woodland at the end of the third millennium BC. This woodland was not, however, the primeval forest, which had been cleared over a thousand years earlier. The hilltop had been abandoned for over 500 years after it had been the focus for a series of Early Neolithic ceremonial monuments. The earliest of these was an enclosure which is now completely covered by the ramparts of the Early Iron Age hillfort. Similar enclosures are found throughout southern England and represent the earliest constructions ever undertaken in the British Isles. The enclosure had a long and complex life before it was succeeded by a monument unique in the British Isles, the Bank Barrow, just visible today as a low bank running east-west across the hilltop.

Sir Mortimer Wheeler

This rich palimpsest of human activity hidden and unsuspected by Hardy was only revealed by the archaeological excavations of Sir Mortimer Wheeler. Wheeler was one of the most significant archaeologists of the twentieth century and spent four summers between 1934 and 1937 at Maiden Castle. He was a great organizer, perhaps because of his military background, and carried out the largest and best-run excavations of the period. His excavation of Maiden Castle was the culmination of his career in Britain, and the standard it set was probably not surpassed for the next thirty years.

He also had a great enthusiasm for generating public interest in archaeological investigations. He was one of the few archaeologists to actually encourage people to come to visit excavations: organizing tours, arranging the excavations so that they could be viewed without disrupting work and having souvenirs on sale. He used the media – newspapers, film and even television – to disseminate news of important discoveries quickly. It was as a result of the latter activities that many people hitherto uninterested in the past came to learn and care about archaeology and in particular Maiden Castle.

The recent survey and excavations

In recent years, however, the number of large scale excavations has increased and the role of the first Maiden Castle results has been overshadowed. Only specialists with access to a good library or who are willing to pay a substantial sum for the rare but authoritative publication of Wheeler's archaeological excavations could up till now even attempt to understand the complexity and longevity of the occupation of this hilltop.

To a certain extent this was one of the principal archaeological motivations for starting a new programme of excavation on the hilltop. More important, however, was the absence of information which is now regarded as essential to any interpretation of the past. The fifty years that separate Wheeler's excavations from more recent ones have seen a considerable advance in the techniques available to archaeologists. The most obvious and important one being the use of radiocarbon and other scientific dating techniques. Since their discovery in the fifties these techniques have revolutionized archaeology by allowing archaeo-

logists to establish an objective chronology for prehistoric activity. In Wheeler's day an enormous effort was required to establish even the most rudimentary chronology and in later years the arguments used were shown to be based on many mistaken assumptions.

Equally important but perhaps less spectacular advances have been made in the development of techniques to recover and analyse the small and very fragile plant and animal remains that tell us what past economies and environments were like. Only cursory attention was paid to these important topics in Wheeler's day. His excavations had, however, exposed the long sequence of monumental construction on the hilltop. This made it possible to plan a relatively limited programme of excavation which could explore areas of the hilltop which the original excavations had shown would contain material for radiocarbon dating and environmental and economic analysis.

The opportunity to carry out these archaeological investigations came when English Heritage realized that the monument was deteriorating and needed urgent repairs. The damage was the result of a number of factors (including

5 *Volunteers from the Princes Trust repair the ramparts of the hillfort, 1986.*

natural erosion, overgrazing and animal burrowing) but the most important factor was the increase in visitors to the site caused by widespread car ownership. Little thought had been given to the problems of public access and visitor facilities since Wheeler's excavations came to an end. The hilltop was covered by a network of fences designed to manage the stock which were necessary to keep the vegetation under control. But they also restricted human access and forced people on to well-established paths that became quagmires in bad weather. There were no facilities at the site and nothing that would explain to visitors what they were seeing, even less what was hidden beneath the ground.

By 1985 it was clearly necessary to do something and a large project was initiated by English Heritage which would repair the damage to the monument, provide facilities and information for the visitors and up date our archaeological knowledge. This book is just one of the more obvious results of the project. There will also be a detailed report on the archaeological investigations of the hilltop and its surroundings; the erosion scars that covered the ramparts will be infilled and stabilized (5); a series of display boards will be in place that explain the history of the monument and point

out important features that can be seen in the interior; and the hilltop will be opened up for people to wander at will. Future changes may involve the construction of a new visitor centre but this is still the subject of some controversy concerning its location and function.

The primary purpose of this book is to present a general description and explanation of the activity that took place on the hilltop at Maiden Castle. It incorporates the results of the new investigations and as a result of this work it can give a much more complete picture of life on the hilltop when it was the focus for activity in the Neolithic and the Iron Age. It also examines the relationship between the activity on Maiden Castle and that occurring both in its locality and in southern England in general. It is only with this wider perspective that a full account of events on the hilltop can be presented. The settlement and activity on Maiden Castle was never self-sufficient. From the beginning the people living there relied upon others: relations, neighbours and ultimately strangers, to provide services, to trade goods and on many occasions to co-operate in activities on the hilltop. Only by understanding the network of relationships can a context and a role for the activity on Maiden Castle be discussed.

2

The environment and agricultural settlement

Any discussion of the history of Maiden Castle must begin with an examination of its location. Only by placing the hillfort in the landscape (**6**) and understanding how this has changed in the last 6000 years is it possible to suggest why this small but prominent hilltop was repeatedly chosen for occupation and why the monuments thus created were the focus for communities many miles from the hilltop.

Maiden Castle lies in the centre of south Dorset only 2.5 km (1½ miles) south of its county town, Dorchester. The landscape of Dorset is best understood by an analysis of the underlying geology (**7**) as this has a direct influence on the topography and soils and thus influences the agricultural potential and the settlement history of any area. The geology also influences the acidity of the soil. This in turn dictates what materials survive and so adds to the process of selection of data which form the archaeological

6 *The landscape around Maiden Castle viewed from the South Dorset Ridgeway.*

record. In this way, our present-day understanding of the past is bounded by the ability of the natural world to preserve evidence of various kinds.

The most important geological formation in Dorset is the chalk. This is the south-western end of the great expanse which spreads across Wessex to Salisbury Plain and, further east, forms the Sussex Downs and northwards runs through the Berkshire Downs to East Anglia. The chalk forms an undulating upland landscape broken by wide steep-sided valleys, which often drain from the north-east to the south-west (**8, 9**). The valleys in the high uplands are now largely without water and are likely to have been formed in a period when the water

table was much higher than it is today. The lower valleys in contrast have plentiful springs and in many areas are occupied by clear streams.

To the east the chalk is covered by the mixed sands and gravels which mark the eastern extent of the tertiary deposits of the Hampshire Basin. These form a low-lying landscape with little topographic variation (**10**). The most important features are the major river valleys of the Frome, Piddle, Stour and Avon (which marks the border with Hampshire) that traverse

7 *The geological basis of Dorset.*

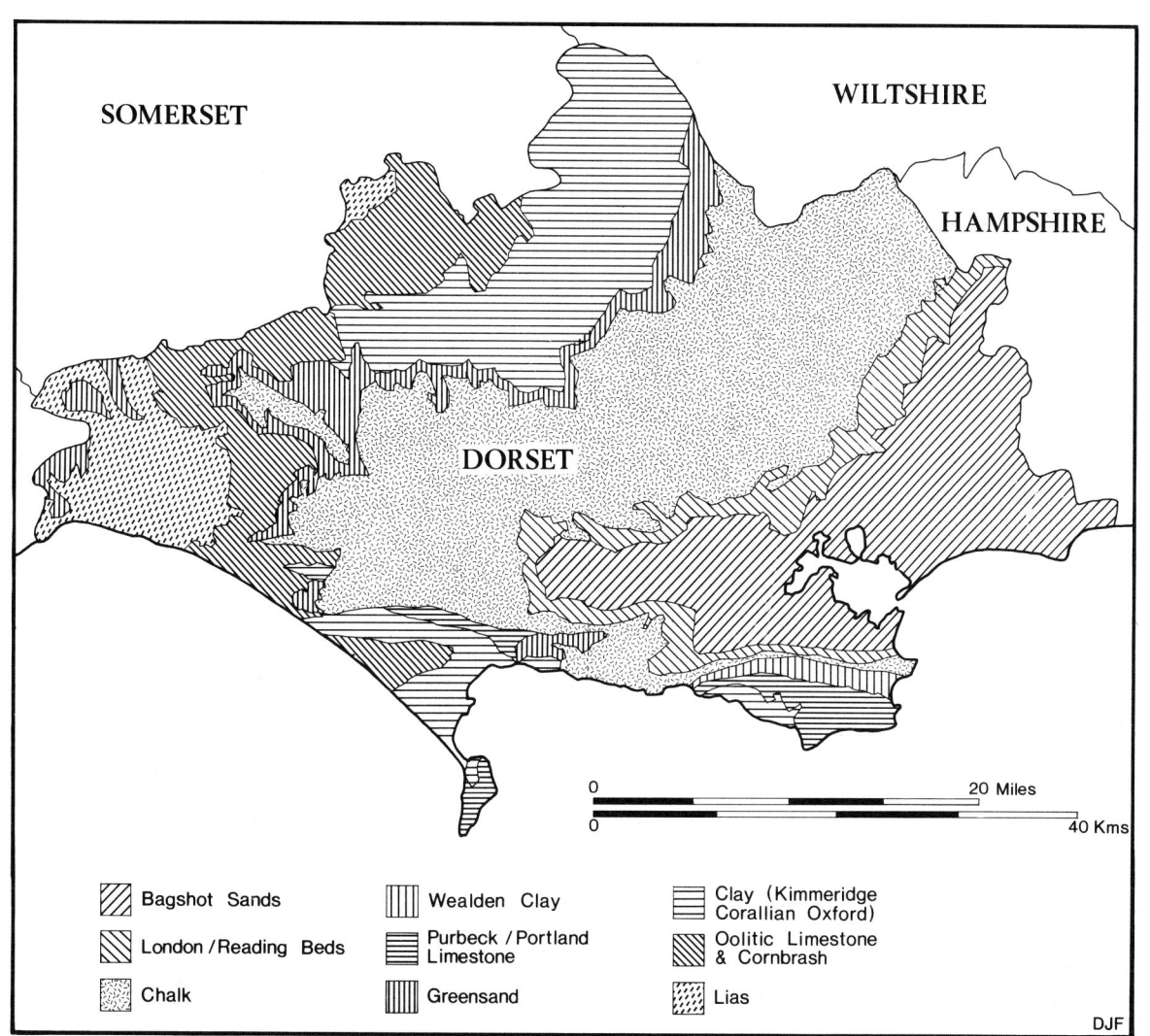

SOMERSET   WILTSHIRE

HAMPSHIRE

DORSET

0   20 Miles

0   40 Kms

▨ Bagshot Sands	▥ Wealden Clay	▤ Clay (Kimmeridge Corallian Oxford)
▨ London / Reading Beds	▤ Purbeck / Portland Limestone	▨ Oolitic Limestone & Cornbrash
⣿ Chalk	▥ Greensand	▨ Lias

DJF

the area linking the streams in the chalk uplands with the sea. Today these rivers meet the sea at Poole and Christchurch harbours.

To the west and south of the chalk the geology and topography is much more complex and is formed from older rocks. The area can be divided into five regions which are separated by the sea and the irregular western edge of the chalk. Erosion of this edge has created a sharp escarpment which is a noticeable feature in many areas. These regions are Purbeck, the coastal plain around Weymouth, Portland, the

Marshwood Vale and the Blackmore Vale (**11, 12**). The geology of these areas consists of a contorted mixture of clay, limestone, greensand and shale.

The Blackmore and Marshwood Vales are dominated by clay with only small patches and narrow bands of limestone. The Blackmore Vale is a wide expanse of low-lying and very damp land in north-west Dorset bounded on its west side by low limestone hills which extend into Somerset. The Marshwood Vale, in west Dorset, is a much smaller pocket of damp ground surrounded by an arc of greensand and limestone high ground. The coastal plain around Weymouth is another clay area but larger outcrops of Oolitic and Purbeck limestone create some relief. In contrast Portland is an upland limestone plateau surrounded by steep cliffs and only connected to the mainland by the shingle beach of Chesil Bank. Purbeck is a very distinctive region on the south-east coast which is dominated by steep-sided valleys and exposed hilltops. It is largely limestone but has significant outcrops of shale and clay. It is separated from the tertiary sands and gravels to the north by a deep clay valley and a thin but pronounced chalk ridge.

The agricultural potential of these different regions is very variable and depends on several

8 *(left) A typical chalk landscape to the west of Dorchester, near Winterborne Abbas. Note the round barrows and relict field systems.*

9 *(below left) The Valley of the Stones in the South Dorset Ridgeway. Clearly visible are the lynchets of one of the best preserved Celtic field systems in southern England.*

10 *(below) A view from the chalk ridge that defines the Isle of Purbeck towards Poole Harbour. The heaths in the foreground have very poor soils and today are mostly covered by conifer plantations and housing developments.*

factors. The soils largely reflect the underlying geology, but the ability and agricultural technology of the farmers and the previous effects of human activity also have a part to play. This disparity is not so noticeable today because the use of chemical fertilizers has made less productive land capable of bearing a crop. However, a glance at the agricultural records of the early twentieth century indicates that there were substantial variations between the geological regions.

The chalk was amongst the richest agricultural land in Dorset. In recent years the agricultural regime has been one of mixed arable farming with sheep. In 1929 one third of the land was under permanent pasture, over one third was cultivated and the rest was unfarmed. This was the highest proportion of cultivated land in Dorset at this time. The landscape was split into valleys which produced hay and meadow grass practically all the year, the downlands which were used for summer and winter grazing, and the intervening land which was cultivated for fodder and grain.

The tertiary sands and gravels were the poorest agricultural land in Dorset and in historical times were regarded as waste land. Only the river valleys provided any soil capable of sustaining a good crop. The area of mixed soils, however, between the sands and gravels and the chalk can be distinguished as a distinct agricultural region which is an important arable area with greater potential than the chalk itself.

Generalized statements about the agricultural potential of the other regions are much more difficult to make. The clay lands of the Marshwood and Blackmore Vales have in recent years proved to be very rich areas, and they have the smallest proportion of unused land in the county. The great majority of this land is under permanent pasture and this is one of the most important dairy cattle areas in

11 *(top left) A view from the western chalk escarpment across the Blackmore Vale. This is now an important agricultural area, but the heavy clay soils would have been difficult to cultivate in prehistory.*

12 *(below left) A view along the western chalk escarpment towards the hillfort of Dungeon Hill which sits on the isolated knoll in the centre of the photograph.*

southern England. Within this area, however, the small outcrops of limestone and the high ground which extends into Somerset provide very good arable land which is extensively cultivated. A similar situation exists in the area around Weymouth but here there is more unfarmed land (partly as a result of the Weymouth conurbation) and a greater proportion of arable on the limestone. Portland cannot be fully appreciated as an agricultural resource due to extensive quarrying and urban settlement. It is likely, however, to be similar to the high chalk downs, though even more exposed. Purbeck has the highest proportion of unfarmed land in Dorset and there is very little land suitable for arable because of considerable small scale variation in the soil conditions.

These regional patterns have considerable historical validity and travellers' comments on the agricultural landscape of Dorset allow them to be extended back to the Medieval period. Individuals consistently draw attention to the number and quality of sheep on the chalk downs, the cattle in the Blackmore Vale (though dairy herds were not so important before the introduction of the railways opened up the London market) and the waste lands of east Dorset. It is clear, however, from any cursory examination of the archaeological record and an analysis of the reasons for the present agricultural regime that this pattern is not likely to represent the situation in the prehistoric period.

The most obvious evidence for change concerns the waste lands of east Dorset. Archaeological work has demonstrated that this area was intensively settled between 2000 and 1000 BC. Field systems are regularly identified in developments around the large conurbations of Bournemouth and Poole and there are large numbers of barrows and cemeteries from this period scattered across the heath. It seems that the soils were originally capable of sustaining a large agricultural population but that this period of cultivation so depleted the fragile soils that they became an agricultural wasteland that has scarcely recovered even up to the present day. The situation in the clay vales is somewhat different. It seems unlikely that these areas would, in the prehistoric period, have been regarded as the rich agricultural lands that they have been in recent years. The very heavy clay soils require extensive drainage and to create the permanent pastures seen in the

Medieval and post-Medieval period required a considerable investment of labour and technology. It is unlikely that early prehistoric farmers would have been capable of farming these areas and there is no evidence for extensive early occupation. It is not clear exactly when these areas were cleared but even in the 500 years before the Roman invasion most of the settlements appear to occupy only the small pockets of more tractable soil in these regions.

The soil on the chalk was probably more fertile than it is today. The present soil regime is dominated by large areas of poor, shallow soils which need extensive fertilizing to produce a decent crop. The areas of fertile soil are restricted to patches of clay with flint, which occur within the chalk, and the valley bottoms where thick accumulations of soil have been deposited by erosion of the chalk uplands. At the beginning of the Neolithic the chalk would have been covered by a thick, rich, brown earth created by the accumulation and decay of thousands of years of leaf litter. It is likely therefore that the chalk would have been an even more important agricultural resource than it was in more recent historical times.

Environmental history

The above analysis of the geology and the recent agricultural history of Dorset has indicated the agricultural potential of the landscape. It does not, however, tell us how this land was used by the earliest agricultural inhabitants of the British Isles. It has also already been shown that there are clearly visible changes in the exploitation of the clay and the heath and it is likely that the vegetation and soil regimes that developed after the last Ice Age would be very different to those visible even in later prehistory. Consequently the recovery of material which would give an indication of the environment of 5000 years ago was one of the major priorities of recent work in this area.

Pollen analysis is the best and most direct evidence for the original vegetation of an area, since practically all plants produce large quantities of distinctive pollen grains which are readily identifiable when seen through a microscope. These are relatively resistant to decay and though best preserved in acid waterlogged bogs they can be analysed from any ground surface which has been sealed by later soil deposition. The best results are obtained by examining columns from sediments which have

accumulated over thousands of years as these can chart any vegetational changes which have taken place over that period. The obvious sources are peat bogs and natural ponds which are being infilled by sediments brought in by streams. Unfortunately pollen does not survive on well-drained alkaline soil and this means that there are no representative samples from the chalk.

Mollusc analysis is the principal means of identifying vegetation changes on the chalk. This is based on the principle that most species of snail have a favourite habitat and therefore if one counts the numbers of different species found in any area these will provide evidence for the environment of that area. Shells will survive long after the death of the snail on alkaline soils which are not subject to excessive disturbance. They do not survive on acid soils and thus give complementary evidence to that recovered by the pollen analysis. The main archaeological technique is to take a measured volume of soil from every 10 cm (33 in.) of a soil sequence that has built up gradually, such as that found filling a ditch, and to count the numbers of each species in the sample (**13**). Species of snail can be broadly grouped into three categories: those favouring open country; those with woodland habitats; and those which have no ecological preferences. The relative proportions of each species will give a picture of the environment of the period when the soil was accumulating (**14**). By taking a column of samples through a ditch the variation in the species present will give an impression of the way in which the environment has changed. This general principle glosses over a number of important caveats which considerably complicate the basis of the study but which cannot be discussed in detail in the limited space available.

13 *(above right) Sampling the Bank Barrow ditch for snail shells.*

14 *(below right) A diagram showing the numbers and species of snails found in the Causewayed Camp ditch. The species are grouped by habitat: woodland, open country and intermediate species that can live in both. There are very few open country species; woodland species are particularly important at the bottom of the ditch.*

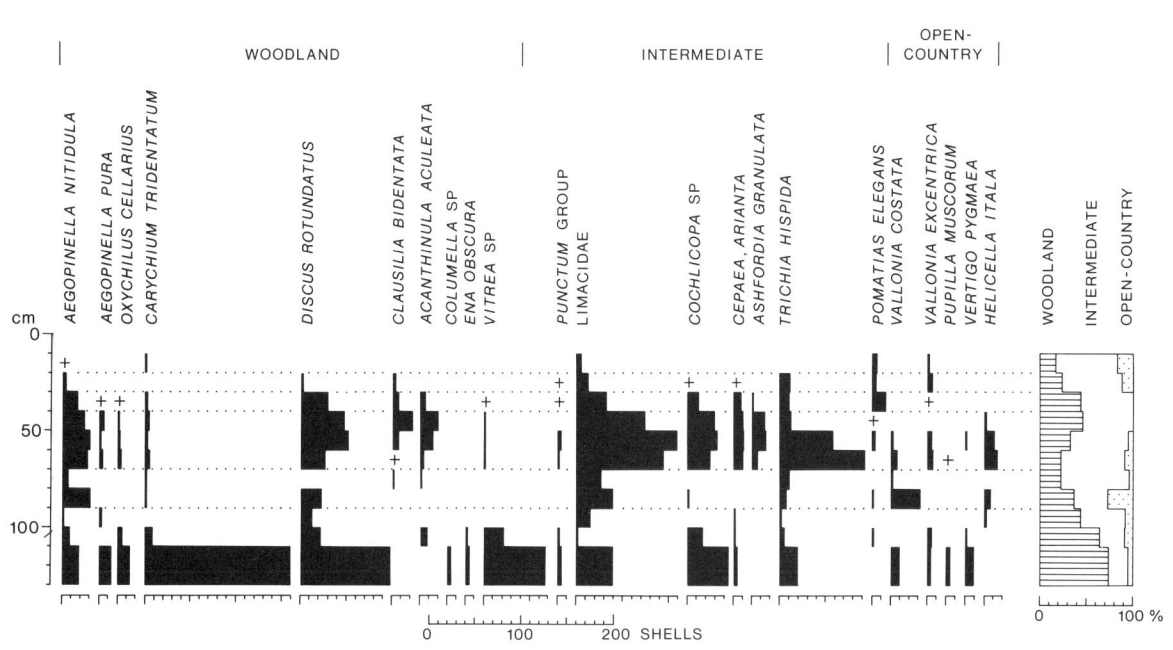

MC III : NEOLITHIC ENCLOSURE DITCH (TRENCH II, N. SECTION)

Other sources of information on the ancient environment include the analysis of buried soils, animal bones, wood charcoal and other carbonized plant remains (particularly seeds). Some of these techniques provide information specifically about the local environment but others give a broader picture of the general area. Snails for instance will only provide information on the land immediately adjacent to the ditch that is sampled but pollen can be blown for many miles before it settles. Many of the results are dependant, directly or indirectly, on human action. Charcoals are largely the result of human exploitation for fuel and do not give a representative selection of the wood species present. Small mammals are not brought to the site by human action but many species are attracted by human presence. These and many other problems have to be borne in mind when analysing the different strands of evidence. The analyses do, however, provide clear evidence for change in the environment on and around Maiden Castle which will be discussed in the following chapters. The purpose of the rest of this chapter is to discuss what the environment was like in Dorset, around Maiden Castle, and on the hilltop itself before Maiden Castle was occupied.

It is now generally accepted that the lowlands of southern England were covered by forest between ten and twelve thousand years ago. In the following four thousand years these forests went through a natural progression from birch to pine (similar forests are now found only in isolated areas of northern Scotland), to deciduous forests characterized by elm, oak, alder and lime. Evidence from southern England is, however, scarce as pollen diagrams are not available from the extensive areas of chalk and are only rarely available from the other soils. The only area of Dorset where pollen analysis has given a detailed picture of the environment is in the east of the county around Poole Harbour and Bournemouth. This area was extensively studied by L.E. Haskins for a Ph.D. at the University of Southampton. Around 5000 BC the region was covered by open woodland and the dominant species were oak, elm and hazel. The damp soils of the river valleys were, however, dominated by alder and lime and on the more infertile acidic soils there were small patches of pine and birch.

The absence of pollen cores from the chalk does make it difficult to reconstruct the environ-ment of Dorset in the Mesolithic, the period immediately preceding the Neolithic occupation. Snail columns and soil analysis from the excavations at Maiden Castle, however, confirm that this area was wooded and analysis of the charcoal indicates which species were present in the woodland (15). The most common species were oak, hazel and ash; oak and ash are likely to dominate the woodland with hazel present as undergrowth or in clearings. The woodland margins are represented by members of the pomoidaea and prunus groups; which include hawthorn, blackthorn, white beam and crab apple. The relatively frequent discovery of ash in the enclosure ditch may indicate that the enclosure at Maiden Castle was created some-time after the hilltop and its area were orig-inally colonized by agricultural settlers since ash is thought by ecologists to be a species only common in disturbed woodland.

Local variation in species would have been crucial to the exploitation of the forest by hunter-gatherers. Certain species such as hazel, whose nuts were a rich and important source of protein would be a required food source at certain times of the year. The density of the plants in the undergrowth under the forest canopy would also have a direct effect upon the food supply. A relatively open woodland would be an advantage as it allows a hunter to identify, attack and follow game. Consequently the density of hunter-gatherer communities can be used as a guide to the vegetation of southern England.

In Dorset sites characterized by microliths, which are a tool type found before the Neolithic occupation, are concentrated on the tertiary sands and gravels and the coastal strip around Weymouth and Portland. There are also settle-ments on the greensand, limestone and the deposits of clay with flints in north Dorset but extensive fieldwork in south Dorset has failed to locate any definite Mesolithic settlement on the chalk.

This distribution has been used to argue that the sandy soils of the eastern part of the county supported a dry open woodland which was favoured by hunter-gatherers. An open wood-land could be the result of the poor quality of the soils in this area. The large deciduous trees, such as oak and elm with their extensive root systems would absorb much of the moisture and nutrients of the topsoil and this would reduce its capacity to support a dense undergrowth. In

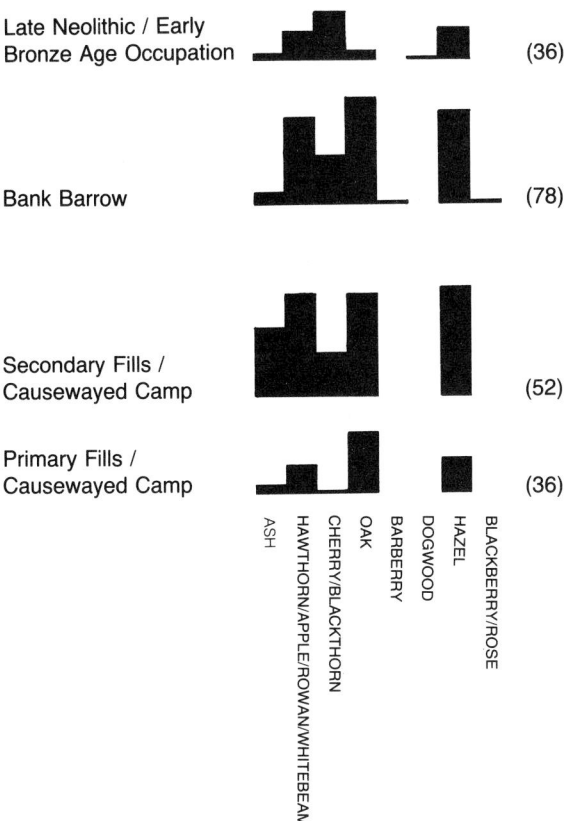

Late Neolithic / Early Bronze Age Occupation (36)

Bank Barrow (78)

Secondary Fills / Causewayed Camp (52)

Primary Fills / Causewayed Camp (36)

ASH
HAWTHORN/APPLE/ROWAN/WHITEBEAM
CHERRY/BLACKTHORN
OAK
BARBERRY
DOGWOOD
HAZEL
BLACKBERRY/ROSE

15 *A diagram showing the charcoal species found in the Causewayed Camp and Bank Barrow ditches. This gives some idea of the types of species available in the woods of this period. The increase in blackthorn/cherry and the appearance of species such as barberry, dogwood and blackberry/rose is a result of the clearance of the original primary forest and the appearance of secondary woodland.*

contrast the fertile soils of the chalk and especially the clay would be capable of supporting the major trees and a dense undergrowth. This undergrowth though made up of species exploited by man would be very difficult to penetrate and appears to have actively discouraged occupation by hunter-gatherers.

It has also been suggested that the limited undergrowth in the dry lands of the east could have been regularly burnt off by hunter-gatherers to encourage nut and berry production and to clear away killing grounds. If this was done repeatedly it would reduce the fertility of the soil and make it more and more difficult for the vegetation to reproduce. This might explain

the patches of pine and birch woods which are known to exist in this area and which are normally found on acidic podzol soils. Pollen diagrams from the area also show a slight rise in the occurrence of gramineae (grasses) and ericaceae (heather) which indicate more open conditions. It would be much more difficult to clear the damp undergrowth of the woods on the chalk and clay by fire.

Neolithic settlement
The distribution of Neolithic sites in Dorset (**16**) is very different from that of the preceding Mesolithic period. Long barrows, enclosures and settlements are largely concentrated on or near the chalk. The only sites known in east Dorset are settlements and long barrows situated in the Stour valley. The large expanses of open forest which were so important in the Mesolithic were avoided. The fertile but damp heavily-forested clay soils of west Dorset were also avoided though there was occasional occupation of the limestone and greensand outcrops. This suggests that the soils of the tertiary sands and gravels were quickly recognized as too poor to be worth farming. The presence of a significant hunter-gatherer population might also have discouraged agricultural settlement of the area. The chalk would have been a visibly more fertile region and would be better drained than the soils of the clay lands to the south and west.

The Neolithic colonization took place about 4300–4000 BC (3450–3100 bc). It is likely the hunter-gatherers of southern England had been in contact with the farming communities of the adjacent areas of the continent from the beginning of the fifth millennium BC and it is even possible that small groups of farmers had been crossing the channel from this period, but there is little sign of a significant influx before 4300 BC (3450 bc). The colonization of the British Isles appears to have been a relatively swift and expansive phase which coincides with the colonization of southern Scandinavia, north Germany and many previously unoccupied areas of France. Radiocarbon dates from northern Scotland, Ireland and southern England show little evidence for a gradual spread northwards and would indicate that the areas of fertile soil in the British Isles were searched out and settled fairly rapidly.

The main characteristics of Neolithic settlements are the presence of domestic crops and animals, the appearance of different types of

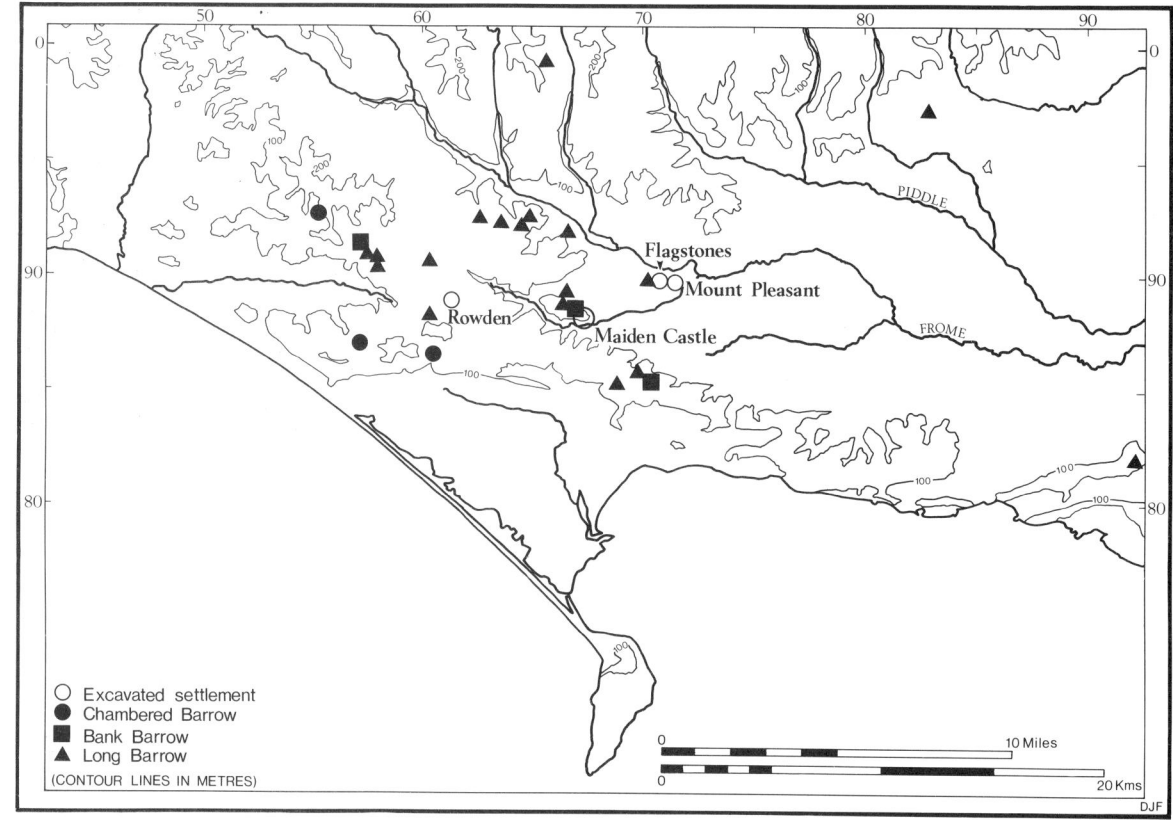

16 *The distribution of Early Neolithic settlements and monuments around Dorchester.*

tools and the construction of monuments (which were completely unknown to the hunter-gatherers). The new mode of subsistence is the most significant change as it indicates a dramatic change in the way of life of the inhabitants of the British Isles. The most important crops were barley and wheat and it seems likely that both of these were domesticated in south-east Europe and the Middle East and spread across Europe as part of a package of agricultural innovations. The sheep is also believed to have been domesticated in the Middle East but it is possible that its prehistoric ancestors were more widely distributed in Europe. Cattle, in contrast, could easily have been domesticated in Europe as wild cattle occur throughout the area. There is no evidence that the wild cattle in Britain were domesticated but as animal bones from the crucial period of colonization are very rare it is not possible to prove this is the case.

The changes in the material culture of the inhabitants do not seem to be the result of direct importation from the continent. The culturally distinctive items are ground stone axes (which

differ from the flaked stone axes of the Mesolithic), ceramics (a particular type of round based bowl) and leaf-shaped arrowheads (previous arrowheads were composite, using several small flint blades). Only vague parallels for this material can be found in Europe.

Similar problems arise when attempting to discover direct parallels for the distinctive monuments of the Neolithic. These include burial mounds (the earthen long barrows with wooden graves in southern and eastern Britain and the chambered tombs of northern and western Britain) and enclosures (normally defined by ditches but including walled enclosures in the west). Similar monuments are known in Europe but the relationship with the British monuments is not close enough to suggest they derived from them and there are none which clearly precede the British examples.

It would appear that the objects and monuments of the first farmers were innovations which, though based on existing material, were radically altered to support a society involved in the rapid colonization of large areas of sparsely populated woodland. Many people have argued that the monuments could not have been built in the early period of colonization as labour in this period would have had to be concentrated on basic subsistence activities such as clearing the forest and planting crops. However, this view fails to appreciate the social importance of these monuments. They are the only visible manifestations of what would have been a widespread network of social and religious relationships linking the widely dispersed settlements. These would create a community which provided support when individual families were in difficulty.

The landscape around Maiden Castle

Maiden Castle is situated on an isolated chalk ridge on the north side of the valley of the South Winterborne, a tributary of the Frome. The highest point of this ridge (Hog Hill) is 133 m (435 ft) above sea level and occurs roughly at its centre. The archaeological monument known as Maiden Castle occupies an eastern lobe of the ridge which rises to 132 m (431 ft) above sea level at its extreme eastern end.

The ridge is an outlier of the South Dorset Ridgeway which lies to the south of the South Winterborne. The Ridgeway is part of the high escarpment which forms the southern boundary of the chalk (Maiden Castle lies only 3 km (2 miles) from the limestone outcrops which define the coastal plain around Weymouth). To the north of Maiden Castle there is an undulating chalk plain which is broken by the valley of the River Frome. Across the Frome the chalk rises gradually to the uplands of central Dorset. This is one of the most extensive areas of low-lying chalk in Dorset and was a very rich agricultural region in recent times. The fertility of the land is helped by the regular occurrence of clay with flints, plateau gravels and river gravels which provide much needed minerals to the chalk soils.

Our knowledge of the Early Neolithic settlement of this area is based on three factors: the distribution of Neolithic monuments (long barrows and enclosures); the results of intensive field survey (which was designed to identify Neolithic settlement by the collection of diagnostic stone artefacts from ploughed fields); and the chance discovery of settlements and monu-

ments by rescue excavation. The distribution of the surviving monuments in south Dorset is very distinctive (see **16**) with four clusters of long barrows around Maiden Castle; three of these lie along the South Dorset Ridgeway. There are two long barrows and a bank barrow near Came Wood, 4 km (2½ miles) south-east of Maiden Castle; three long barrows and a bank barrow clustered around the enclosure at Maiden Castle; and, about 11 km (7 miles) to the west, are three long barrows and a bank barrow on the hill above Long Bredy. The only cluster away from the Ridgeway is around the dry valley leading into the Frome valley at Bradford Peverell.

Isolated monuments are also known but it is possible that these were originally part of monument clusters which have been partially destroyed by later activities. The Grey Mare and her Colts (**17**) and the Hell Stone are isolated chambered tombs found on the southern edge of the Ridgeway. There is a single long barrow at Black Down (**18**) and rescue excavations have recently discovered a long barrow on the eastern edge of Dorchester. Close to the latter was an enclosure which may also be of Early Neolithic date.

Intensive field survey is the only means by which these monuments can be related to the settlements of the period. The most important aspect of such field survey is the controlled collection of flint artefacts from ploughed fields. Amongst these artefacts may be tools which were only used in the Early Neolithic and which identify settlements of this date. The only extensive area in south Dorset which has been subject to detailed field survey is the area around Maiden Castle. A large area was surveyed as part of the recent research project extending from the valley of the South Winterborne to the ridge on the south side of the Frome. This survey revealed that Early Neolithic activity contemporary with the long barrows was quite restricted and was concentrated in the valley of the South Winterborne. There was probably some exploitation of the lowlands to the north of Maiden Castle, and it is likely that flint gravels in this region were an important and useful resource, but this area was not settled or farmed until later. Unfortunately it was not possible to explore the area around the long barrows on the edge of Dorchester as this is now extensively built up. The discovery of settlements during rescue excavation in

Dorchester would, however, seem to indicate that it was also occupied early in the Neolithic.

It seems then that Early Neolithic settlement was relatively restricted to small clearings in an otherwise dense forest. Two features of this settlement pattern are, however, noticeable. The clusters of long barrows in south Dorset are exceptional; the nearest similar cluster is in north Dorset and there is a large expanse of cultivable land between these two areas. The second feature is that the settlement zone around Dorchester is not concentrated on what should have been the best agricultural land, the plain around Dorchester. It occurred either on the high ground or in small steep-sided valleys. Both of these features may be due to the colonization process of the early farmers. The overall distribution would be explained if the settlers moved into the chalk area along the major river valleys and we have already seen that the distribution in south-east Dorset was indeed concentrated along the river valleys. The local distribution is probably related to the occurrence of natural clearings within the landscape. The uplands and steep valley sides may have been relatively open areas within what was otherwise a densely wooded landscape.

17 *The chambered tomb the Grey Mare and her Colts on the South Dorset Ridgeway. The large upright stones mark the east end of the barrow and define a forecourt where activities would take place. Behind the large central stone is the chamber where the dead were placed.*

18 *The isolated Early Neolithic long barrow at Black Down on the South Dorset Ridgeway.*

3

The Causewayed Camp

The earliest evidence for human activity on the hilltop at Maiden Castle can be dated to roughly 6000 years ago. The hilltop was cleared of a dense deciduous woodland and an oval enclosure was created by the digging of two concentric ditches. The area enclosed was deliberately situated on the eastern edge of the ridge occupied by the present hillfort of Maiden Castle. From the centre of the enclosure much of the surrounding countryside is visible on a clear day and it is likely that this view was an important reason for the enclosure's location (**19**). The southern horizon is dominated by the uplands of the South Dorset Ridgeway. To the east is the valley of the South Winterborne, winding past the low ridge known as Conygar Hill, to the point where the valley meets the River Frome. The vista to the north is perhaps the most impressive and extensive. Today, there is a splendid view of the town of Dorchester and the rich agricultural land that surrounds it and in the distance are the chalk uplands which form the heart of Dorset. It is only to the west that the views from the centre of the enclosure are seriously restricted. One has to move to the western edge, amongst the ditches of the enclosure, before it is possible to see any distance and even then the views are impeded by the summit of Hog Hill.

Perhaps as important as the views from Maiden Castle were the views which could be obtained *of* Maiden Castle from the surrounding countryside. It is often possible to have clear views of the surrounding landscape from an area which is almost invisible to other people. The enclosure at Maiden Castle, however, was placed on the side of the hill, so that it could be seen from many miles away. The ditches on the western edge of the enclosure cut across some of the highest ground of the area enclosed, most of the interior slopes from west to east, and the ditches on the east side are well to the east of the break in slope which marks the top of the hill. When the ditches were originally dug the area would be particularly prominent as they would have stood out as white scars in the predominantly green landscape. It is possible to interpret the ditches as a clear signal, which demanded attention and attracted people as surely as a neon sign today. The enclosure was designed to be seen from the east, and to focus attention to the area.

Another factor in the positioning of the enclosure is the proximity of the South Winterborne valley. The southern ditches of the enclosure run along the top of the scarp down to this valley and it is only five minutes walk from here to the stream in the valley bottom. It would have been possible to enhance the visibility of the enclosure by situating it on several more prominent hills, most noticeably any part of the South Dorset Ridgeway, but these were much further from a valley as sheltered and agriculturally rich as the South Winterborne. At present this is an unimpressive little stream which dries up completely in the summer months. It is, however, likely to have been a much more powerful and constant source of running water in the past and was a focus for early settlement. Today the traces of abandoned Late Medieval water-meadow systems give some idea of the former importance of the valley, but this is perhaps best expressed by the number of sixteenth- and seventeenth-century manor houses scattered along its length.

By analysing the siting of the enclosure we can, therefore, obtain an idea of its function even before we have begun to examine the

nature of its construction and the activities that took place in and around it. It was probably closely tied to the agricultural community cultivating the valley of the South Winterborne and was intended to draw people from the surrounding agricultural settlements to the north and east.

The area enclosed

Our knowledge of the nature of the Neolithic enclosure is restricted for a number of reasons. The most obvious and significant of these is the presence of the later hillfort. The original features of the enclosure are now completely invisible as they were covered by the massive banks and ditches of the fort. The existence of this early enclosure was indeed a completely unexpected discovery during the work of Sir Mortimer Wheeler in 1934. A trench through the rampart of the first hillfort revealed that it was built over the inner ditch of the enclosure (**20**). Wheeler went on to excavate several trenches through the defences of the early hillfort and found the same ditch in every one. (**21**). It was only when he excavated the entrance to the hillfort, however, that he discovered this ditch was just one of a pair. The outer ditch of

19 *The view from Maiden Castle looking towards Dorchester in 1985. The landscape is now disrupted by the construction of the Dorchester bypass.*

the enclosure lay on the line of the much larger hillfort ditch and had been almost completely removed when this was excavated.

It is now clear from the recent excavations that the line of the early hillfort defences was based on the presence of a small bank which lay between the two ditches of the earlier enclosure. Whereas the ditches of the enclosure were by then almost completely infilled, and invisible, the bank was still clearly visible and was used to mark the front of the hillfort rampart. The direct juxtaposition of the early hillfort and the enclosure is important, as it identifies the location and plan of the enclosure. The presence of the hillfort rampart has, however, restricted the examination of the enclosure ditches as only determined and costly excavations could afford to remove even small areas of the hillfort defences.

The occupation of the hillfort has also considerably obscured any evidence there was for the occupation of the enclosure. As will later

become clear, the interior of the hillfort was densely populated and one of the most characteristic activities during the later period was the digging of large pits. These literally honeycomb the surface of the hill and have resulted in the almost wholesale destruction of evidence for previous occupation. Only one part of the earlier deposits survived this destruction intact: the area under the mound of the Bank Barrow. This barrow was avoided during the use of the hillfort and as a result the surface of the hill, sealed beneath it, is the only part of the

20 *The first trench excavated across the Causewayed Camp. (The Society of Antiquaries.)*

21 *The Causewayed Camp: (A) A hypothetical plan showing the trenches where the ditches have been discovered; (B) Wheeler's excavation of the western entrance to the Early Iron Age hillfort showing the extent of the underlying Causewayed Camp ditch; (C) Wheeler's excavation in the eastern entrance of the hillfort showing the location of the Causewayed Camp ditch.*

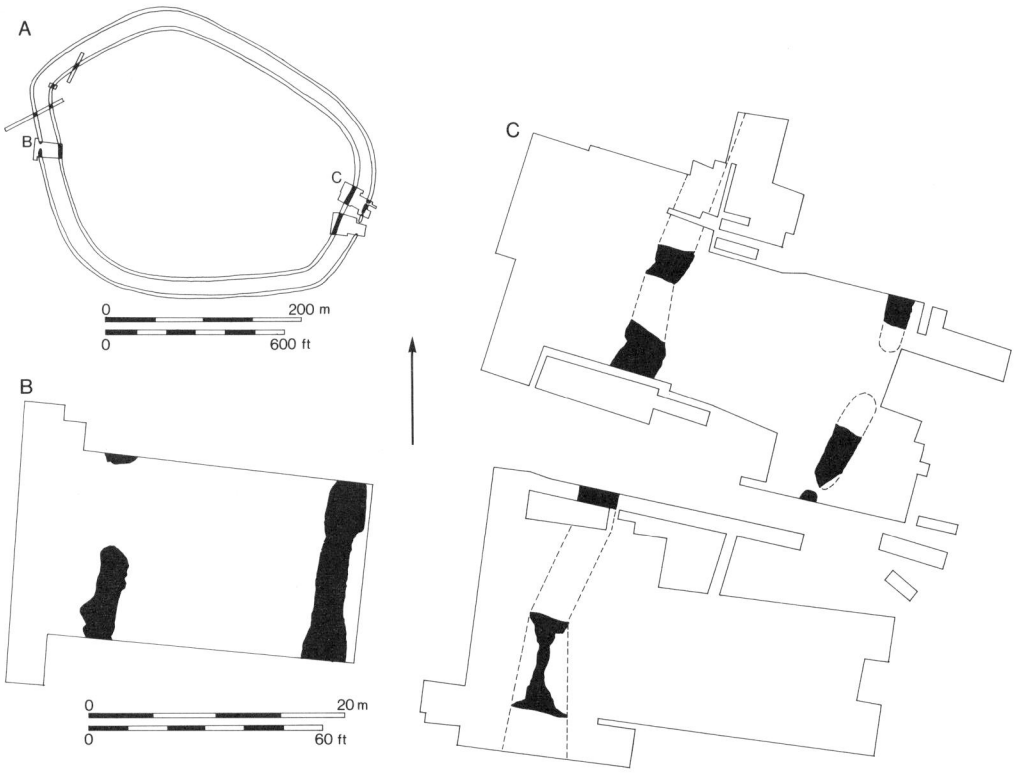

hilltop where undisturbed evidence for the occupation of the enclosure may survive.

The importance of this undisturbed portion in the interior of the enclosure is highlighted by consideration of other enclosures in southern England, contemporary with Maiden Castle. It is clear that conditions of preservation at Maiden Castle are exceptional as most enclosures have been very badly damaged by activities in the 6000 years since their use, and in particular by the intensity of agricultural practices in the last thirty years. It is important to emphasize that the recent advent of ploughing on areas of chalk downland undisturbed since the Medieval period has been a disaster for our archaeological heritage.

The evidence from Wheeler's examination of the centre of the enclosure is consequently a very important source of information for what took place here and in many similar enclosures scattered across southern England. It is all the more disappointing then that the evidence perhaps tells us more about what did not happen in the enclosure than what did. A large area was examined and yet only a scatter of shallow pits, an area of burning (perhaps a hearth) and a handful of post-holes, not obviously indicating a building, were discovered. However, the findings are important for two reasons. Firstly, the absence of continuous and intensive occupation is significant in itself and secondly, though the evidence is sparse it nevertheless indicates that certain activities did take place. Amongst the discoveries two features of particular interest were a pit dug into the surface of the hill and the grave of two children.

The pit was of interest because it contained a large quantity of broken pottery, fragments of animal bones and a collection of limpet shells. It would normally be assumed that the limpet shells were the remains of food debris but Maiden Castle is over 8 km (5 miles) from the sea and limpets are not a very desirable food source. In the historical period they were only ever eaten during times of famine and though archaeological evidence suggests they were eaten in prehistoric times this was only by communities living near the sea shore. It would also seem sensible to shell them at the shore if they were collected as a food source as the shell makes up a large part of the weight. The presence of these sea shells would seem to indicate that the deposit is not simply domestic rubbish. The large number of vessels and the high quality of the pottery in the pit are also unusual.

The grave contained two small children, about six or seven years old. The bodies had been placed in a crouched position with the knees tucked up against the chests and the arms folded as if in prayer. They were arranged so that the head of each child faced the legs of the other. At the shoulder of one child was a small, plain bowl which may have contained food or drink. Burials of children are not common discoveries in this period, but they do seem to occur with some frequency in enclosures similar to Maiden Castle.

The nature of these two features therefore suggests that the activities taking place inside the enclosure were rather unusual. They included the burial of deposits of special (not easily obtainable) objects, and children. Perhaps the most important point, however, is the relative absence of evidence for anything that could be regarded as 'normal' domestic activity. In particular there is nothing that could possibly represent a house. It may be argued that the evidence is so inadequate that we cannot make any statements about activities inside the enclosure. However, when we compare Maiden Castle with other sites, especially the nearby enclosure at Hambledon Hill, these three points, burials, special deposits and scarcity of occupation, recur. It is clear, therefore, that these enclosures cannot be regarded as simply enclosed settlements; they must have had a different and more specialized role.

The ditches

The ditches themselves (**22** and **23**) are the most important features of the Neolithic enclosure at Maiden Castle. Obviously they define its size and shape but they also act as a sign to focus the attention of people to this point in the landscape. In marked contrast to the paucity of evidence from the interior, the ditches were prominent features which have yielded a wealth of evidence. Despite the very small area of ditch examined, the evidence obtained can help to explain the use of the enclosure and also its status.

A striking feature of the ditches is the manner in which they were created. The easiest way to dig a ditch in chalk is to start at one point and work at a vertical face until the desired end is reached (in the case of an enclosure the end is the point where the ditch was begun). It is much

quicker to work at a vertical face than to dig down from the surface. To create the enclosure at Maiden Castle, however, a very different method was employed. The ditch was created by digging a series of flat-bottomed and vertically-sided pits, elongated and curved to create the shape of the enclosure. The pits were originally separated by undug areas of chalk but at a later date the areas separating the pits of the inner ditch were removed. The positions of the original pits show up clearly as they were deeper than the later ditch which joined them. The pits of the outer ditch were left largely unconnected and were smaller and narrower.

This type of 'segmented' ditch is a common feature of monuments constructed in the period around 4000 BC. It is so characteristic that the enclosures similar to Maiden Castle are collectively referred to by archaeologists as 'cause-

22 *The recent re-excavation of Wheeler's trench A, showing the inner ditch of the Causewayed Camp.*

23 *The outer ditch of the Causewayed Camp exposed by the 1986 excavation of the eastern entrance.*

wayed enclosures' because of the gaps or 'causeways' in their ditch circuits. 'Segmented' ditches are also a feature of other contemporary monuments. Many of the barrows, constructed as monuments to the dead during this period, were flanked by parallel ditches which were dug as pits and then joined together.

This method of ditch digging is significant and must indicate not only something about the use of the enclosure but also about the organization of the labourers who created it. It would have been more sensible to dig the ditch as a continuous trench if a small labour force was present. It would, however, have taken a long time to define the area enclosed. The technique of pit digging, in contrast, is more efficient when a much larger labour force is available but only for a short period. The evidence would therefore suggest the enclosure was created by the small agricultural communities dispersed around Maiden Castle. Each community could only provide a minimal amount of labour but this would be at specific times in the year when agricultural activities required less labour. Consequently there would be a large number of people available at these times. It may be surmised that each community acted separately and was assigned a specific part of the circuit of the ditch to dig. Furthermore it suggests that the communities regarded themselves as relatively independent, otherwise it would have been more practical to organize a specialist team to dig the ditch. The tradition of ditches dug as lines of pits is a feature which disappeared in the later periods when the landscape was more densely populated, and separate communities were more closely integrated.

If the ditch was intended to be used as a boundary physically to prevent people entering the enclosed area then one would expect it to be continuous. It is evident therefore that the principal purpose of the ditch was not to act as a barrier but to define the area enclosed and the activities which took place within it. This appears to be confirmed by the absence of a substantial bank. The only bank identified in the recent excavations was insignificant, a mere 17 cm (7 in.) high. This was well preserved by its incorporation within the later Iron Age rampart, and it was originally no more substantial than it appears today. There was no evidence for any other bank either inside or outside the enclosure ditches. As much of the area immediately inside the ditch was protected by the later

ramparts of the hillfort it is fairly certain that there was no large bank – an absence which is difficult to understand. The spoil from the ditch might be expected to have formed a bank and a lot of effort would have had to be invested to remove the chalk from the enclosure.

As soon as a ditch is dug it begins to fill up. Initially the loose soil created by digging is washed in by rain. Then, with the advent of winter, frost starts to break up the rock that forms the side of the ditch. A soft rock such as chalk breaks up easily, particularly when the ditch sides are vertical. As the sides break up the turf at the edge of the ditch is undermined and soon large lumps break off and fall into the ditch. This process may continue for several years until the ditch is grassed over and the sides are gentle slopes. Then, much more gradual and imperceptible processes take over. Soil creep down the slope will continue for many years until the ditch is an insignificant depression.

There is normally therefore an accumulation in the ditch of very distinct layers of soil and rubble which are easily identifiable and quite different from the solid material from which the ditch is cut. As the layers accumulate they trap any objects or material which are dropped in the ditch and seal them in position, in chronological order. Excavation aims to remove each layer of soil carefully in the reverse order of deposition and to recover the archaeological information that reveals the sequence of activity that occurred in, and around, the ditch.

The general sequence of deposition outlined above is clearly visible in all the cuttings through the inner ditch at Maiden Castle (**24**). The lowest chalky layers would have accumulated very soon after the ditch had been dug, perhaps within only five years, so that the material in the silt and rubble would have been trapped in the ditch from the beginning of the enclosure's use. Objects in these deposits are rare. The most noticeable find in the recent excavations was large quantities of charcoal. This was mixed up amongst the chalk rubble, some of which was also burnt. This suggests that fires were actually lit within the ditch or close by, and then swept into the ditch while the wood was still burning. These fires may have had something to do with the clearance of the woodland covering the hilltop. One of the methods of clearing woodland is to ring-bark the trees and then burn the dead wood. Most of

the charcoal identified was oak, the dominant species in the natural woodland 6000 years ago.

Another very important discovery in these early ditch fills was the skeleton of a child about three or four years old (**25**). This is the third child burial which can be associated with the use of the enclosure and confirms the earlier impression that rituals of burial were important to its function. Various fragments of animal bones, pots and flint tools were also found but these were relatively insignificant at this level.

In contrast to the inner ditch, the outer ditch (see **23**) does not contain these natural ditch fills since it was deliberately and completely filled with small chalk rubble. This rubble sealed a layer of material which had been placed on the base of the ditch. In one of the trenches examined in 1985 there were the disarticulated remains of three people, two children aged three to five and five to ten years old and an adult

24 *A section through the inner ditch of the Causewayed Camp. Exposed by Wheeler in the eastern entrance to the hillfort. (The Society of Antiquaries.)*

about 45 years old, scattered with animal bones, flint tools and a broken stone axe, on the base of the ditch. In a trench examined in 1986 there were carved lumps of chalk and slabs of high quality pottery in a similar situation. The size and character of this outer ditch have already indicated that it was not the same as the inner ditch; either it was only open a few years or it was deliberately cleared out before being filled in again.

Above the primary layers of the inner ditch were the silts which accumulated slowly after the sides had collapsed. It was amongst these that the natural sequence of soils was seriously disturbed by intensive human activity in and

interpretation of this deposit before the final fill of the ditch is discussed. It might be thought that the presence of such a layer of rubbish, full of domestic debris, indicates the enclosure was a settlement and this theory has been persuasively argued by many archaeologists. It was once suggested that people actually lived in the ditches. Most people do not, however, live on top of their rubbish; it is normally taken away and disposed of in specific areas that are set aside for this purpose. It is also clear from the anthropological study of present day societies that rubbish deposits are used to emphasize important distinctions in social relationships. Some of the more extreme manifestations of this

25 *The human burial discovered in the fill of the Causewayed Camp ditch in 1985.*

26 *The Causewayed Camp ditch in trench II showing its location under the hillfort rampart that cuts across the interior of the hilltop.*

around the enclosure ditches. Activity was represented by a charcoal-rich layer full of animal bones, fragments of pottery and massive amounts of debris from the manufacture of flint tools. This layer has been identified in all the sections of the ditch that have been examined. Detailed analysis of the soil suggests that the layer originally had a large organic component, including plant remains, flesh and faeces, which has subsequently decayed away. It would therefore have been a foul-smelling rubbish dump which completely surrounded the enclosure (**26**).

This deposit is an important source of material for reconstructing the everyday life of the community that used the enclosure. The animal bone and plant remains provide information on the environment at this time, as well as about agricultural practices and diet, whilst the ceramics and stone tools are indicators of trade, technology and social conflicts. These will be discussed in detail in the next chapter. It is important, however, to be clear about the

practice involve smearing dung on the body and possessions of individuals. More commonly rubbish is used to mark a barrier, and this may explain the deposits in the enclosure ditches at Maiden Castle. The presence of a ditch filled with foul-smelling rubbish would certainly emphasize the significance of the enclosure at Maiden Castle and yet it would not physically inhibit access.

The final layers in the inner enclosure ditch are only recoverable where the ditch was sealed by the Bank Barrow mound. Elsewhere later activity on the hilltop has disturbed the upper fill and it is not clear what happened subsequent to the enclosure's abandonment. Where the ditch was sealed by the Bank Barrow, however, the presence of a thin soil horizon suggests the Bank Barrow was erected soon after the enclosure was abandoned.

Other enclosures

Enclosures similar to Maiden Castle are found throughout the Midlands and southern England (**27**). Isolated examples are known from Ireland and Scotland and it is likely that they are a feature of early agricultural settlements throughout the British Isles. Similar enclosures are also known in other areas of western Europe and there are particularly dense concentrations in western France and Denmark.

In England the enclosures were split into four topographically defined areas by Palmer: the south-west – ranging from Hembury in Devon to Windmill Hill in Wiltshire; Sussex – with sites found exclusively on the chalk of the South Downs; the Thames Valley – which ranges from Crickley Hill on the Cotswold scarp to Staines on the west side of London; and the Midlands and East Anglia, which ranges from Orsett on the Thames estuary to Mavesyn Ridware on the River Trent in Staffordshire. These regions are not rigidly defined and there are areas of ambiguity. It is possible for instance that the enclosures around the site of Avebury belong in the Thames Valley group and the site at Orsett

27 *The distribution of Early Neolithic enclosures in southern England (after Palmer 1976).*

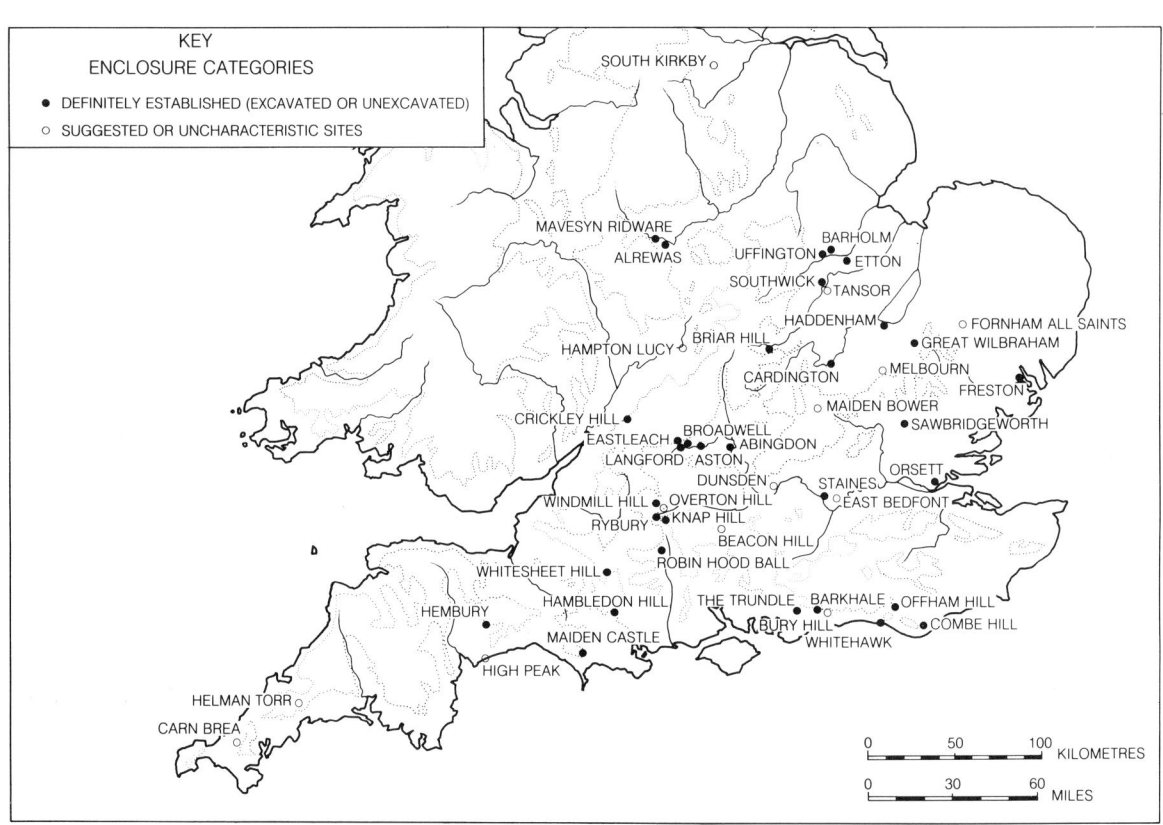

has been placed both in the Thames Valley and Midland/East Anglia group. Nevertheless there do seem to be significant gaps in the distribution between most of the clusters, and the Sussex group is particularly isolated. The common feature which unites these enclosures is the interrupted ditch and this almost always indicates an Early Neolithic date. There are, however, considerable differences between these enclosures arising from variations in the number of ditches, the spacing between each ditch and the area enclosed by the ditches. A comparison of the enclosures of Windmill Hill in Wiltshire, Whitehawk in Sussex, Whitesheet Hill in Wiltshire, Haddenham in Cambridgeshire and Briar Hill in Northamptonshire will highlight these differences (28).

Windmill Hill is one of the largest enclosures with three widely spaced ditches. The inner ditch encloses an area of only 0.50 ha (1.2 acres) and the outer ditch encloses an area of 9.60 ha (23.7 acres). These ditches are not arranged concentrically and show considerable variation in the length of the ditch between each causeway. The inner ditch has a noticeable inward kink on the north-west side which might indicate an entrance. Whitehawk is similar with four or possibly five widely spaced ditches. The inner ditch encloses an area of only 0.64 ha (1.6 acres) and the fourth (the fifth may never have been complete) encloses 5.50 ha (13.5 acres). The ditches are only loosely concentric with considerable variation again in the intervals between causeways. The enclosure at Whitesheet Hill is very different from these sites. It has a single ditch enclosing an area of 2.39 ha (5.9 acres). Haddenham is a very large enclosure with a single ditch and internal pallisade enclosing 8.5 ha (21 acres). It has an unusual D-shape and excavations suggest the straight side was the focus for activity. A more complicated monument is the enclosure at Briar Hill which has two closely spaced ditches enclosing an area of 3.15 ha (7.8 acres). Inside these was a smaller, single-ditched enclosure which lies on the east side of the double-ditched enclosure and overlaps its inner ditch.

Unfortunately the variation in the form of the enclosures does not seem to conform to the regions as defined by their distribution. The most noticeable distinction is that closely-spaced ditches were a feature of the Midlands/East Anglia group and widely-spaced ditches were a feature of the south-west and Sussex groups with both types occurring in the Thames Valley. There are, however, several examples which undermine this generalization. The most obvious is Maiden Castle, in the south-west, which has two closely spaced ditches. Single-ditched enclosures are known in all the areas except the Thames Valley; in the south-west there is Whitesheet Hill, in Sussex there is Barkhale and in the Midlands/East Anglia, Etton.

The major distinction between the regions is in the choice of topographic location. Examples in the south-west and Sussex groups are all situated on high ground on the summit or shoulder of chalk hills. The Thames and Midlands/East Anglia group in contrast are situated on low ground immediately adjacent to important rivers. This may, however, reflect archaeologists' ability to recognize these enclosures. The latter two groups have largely been identified in recent years because the gravels of the river valleys are highly receptive to the formation of crop marks. The former two groups include examples which survived as earthworks until recent years because the high chalk downland on which they lay was not cultivated. The chalk is also conducive to crop mark formation and this has revealed a small number of new sites. The valleys in the south, which tend to be covered by alluvium, and the high ground in the Midlands are areas of clay not conducive to crop mark formation. This distribution is, however, likely to reflect the desirable settlement areas in each region as the clay and alluvium which inhibit crop mark development are also not easily worked by simple cultivation methods.

Conclusion

This chapter has outlined the various features which define the earliest occupation of Maiden Castle. These are now completely invisible, buried by the earthworks of the hillfort, and have been discovered only during the excavation of the later structures. These ditches and pits may not appear very impressive especially when compared to the enormous banks and ditches of the hillfort. Nevertheless the enclosure is important because it is part of a group of similar monuments, the earliest created in Britain, and their creation represents the first attempt to divide the natural landscape. The importance of the enclosure is also clearly indicated by the quantity and quality of objects

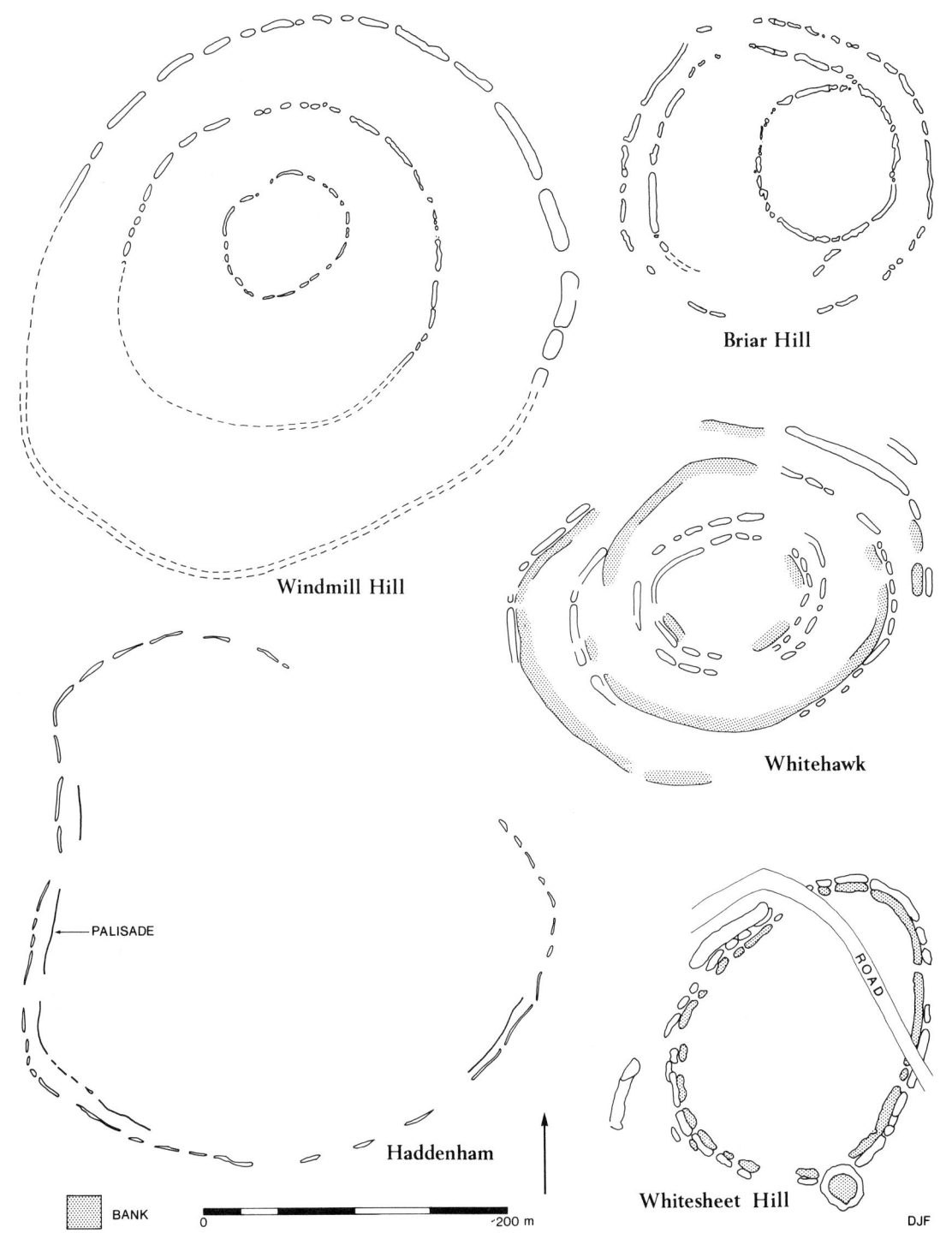

Windmill Hill

Briar Hill

Whitehawk

PALISADE

Haddenham

Whitesheet Hill

ROAD

BANK

0   200 m

DJF

deposited in the enclosure ditches. Only by the analysis of these deposits will it be possible to suggest the reasons behind the creation of the monuments.

28 *Comparative plans of the causewayed camps at Windmill Hill, Briar Hill, Whitehawk, Haddenham and Whitesheet Hill (after Evans 1989, Mercer 1980 and the RCHME).*

4

Activity at the Causewayed Camp

The function of these Early Neolithic enclosures has been a matter of some debate since the excavations at Knap Hill, Wiltshire in 1908. Seven of the best preserved examples were extensively excavated in the period between the First and Second World Wars and in the last twenty years there has been renewed interest with extensive excavations at six enclosures and more restricted sampling at many more. It is clear, however, that in the 80 years since the Knap Hill excavations, archaeologists have come no closer to an agreed interpretation of these monuments. Indeed it sometimes seems that the growth in information simply increases the number of interpretations that can be applied to them.

During the discussion of the excavations of the enclosure at Offham, in Sussex, Peter Drewett identified seven possible functions that had been or could be applied to the enclosures. These were: settlement, defence, cattle compounds, trade centres, communal meeting places, cult/ritual centres and burial sites. Settlement and defence were the favoured interpretations of early archaeologists but their reasoning was dismissed by Stuart Piggott in the fifties who argued that they were cattle compounds. This interpretation was, however, discounted by Isabel Smith when she published the excavations at Windmill Hill in the sixties. She favoured a more complex explanation of a ceremonial centre where people met and conducted trade, thus combining three important functions in one place. Drewett in his assessment, however, could find no evidence that the Sussex enclosures acted as trade centres and he preferred to see all the enclosures as primarily concerned with death and the complex rituals which surround this event. This interpretation

was given some considerable support by the excavations at Hambledon Hill where large numbers of human burials were found. However, in recent years there has been a renewed interest in the original interpretations of defence and settlement and in the most recent synthesis of British prehistory Richard Bradley has argued that these interpretations may be essentially correct.

We have already noted in the previous chapter that human burials were found in the ditch and inside the enclosure at Maiden Castle. By examining the objects recovered from the excavations it should be possible to identify the activities that took place on the hilltop. Large quantities of artefacts were recovered from the enclosure in both the previous and the more recent excavations. This material is, however, limited in its range, for it consisted largely of ceramics, stone tools and animal bone. It is obvious that there would be none of the metal tools of later periods but there are also very few bone tools, clay objects or stone tools other than those made by flaking local flint. Nevertheless the pots and stone tools are very well made. The quality of production and aesthetic of design revealed in a large number of pots is considerably superior to the majority of the pottery in the periods after the Neolithic. Similarly the control that went into the production of the flint tools was also at its peak in this period.

The pottery
The ceramics discovered in the ditches belong to a style of Early Neolithic pottery known as the Hembury or South-Western style (**29**). This style is found on Early Neolithic sites ranging from the walled enclosure of Carn Brea in west Cornwall to the ditched enclosure at Hamble-

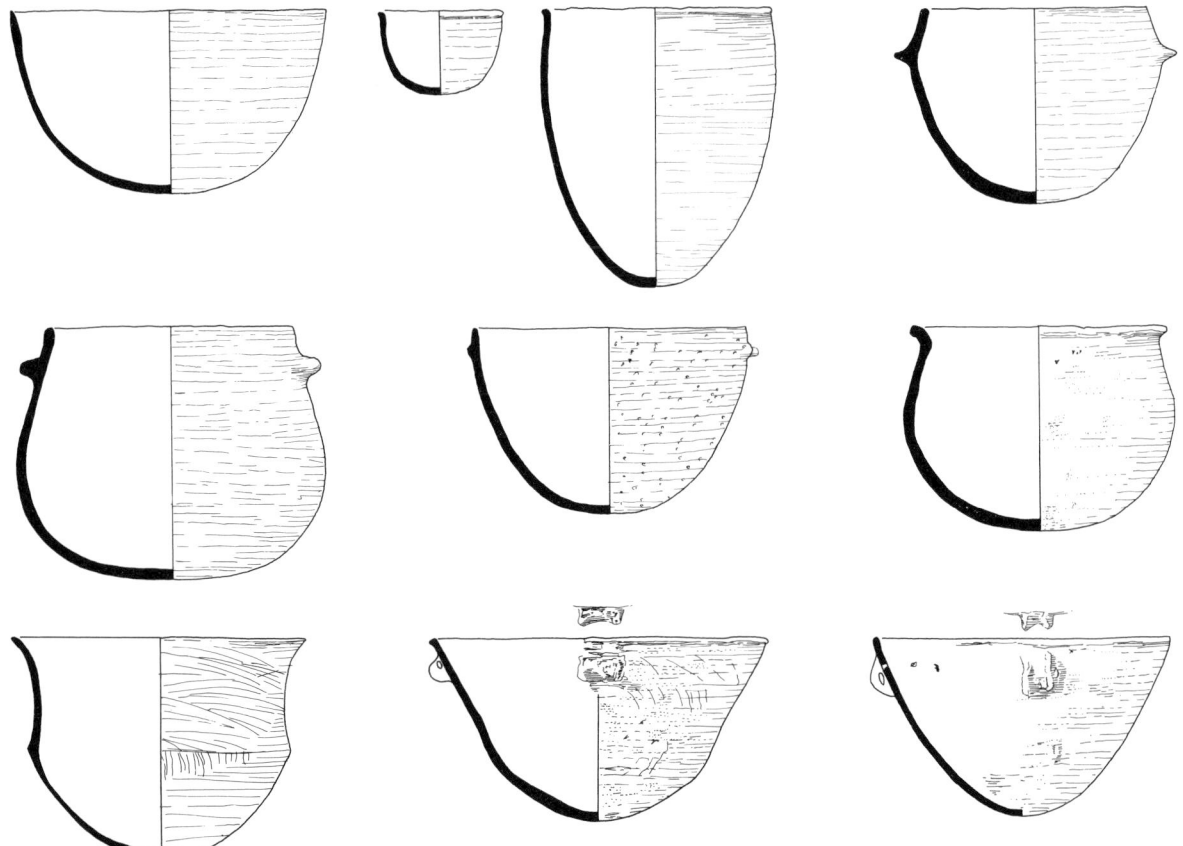

29 *Neolithic pots of the Hembury or South-Western style found at Maiden Castle.*

don Hill in north Dorset and it influenced the assemblages of sites as far away as Windmill Hill in north Wiltshire. Within this large area there are differences between the variety and styles of pottery of particular sites and it is possible to identify an assemblage as coming from a site on the western or eastern edge of the region by a number of features. For instance the number of decorated vessels increases and the number of carinated vessels decreases, at sites towards the eastern end. Nevertheless there are strong similarities between the ceramics used at all, which indicates that they were produced and used as part of a common tradition. There are two other distinct regional styles in southern England: the decorated style of the southeast, which includes Sussex and the Thames Valley enclosures and the eastern or Mildenhall style of East Anglia and the Midlands.

The most important feature of the Early Neolithic pottery from Maiden Castle is that all the vessels have round bases, with shapes ranging from small cups to large globular jars.

The bulk of the vessels (52 per cent) were bag-shaped open bowls and most of the rest (21 per cent) were shallow open bowls. There were only five carinated bowls and six decorated vessels; their decoration would have been almost invisible during the vessels' use. The rims are very simple, they are almost always cut off square or slightly rounded. One of the most distinctive features of the assemblage is the use of stubby handles stuck on to the sides of vessels and known as lugs. Most of these are simple oblong or rounded knobs of clay but some have been perforated which would allow the pot to be suspended from the rafters of a house. A very distinct type of lug known as the trumpet lug is also found at the enclosure, this was restricted to the Hembury style and was carefully shaped.

Most of the pots appear to have been made from local clay, not actually on the hilltop but in its immediate vicinity. The presence of distinctive geological types in the clays of a small number of pots allows a more precise location for the source of the clay used in their manufacture. Several vessels contained fossil shells which came from the area of Burton Bradstock and Shipton Gorge about 14 km (8½ miles) to the west of Maiden Castle. Another group of vessels had a distinct type of calcite which was most likely to come from outcrops of the Purbeck Beds at least 5 km (3 miles) south of Maiden Castle.

The most interesting group of vessels comes from over 215 km (133 miles) to the west of the site. These were made of clay from the Gabbro outcrops of the Lizard peninsula in south Cornwall. Clay from this area was valued for its ability to withstand primitive production techniques and this made it a favoured source throughout the prehistoric period. Vessels made from this clay occur throughout the south-west, but, as might be expected, their importance decreases according to the distance from the production source. In west Cornwall the industries provided all the pots found on the enclosure at Carn Brea but in Wiltshire the enclosure at Windmill Hill had only a few vessels. At Maiden Castle only between 5 and 10 per cent of the vessels were from Cornwall.

The ability to distribute these vessels over such long distances is quite extraordinary, particularly as many of the vessels are enormous. One of the largest bowls found in the recent excavations at Maiden Castle was 28 cm (11 in.) in diameter and would have weighed over 1.5 kg (3.3 lb). If these vessels were distributed direct from the production centres it is likely that they were moved by sea along the coast and then up the river valleys. It is difficult to believe, however, that there were specialized traders in operation at this period and it is more likely that the items were passed between communities as part of the system of reciprocal gift exchange. This was possibly in return for commodities such as cattle or sheep but more probably in ritualized exchanges involving brides or marriage which did not necessarily involve immediate remuneration.

These vessels were distinguished from the rest of the pottery at Maiden Castle by the considerable amount of effort that had gone into their production and finishing. It is possible that their owners would have had considerable prestige in the community. It is noticeable that at the contemporary settlements near Maiden Castle such as Rowden and Flagstones there are no vessels of Gabbroic type. This would suggest that activities taking place at Maiden Castle had more significance than the usual domestic ones and it is possible the site played a pivotal role in the distribution of status goods.

The flint

Very large quantities of stone tools were found in the ditch. Over 21,000 pieces of worked stone were recovered and though most of these were waste (see **32**), discarded after the production of tools, there were about 180 tools which had been carefully worked to a predetermined shape and many of the other flakes were probably also used as tools without being deliberately modified. The most common tool was a flint flake whose sharp edge was modified by very small flaking to create a serrated edge. These were only found in the Early Neolithic enclosure and were probably used with unmodified flakes as the basic cutting tool for butchering animals.

The next most common tool was the scraper which was probably a multi-purpose tool used for woodworking, cleaning hides and a variety of other tasks. The other tools included piercers (probably part of leather working), more elaborate knives, axes, picks, arrowheads, and a large number of pieces of less obvious shapes which could not be allocated a clear function.

The arrowheads (**30**) are important as there is a concentration of these in the enclosure ditch in trench II and from Wheeler's excavation in the same area. Most of these were broken, and the manner in which the breakage occurred indicates that it was as a result of their use. It suggests the enclosure at Maiden Castle was attacked by archers. This might seem a rather extreme hypothesis on the basis of a few broken arrowheads but it does fit into a pattern known from the other causewayed enclosures. Extensive excavations at Crickley Hill in Gloucestershire recovered large numbers of arrowheads along a palisade just inside the ditch, with a concentration around the entrance. At Hambledon Hill extensive excavation revealed that the site was fortified by large banks which were pulled down after an assault on the hilltop. In the enclosure ditch, sealed by the rubble of the collapsed rampart, was a defender killed by an arrow whose flint head was found next to his backbone (**31**). In the arms of the defender was a child crushed by his fall.

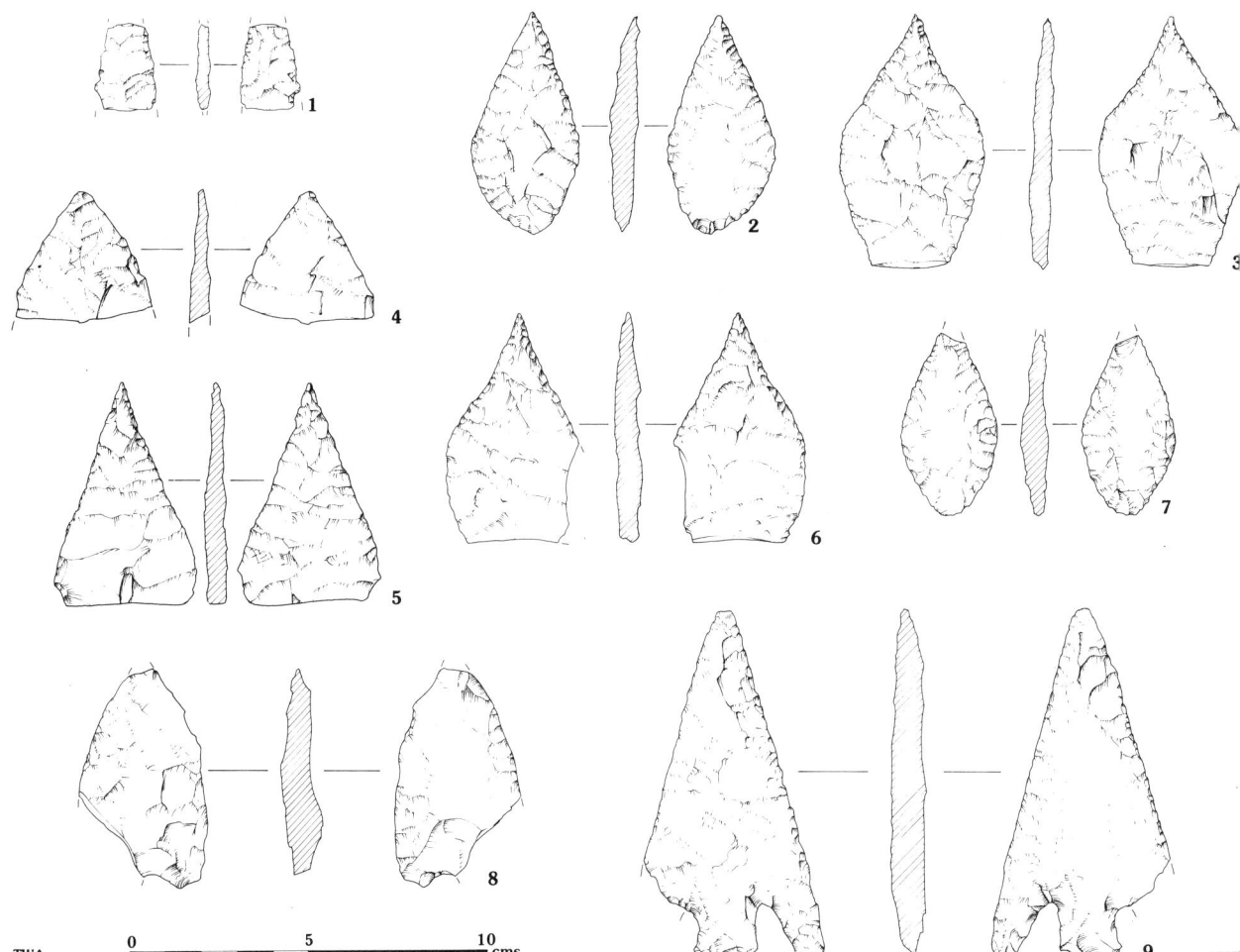

30 *Arrowheads found during the recent excavations. The high proportion of broken leaf arrowheads suggests that the enclosure might have been attacked.*

It is likely that more extensive excavations at Maiden Castle would reveal similar evidence for a major confrontation on the site. The developing importance of warfare in the Early Neolithic period is emphasized by the design of the arrowheads. These were very different from those of the earlier period, which were composite with many barbs, and the later arrowheads, which had a very wide cutting edge. Both of these would have been most effective when hunting animals. The former would stay in an animal and slow down its escape, the latter would cut a wide gash in an animal to make it bleed to death. The leaf shape of the Neolithic arrowhead does not make sense as a hunting implement and could only be designed for warfare and killing people.

Most of the flint found at Maiden Castle was waste from the production of tools (**32**). The

amount recovered suggests that the hilltop was a focus for a considerable amount of production activity. The bulk of the flint was collected in the immediate vicinity of the site either from shallow pits dug into the chalk or from surface collection on the tertiary gravels. A detailed analysis of the waste indicates what was produced at the enclosure. One of the most important activities on the site was the preparation of cores from which tools could be manufactured. Most of these appear to have been taken away from the site and it is likely they were distributed to settlements in the immediate vicinity.

31 *A young man found in the ditch of the Neolithic enclosure at Hambledon Hill. He appears to have been killed by an arrow and collapsed onto a child.*

32 *Flint waste. This occurred in enormous quantities in the midden filling the inner ditch of the Causewayed Camp and probably results from the production of axes.*

The cores would be used to produce tools as and when they were needed. Another process taking place on the site was the production of large tools, most probably axes (**33**). Large numbers of these were broken in the final stage of production and were discarded at the enclosure.

The assemblage from the enclosure can be compared with some contemporary assemblages from excavations in south Dorset. At Rowden on the Ridgeway (**34**) a pit was found which contained large quantities of flint debris from the production of cores. There was no evidence for the production of axes, however,

33 *Flint and stone axes from the Causewayed Camp.*

34 *An aerial view of the Bronze Age house at Rowden on the South Dorset Ridgeway. On the edge of the trench is a large Early Neolithic pit which produced an assemblage of pottery and flint.*

and there were few tools or implements which would indicate domestic activity. In contrast a pit found on the edge of the South Winterborne valley (actually within the hillfort but well outside the Neolithic enclosure) contained a large number of flakes which were clearly intended, or had been used, as tools. There was no evidence for the primary flaking debris necessary for the creation of these tools.

On the basis of these three sites it is possible to suggest a threefold division of activity. 'Consumption' took place when tools were used and discarded, such as in the settlement indicated by the pit at Maiden Castle; production, when tools (or more precisely blanks for the production of tools) were created, is indicated by the pit at Rowden. The more restricted and prestigious activity of making axes was carried out only in enclosures such as Maiden Castle, though here tools were also used (consumed) and produced.

It is perhaps significant that the only stone tools on site that were not made of flint were axes (see **33**). Seventeen axes have been found and ten of them can be traced to four specific sources in Cornwall. Three of these came from two sources at the western end of Cornwall on the north coast near Camborne, but most came from a source on the eastern edge of the county at Balstone Down near Callington. This is a rather rare source but axes from it are found at the Early Neolithic settlements of High Peak, South Cadbury and the enclosure at Hembury. They are always found in association with axes from the sources at the western end of Cornwall.

The discovery of these axes confirms the suggestion that the enclosure had an important role in the exchange of commodities. It is interesting to note, however, that though the axes and the Gabbroic pottery are both from Cornwall, they are not from the same region. Indeed it is noticeable that the one type of axe produced close to the Gabbroic source of pottery is not generally found in these Early Neolithic enclosures. This production centre, in Mounts Bay, was only of local importance in this period but became very important in the Late Neolithic. This could be taken as an indication that the distribution of Gabbroic pottery was not by means of trade as such but by a more complex interrelationship of gift transfer which can move goods gradually across many miles by small-scale inter-group exchange.

The only other tools associated with the Early Neolithic occupation were three saddle quern fragments and a handful of simple bone points. The latter were probably used for leather working and the former were used to grind seeds into flour ready for baking. Both indicate that a range of strictly domestic activities took place in the enclosure and that it was not only connected with more elaborate purposes of exchange and ritual.

The animal bones
Another frequent discovery in the midden layers of the enclosure ditch were animal bones. Cut marks from stone tools, such as the serrated blades mentioned above, were found on many bones and suggest they largely derive from food preparation. The animals were first skinned then the backbone and rear end were cut off and the major meat-bearing bones filleted. The bones were also heavily fragmented probably because they were broken to extract marrow. All of the butchery took place on site and the animals must have arrived on the hoof.

The most important animals were cattle which contributed up to 52 per cent of the bones recovered from the recent excavations. The only other domestic species were sheep and pig and they contributed 26 per cent and 17 per cent of the bones recovered. Cattle would be even more important when one takes into consideration that the amount of meat provided by the carcass was considerably more than that provided by a sheep or a pig. Similar considerations would indicate that pig and sheep provided roughly the same amount of meat.

Judging by the bones recovered and examined, it might appear that wild animals were not of great importance to the economy. Bones of red deer, roe deer and wild cattle were present but only in small quantities. It is possible, however, that these animals were more important than the bones suggest as the animals may have been butchered where they were killed and only the meat brought to the enclosure. Red deer were certainly valued for their antlers, which were brought to the enclosure to be used in the production of tools.

Most of the cattle and sheep were relatively old animals (over 3–4 years) and this suggests that they were not simply kept as a source of meat. The cattle could be milked and the sheep could provide wool. It is, however, important to note that the quality of the fleece on the sheep of this period may not have been high: the proportion of wool to hair may well have been such that wool production was unlikely to be of great significance. It has also been argued that milk would not be important as the taste for animals' milk, or even the ability to drink it, was only acquired later in human history. It is often forgotten that many races are physically incapable of drinking milk. There is, however, no clear reason why northern Europeans should have acquired a taste for milk after the Neolithic, moreover milk could have been turned into butter and cheese which are palatable to almost everyone.

The crops

One of the primary objectives of the recent excavations was the recovery of crop remains from the enclosure. These only survive if they have become carbonized and the quantities of charcoal visible in the ditch suggested that the excavation might recover enough to allow an analysis of the arable agriculture of the community. This charcoal, however, was almost exclusively from trees and from the sieving of 2262 litres (about 80 cu. ft) of soil (35)

only 631 seeds were identified. This was a disappointingly low total, and significantly lower than that from the Iron Age deposits (see p. 102).

The assemblage recovered consisted of roughly equal quantities of cereals, edible weeds and hazelnuts and can be characterized as a sort of prehistoric muesli. The cereals included bread wheat and naked and hulled barley but emmer wheat was the dominant species. The weed assemblage contained a narrow range of species but these came from a wide variety of habitats. Some of the seeds such as those from Atriplex Littoralis (Shore orache) were brought to the site from the coastal lowlands, presumably around Weymouth, and again indicate the extensive contacts of the occupants of the enclosure. The main species were Chenopodiaceae (such as fat hen) and

35 *Sieving soil on the hilltop. Only by washing soil through very fine mesh sieves is it possible to recover the small seeds and plant remains which tell us about the vegetable diet of the inhabitants.*

Polygonaceae (such as knot grass). These could have been collected as food stuffs but it is more likely that they were the accidental inclusions from the cultivation of weed infested garden plots.

However it is not so much what is present as what is missing from the assemblage that is of interest. There is no sign of the chaff fragments which have to be removed by threshing and winnowing the crop and which dominate the assemblage of plant remains found in the Iron Age. It is possible that these more fragile remains have decayed so far as to become unrecognizable but it is more likely that they were never present on the site and that unlike the animals the crops arrived at the enclosure in a cleaned state, ready for the final stages of food preparation.

It is difficult to compare the importance of cereals and animals in the economy of these early agricultural settlers as their recovery and deposition are the result of completely different processes. Every animal which is culled leaves a physical record of its existence, since the skeleton is seldom completely used. Cereals, however, if exploited efficiently will be totally destroyed (the chaff may not be eaten by humans but does make good animal fodder or fuel). Despite this potential imbalance in the archaeological record, it could be suggested that crops were much less important than animals – cattle in particular. If this is true, it has a major impact on how the society of these early farmers should be interpreted. A cattle-based economy is likely to be much more mobile than one concentrated on cereal production. This might explain the rapid colonization of the British Isles at the beginning of the Neolithic. It would also explain why it is so difficult to locate settlements or houses belonging to the Early Neolithic.

The function of Early Neolithic enclosures
Consideration of the function of the Early Neolithic enclosures such as that at Maiden Castle should start out from three basic assumptions, against which the evidence can be tested. To begin with, let us assume that it is inappropriate to expect such enclosures to have a single purpose. It is likely that they had a variety of uses and that each function was given different emphasis or importance by different groups in the surrounding community. Second, it is also inappropriate to think that all enclosures were

expected to fulfil the same function. Some might be more important than others and the environmental and cultural differences that distinguish the Neolithic in Dorset from that in the Midlands would make geographical distinctions likely also. Finally it is likely that the activities carried out in the enclosures changed during their lifetime. The Early Neolithic lasted for over a thousand years and this would be sufficient time for considerable transformation of the economy and society to take place.

The evidence from Maiden Castle certainly indicates that the first assumption is correct. The enclosure contains evidence for many different functions. Burials indicate the importance of rituals at death; exotic imports such as Gabbroic pottery and Cornish axes indicate trade was important and large quantities of domestic refuse such as butchered bones and broken tools indicate settlement. The other suggested uses of the enclosure discussed at the beginning of this chapter are less specific and it is difficult to confirm or deny their importance. The presence of items from the coast and from areas to the east and west of Maiden Castle suggest that it was a meeting place for the surrounding communities as does the quantity of waste from food consumption. It is difficult to believe the enclosure had a mainly defensive function even though the discovery of arrowheads indicates some connection with warlike activities. It is, however, quite possible that a palisade or more substantial defences, such as those at Hambledon, were present but have been missed by the very limited excavations. The large numbers of cattle bones present could also indicate that the enclosure was a cattle compound but only temporarily before the cattle were slaughtered for consumption.

It is also clear from a cursory examination of the other enclosures in southern England that the quantity and quality of evidence from Maiden Castle is exceptional. Many sites have been much more extensively excavated and yet have produced only small quantities of material. The best example is the enclosure at Offham in Sussex. About a quarter of this enclosure was excavated and yet under 7000 flint flakes and 171 sherds of pottery were recovered (the figures from Maiden Castle were 21,000 and 1143 respectively). Similar low quantities of material were recovered from the enclosures of Haddenham in Cambridgeshire and Orsett in Essex. The evidence suggests that only a few enclosures, such as Maiden Castle, Windmill Hill in north Wiltshire and Staines in the Thames Valley, were centres of a range of activities and that sites with limited and restricted uses were more common.

Evidence for the historical development of the enclosure at Maiden Castle indicates that there was a major change during the Early Neolithic. A range of radiocarbon dates (36) was obtained from material recovered from the enclosure. The primary fills of the ditch, which contained large quantities of charcoal and most of the human burials but very little occupation debris, were dated to between 3900 and 3700 BC (3100–2950 bc). The secondary ditch fills, which contained the rich midden layers, were dated to between 3700 and 3500 BC (2950–2725 bc).

It is obviously difficult to generalize about the activities taking place in any enclosure simply on the basis of the material deposited in its ditch, and this is particularly true for Maiden

Castle where such a small area was excavated. Nevertheless generalizations are necessary to make any sense of the evidence we have from the Neolithic and there does appear to be an indication of changing use through the period of its occupation. Initially the enclosure was used only sporadically and activity inside it was restricted and, as suggested by the burials, probably of a religious nature. Later the enclosure became more important and was a focus for a variety of activities. The amount of domestic

36 *A diagram showing the distribution of radiocarbon dates from Maiden Castle. (A) the earliest fills of the inner Causewayed Camp ditch; (B) the midden filling of the inner Causewayed Camp ditch; (C) the fill of the outer Causewayed Camp ditch; (D) the early fills of the Bank Barrow ditch; (E) the bank; (F) the Late Neolithic and Early Bronze Age occupation.*

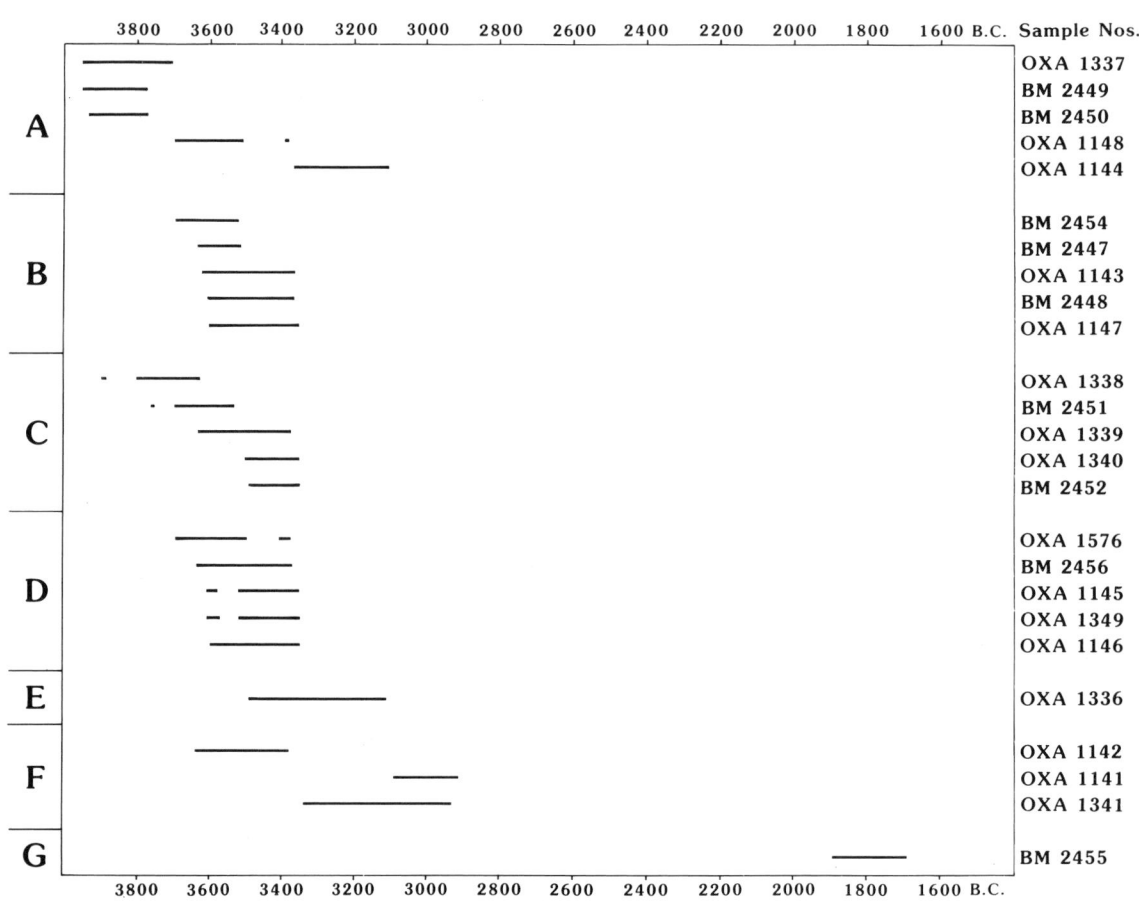

debris deposited in the ditches in this phase may indicate that the enclosure was continuously occupied. The absence of traces of permanent houses should not be treated as conclusive as these are very rarely discovered in Neolithic settlements. During this period the occupants of the enclosure controlled the exchange of exotic items (such as pottery and axes) and the production of many everyday tools.

The sequence at Maiden Castle can also be used to explain the differences noted above between enclosures such as Offham which had very little material deposited in the ditches, and those such as Maiden Castle and Windmill Hill, which were rich in artefacts. The latter appear to have started life with a restricted function but then acquired a more important role not achieved by all the enclosures. It is not clear if the lesser enclosures were abandoned when the enclosures with richer deposits became important. It is possible they continued to carry out their original role but they may have been deserted.

The early enclosures were widely distributed in the landscape and it is possible that all the areas with substantial Neolithic clearances would have contained one. This is certainly suggested by the dense concentrations in Sussex and north Wiltshire but it would imply that in other areas of southern England, such as Dorset, many enclosures are still to be discovered. These enclosures may have been created early in the Neolithic colonization of southern England to establish, through rituals such as those of burial, a series of internal relationships that would bind dispersed families into a community. As these farming communities became more established and secure, the small number of enclosures where occupation became increasingly complex and varied indicate that some communities were becoming more important. It is likely that this pre-eminence followed a period of competition between communities indicated by the increasing importance of prestige goods (such as imported stone axes and pottery). The later enclosures would have served more to regulate relationships between the different communities than to emphasize existing positions of relative status within a community centred on the enclosure itself. It is likely that external relationships were conducted by means of important rituals which will have included the exchange of high quality or status gifts or goods. The increasing importance of the relationships between communities would be a natural result of the increase in population during the Neolithic.

Conclusion

This chapter began with an examination of the interpretations that archaeologists had formerly suggested for Early Neolithic enclosures. An examination of the range of material recovered from Maiden Castle indicates that most if not all of these functions could have been carried out here, though possibly not all at the same time. This evidence does not, however, necessarily explain the creation of the enclosure. It is clear that many of the activities that occurred in the enclosure were also carried out elsewhere.

The primary purpose of the enclosures was to define an area separate from both the domestic landscape of the settlement and the wilderness of the forest. Once they had been so defined, what went on in these enclosures is likely to have become of greater significance because of this location: any such transformation will have been mostly symbolic, and not detectable in the archaeological record. One might suggest, for example, that the circularity and concentricity of the enclosure was a physical representation of the Neolithic settlers' view of their relationship with the outside world – a central settled domestic area surrounded by zones of partially domesticated land and then by undifferentiated wilderness. If this, albeit highly speculative, hypothesis is correct, it would explain the focus on the independence of each community; an independence which would have been seriously threatened when expansion brought adjacent communities into direct contact with each other. It is not surprising therefore that there are signs of an increase in warlike activities at the enclosures, and that they were eventually abandoned.

5

South Dorset 3500-700 BC

The abandonment of the enclosure at Maiden Castle appears to have been a relatively sudden event. It was possibly the result of the violent attack indicated by the broken arrowheads in the ditch but we do not have the evidence of deliberate destruction which was found at the enclosures of Hambledon Hill and Carn Brea. After the last layer of midden had been dumped in the ditch there was a period of between thirty and fifty years when the ditches remained untouched and were grassed over. It is likely, however, that during this period the hilltop retained some importance as the next major monument built in this region, the Bank Barrow, was built over the enclosure.

The Bank Barrow
The Bank Barrow (37) is one of the most unusual monuments known from the Neolithic period

and is unique within the British Isles. It consists of a mound of earth about 546 m (1790 ft) long which was thrown up between two parallel ditches set 19.5 m (60 ft) apart. The mound extends from just north of the western entrance to the fort, to the break in slope south of the Roman temple (38).

The Bank Barrow started life as a much smaller long barrow situated just outside the

37 The Bank Barrow: (A) A general plan showing the extent of Wheeler's excavations; (B) A section across the Bank Barrow where it overlies the Causewayed Camp ditch and underlies the Early Iron Age rampart; (C) The area extensively excavated by Wheeler at the east end of the Bank Barrow.

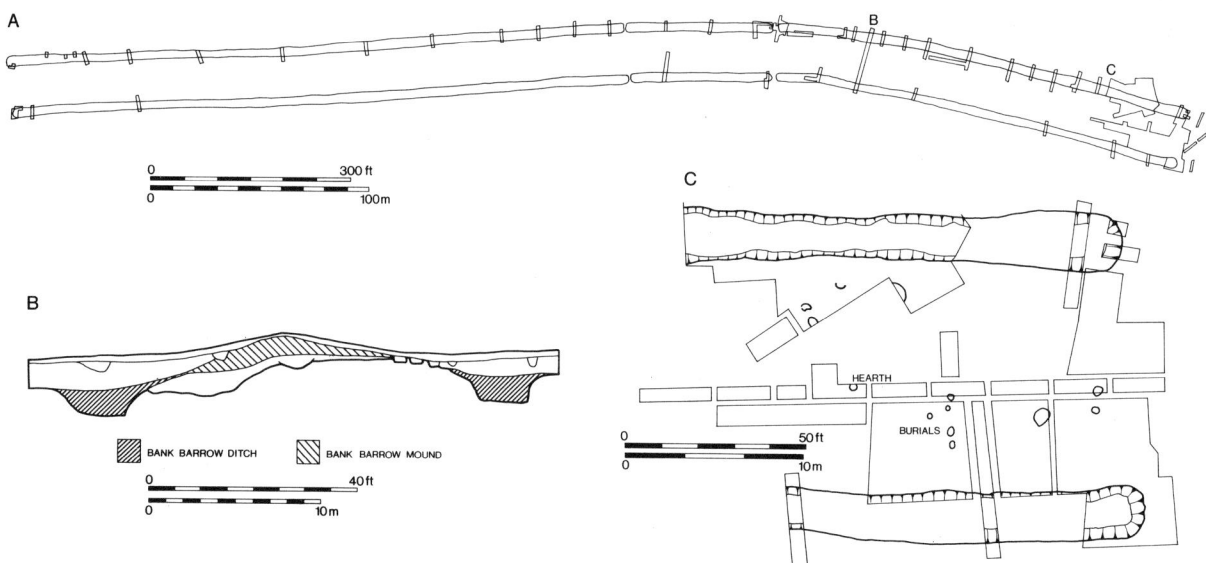

western edge of the enclosure. Barrows similar to this (see **16**) were common throughout southern England and their distribution in south Dorset was shown in chapter 2 to indicate the areas of Early Neolithic settlement. They were constructed over a period of *c.* 500 years starting around the end of the fifth millennium BC (*c.* 3200 bc).

Such barrows were substantial earthen monuments, built over small wooden structures which contained the remains of human burials. It is common to find bones representing several individuals all jumbled together in these structures, only rarely are there complete skeletons. This suggests that bodies must have decayed to a skeletal state before they were deposited in the barrows. The discovery of human bones in enclosures such as the one underlying Maiden Castle and the close relationship of barrows and enclosures suggests that the bodies may have been allowed to decompose at these enclosures. Even though these early barrows are closely

38 *An aerial view of Maiden Castle in 1937. The distribution of Wheeler's excavation trenches highlights the position of the northern ditch of the Bank Barrow.*

associated with human burials it is unlikely that the primary purpose of the mound was as a receptacle for the dead. The burials were never very numerous and could only be a very small percentage of the dead from any community. It is more appropriate to think of these burials as a token which represented the ancestors of a community. They then acted as a marker which symbolized ownership or the right to exploit a certain area of land. The spirits of the ancestors would have played a very important role in the rituals which punctuated the everyday business of subsistence for these early agriculturalists.

There appear to be two distinct types of long barrow in the later part of the Early Neolithic – a time when Maiden Castle was becoming an

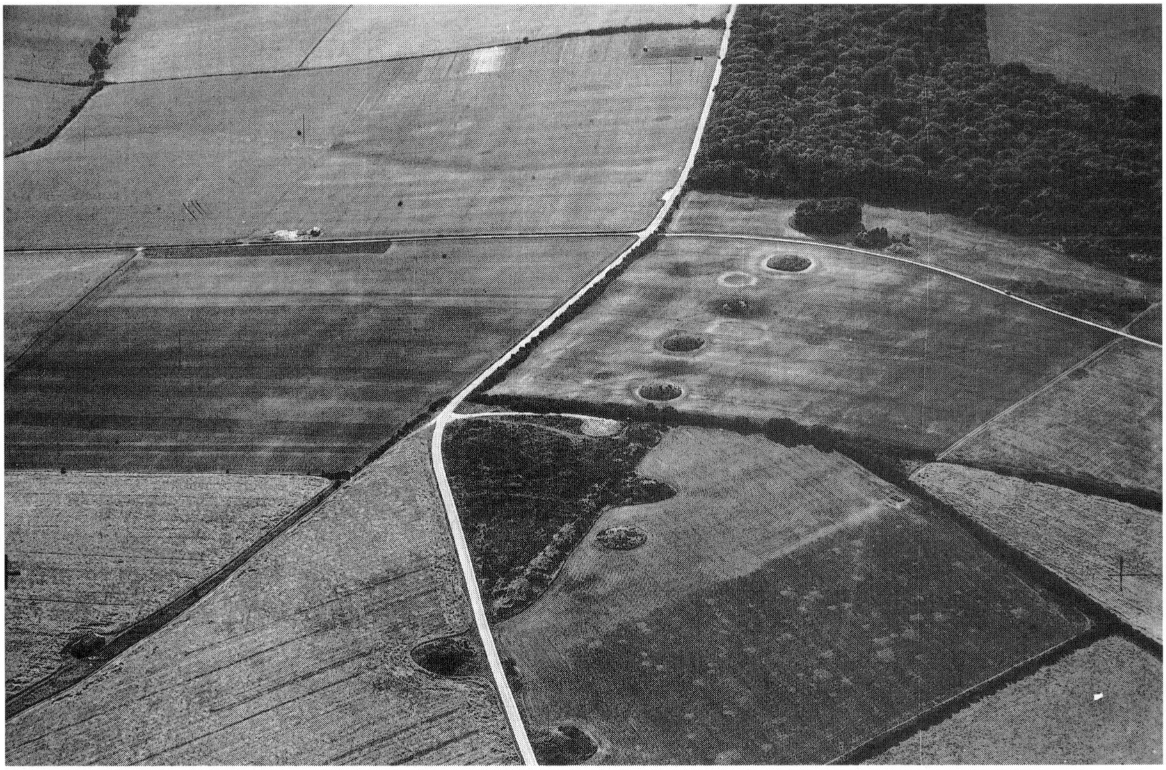

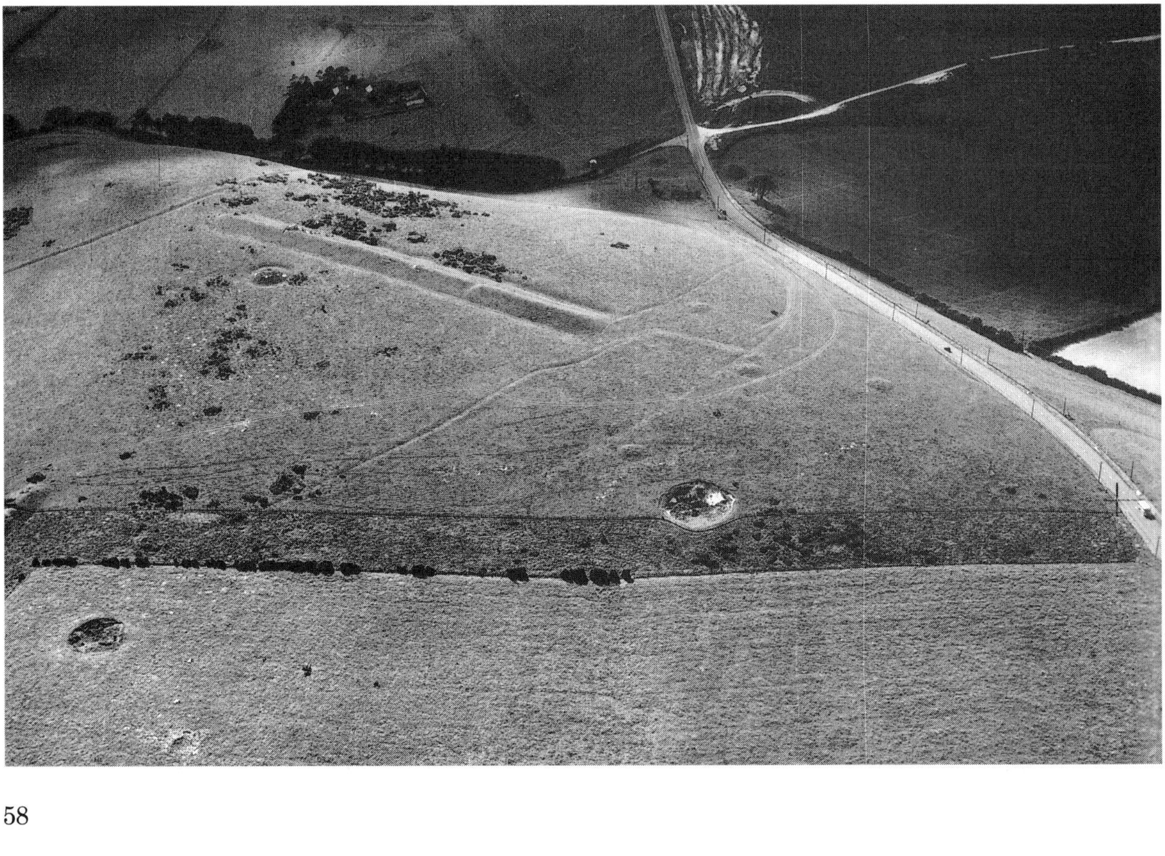

important centre for surrounding communities. Small long barrows, which cover graves containing individual burials, may mark the burial of important members of the community and indicate the development of a hierarchy. Large long barrows, which do not cover any burials, probably mark the territorial boundaries of these communities. The larger barrows are probably the precursors of the Bank Barrow at Maiden Castle. The size of this monument, however, suggests that it can be linked to another contemporary monument type – the 'cursus'. These are found throughout southern Britain in association with clusters of Late

Neolithic monuments and until recently it was thought that they were built in the Late Neolithic period. Recent excavations have shown, however, that several examples date from the end of the Early Neolithic and this would make them contemporary with the Bank Barrow at Maiden Castle.

Though the Bank Barrow is of exceptional size, there are two other similar smaller sites in south Dorset, at Broadmayne (**39**) and Long Bredy (**40**). These barrows were situated at the east and west end of the South Dorset Ridgeway, which would later attract a dense concentration of Bronze Age round barrows (**41**). The ridge actually continues both east and west of these points but it is not such a clearly defined feature and has less archaeological prominence. Maiden Castle lay to the north of the Ridgeway, roughly equidistant between it and the River Frome which also became the focus for Late Neolithic activity.

The location of these three barrows suggests that they may have been used to define different zones in the landscape: an upland area; the South Dorset Ridgeway; and an area of lowland,

39 *(left) An aerial view of the Broadmayne Bank Barrow.*

40 *(below left) An aerial view of the Bank Barrow at Long Bredy.*

41 *(below) The distribution of Late Neolithic and Early Bronze Age monuments and settlements around Maiden Castle.*

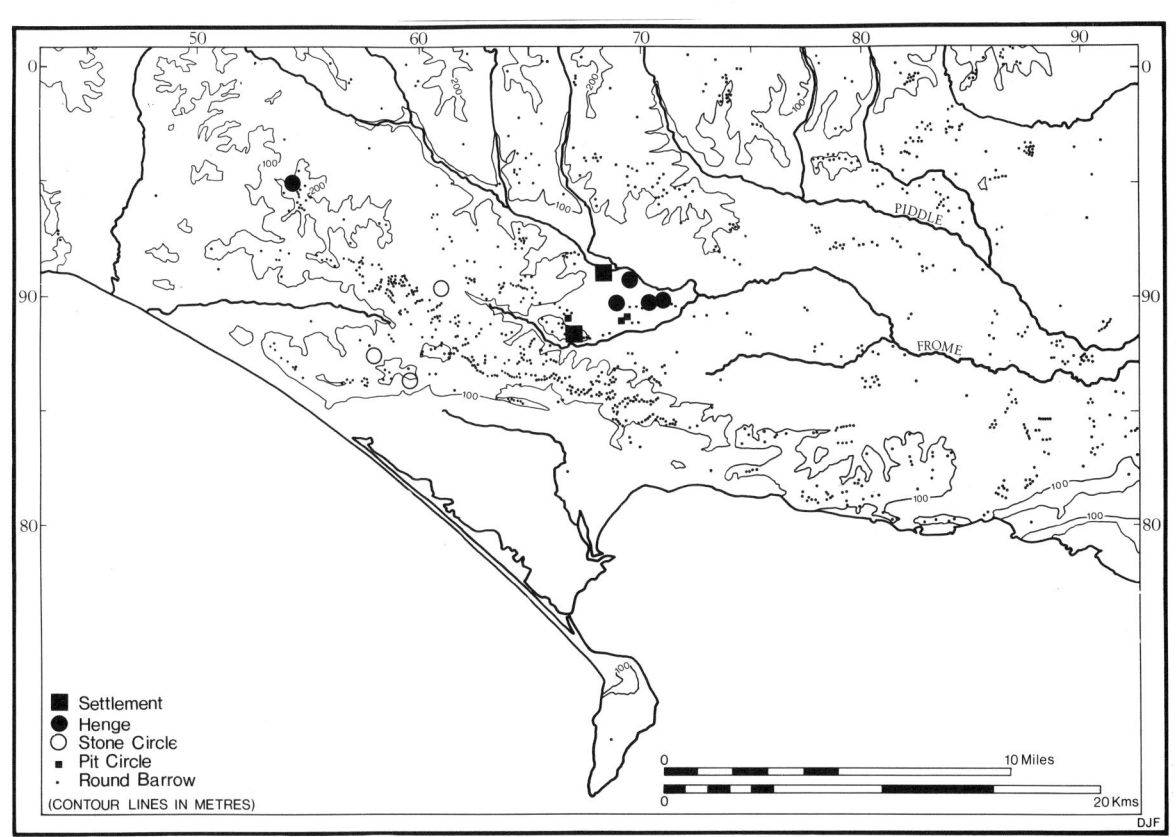

Settlement
Henge
Stone Circle
Pit Circle
Round Barrow
(CONTOUR LINES IN METRES)

the valley of the Frome. This marks a departure from the original role of the hilltop at Maiden Castle as a focus for the surrounding communities. The division of the landscape indicated by the Bank Barrow crystalized the way in which the landscape was organized for the next thousand years.

A similar division of the landscape can be seen in the cluster of Neolithic sites around Cranborne Chase. Here the cursus, which is a much more extended monument, acts as a physical barrier which separates an area of upland on Cranborne Chase from an area of lowland around the River Allen. The difference in the size of the monuments at the two locations may reflect the differences in scale of the topography. In south Dorset the landscape features are topographically well defined but the differences on Cranborne Chase are not nearly so clear.

The Late Neolithic

In the 500 years after the construction of the Bank Barrow there are good reasons for suggesting that the hilltop lay on a boundary and that activity there was restricted and sporadic. The flanking ditches of the Bank Barrow (see **13**) were filled through natural soil processes and there was little evidence of occupation. Only a scatter of flint debris was present and this resulted from the production of tools used in the excavation of the ditches and their subsequent breakage.

Analysis of the microscopic remains of the natural fauna, snails and rodents, and also of what remains of the flora, provides some indication of what was happening on the hilltop at this time. The species of snail which have open country as their normal habitat were relatively abundant in the base of the ditch of the Bank Barrow, but as the ditch fills up these species disappear and species which require shaded conditions become dominant. This indicates that when the barrow was constructed the hilltop had been cleared, either through grazing or cultivation, but that soon afterwards vegetation was allowed to regenerate and the hilltop was either covered in woodland or rank grass and shrubs.

Similar changes are indicated by the finds of small rodent bones. During the period of use of the enclosure the number of species was relatively restricted, only field and bank voles were common. In the ditches of the Bank Barrow,

however, practically all the species native to the British Isles were present: field and bank vole, common and Pygmy shrew and field mouse, and there were also grass snakes. This diversity of fauna shows that the hilltop was not inhabited. It also gives a picture of a varied vegetation cover which is quite different from that of the original natural woodland.

The evidence for the actual trees and plants that grew on the hilltop during this period is very limited as it is only when these plants are carbonized, normally in domestic fires, that they appear in the archaeological record. As human activity is rare in this period, plant remains are rare too. Analysis of the charcoals (see **15**) found in the ditch do, however, confirm the pattern of the animal bones. The species present in the Early Neolithic are those expected to be dominant in primary woodland and they are also those species which would have been actively sought out for buildings and fuel: ash and oak. In the Late Neolithic, species which are common in clearings and areas of secondary woodland, and which are relatively unimportant for human subsistence – hawthorn, blackthorn and hazel – dominate the assemblage; the presence of yew, dogwood, barberry and blackberry/rose also indicates a more open woodland.

The Dorchester monuments

This period of apparent abandonment at Maiden Castle is in marked contrast to what was happening not far to the north on the edge of the valley of the Frome. Intensive examination of many monuments and environmental contexts in this area indicate that the woodland was completely cleared at this time. The evidence from the analysis of snail shells is particularly clear, as the dominant species indicate open conditions, probably cultivated areas, while those which prefer shaded environments are almost completely absent. Examination of the buried soils suggests that cultivation was much more extensive than had previously been thought. Wind-blown soil accumulated in many ditches and could only be derived from the widespread erosion of arable fields.

Evidence for Early Neolithic settlement and monuments in this area was limited to a few pits and an isolated long barrow. In the Late Neolithic period the situation is very different. Several settlements have been identified in the recent field survey (though only one, at Poundbury, has been excavated) and there are large numbers of monuments. The number, size and types of monuments in the area around Dorchester is only paralleled by the rich complexes at Stonehenge and Avebury. Indeed it is a striking feature of these ceremonial centres that they all contain a similar combination of different elements even though the monuments are all themselves unique. Most of the sites are enclosures of some sort but they can be split into three categories by their size. The manner in which the enclosure is defined is also important.

Each region has one large enclosure, up to 472 m (1548 ft) in diameter, defined by a single bank and an internal ditch which can be up to 10 m (33 ft) deep. In the Stonehenge area, the enclosure is Durrington Walls, while at Avebury it is the main circle. The latter is still well preserved, and provides the best example of how these sites originally appeared. In the Dorchester area, Mount Pleasant was very similar to these two, but it has now been ploughed virtually flat, and it is difficult to appreciate its original form.

Several smaller enclosures defined by ditches, pits or stones, belonged both inside and outside these large enclosures (**42**). Inside the enclosure at Mount Pleasant there is a ditched enclosure, 21.5 m (70 ft) in diameter, which enclosed multiple rings of posts. Similar post structures are known within Durrington Walls and immediately outside it was Woodhenge a ditched enclosure with a very complicated sequence of post circles. It is not known whether similar subdivisions existed inside Avebury, as there have been only limited excavations, but a similar complicated series of post circles was found at the Sanctuary, 2.5 km (1½ miles) to the south-east. In the Dorchester region several

42 *Comparative plans of the small enclosures and stone and post circles at Mount Pleasant (Dorchester); Durrington Walls and Woodhenge (near Stonehenge); and the Sanctuary (near Avebury) (after Wainwright 1979 and Malone 1989).*

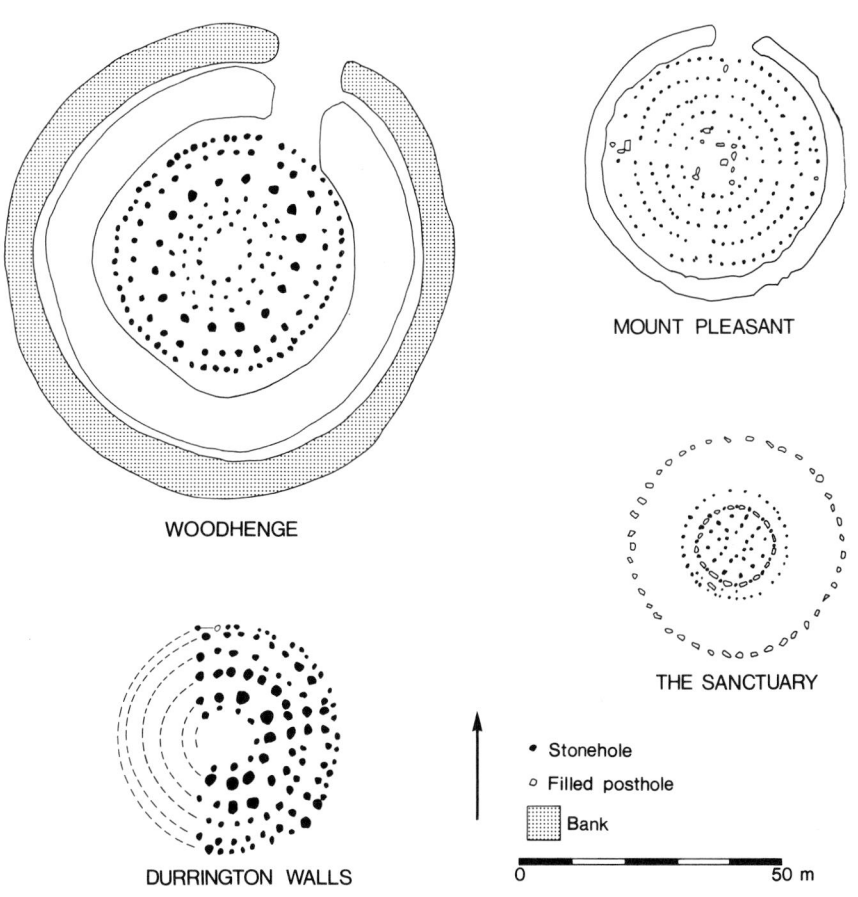

WOODHENGE

MOUNT PLEASANT

DURRINGTON WALLS

THE SANCTUARY

- Stonehole
- ○ Filled posthole
- ▨ Bank

0   50 m

other small pit circles which may have served similar functions have been discovered.

Enclosures lying between these two extremes in size are also common. There are two in the Dorchester area: a pit circle, 100 m (328 ft) in diameter, at Flagstones (43) (within which Max Gate, the house built by Thomas Hardy, was constructed) and a ditched enclosure, 51.5 m (168 ft) in diameter, which lies under the Roman amphitheatre at Maumbury Rings (44). These are similar in size to the ditch around Stonehenge and another enclosure on Coneybrae Hill which lies to the south of Stonehenge. In the Avebury area enclosures of this size are not yet known though it would be possible to compare them to the stone circles inside the large enclosure. The fact that such sites have not been identified at Avebury may be attributed to the lack of any large scale excavations in and around the henge there.

At Stonehenge and Avebury there are also important linear monuments which appear to define processional approaches to the enclosures. The most obvious of these is the stone

43 An aerial view of the Late Neolithic enclosure at Flagstones, Dorchester.

avenue which leads from the Sanctuary to the eastern entrance of Avebury. The ditches of the comparable avenue which lead from the Avon to the entrance to Stonehenge are also visible in places. There is no evidence for such an avenue in Dorchester but it is possible that one awaits discovery under the town.

Barrows – burial mounds – are another feature of all these areas. At Dorchester the earliest monument in the complex was the long barrow at Allington Avenue and both Stonehenge and Avebury were at the centre of distinct clusters of long barrows. Late Neolithic round barrows are also present and these, unlike the long barrows, appear to be primarily burial monuments. Dorchester has the best fully-excavated examples in the barrow at Fordington Farm.

Each of these areas, however, has one unique monument which was probably originally the

44 *An aerial view of the Roman amphitheatre at Maumbury Rings. The shape of this enclosure was dictated by the Neolithic henge on which it was built. (Crown copyright/MOD.)*

most important or the most time-consuming to create. Even these, however, are all elaborate versions of a familiar monument type. The most obvious example – perhaps the most famous prehistoric monument in the British Isles – is Stonehenge, which is a stone circle quite unlike any other in the complexity of its design and the size and shape of the stones used. Similarly Silbury Hill near Avebury is an earthen barrow but it is 40 m (130 ft) high and covers an area of 2.2 ha (5¼ acres). The most elaborate monument in the Dorchester area is the timber circle under the town (**45** and **46**). This has only been partially exposed by recent rescue excavations and the area it enclosed is unknown. The enclosure was defined by a continuous line of posts about 1 m (3 ft) in diameter and spaced 1 m (3 ft) apart. Hundreds of these enormous posts

(which could have been over 5 m (16 ft) tall) were required. They would have to be cut down, dressed, transported and erected. This was an enormous feat of civil engineering and social organization.

We know as much about the monuments in the Dorchester area as we know of any other region but it is still difficult to understand how they functioned and why they were constructed. Some points are clear however. Most of the monuments existed simultaneously but some were short lived while others had a very long life. Of the five sites which have been dated by radiocarbon analysis of organic remains, Flagstones, Allington Avenue, Mount Pleasant, Greyhound Yard and Maumbury Rings, all but the long barrow at Allington Avenue, have returned dates of around 2500 BC (2000 bc). Similar dates are recorded for many of the monuments around Stonehenge and Avebury. The relative longevity of some monuments is indicated by their repeated reconstruction: Mount Pleasant has radiocarbon dates which indicate that it was an important focus for over

five hundred years. It does seem, however, that some sites had a short life. The clearest example of this is the Flagstones enclosure where the pits were deliberately backfilled almost immediately after the enclosure was created.

It is therefore possible to suggest that the smaller enclosures were relatively short-lived centres which were deliberately erased, but that the larger enclosures and the barrows were reused and altered to adapt to changing attitudes and beliefs. This must partly be a reflection of the scale of the monuments. It would have been difficult to ignore something the size of Mount Pleasant but this might also have been a feature which was important to the original creators. Certain monuments may have been created to serve an ongoing purpose, and were therefore in use for centuries but others were created with more limited aims in view.

Barrows and settlement

Contemporary with the later use of these enclosures were large numbers of round barrows. These cover and commemorate burials

45 An aerial view of the Trust for Wessex Archaeology's excavations at Greyhound Yard, Dorchester in 1984. The large post holes of the enclosure which underlies the town are clearly visible in the centre of the excavated area.

and are an indication of the importance that was placed on death within the community. Burials of this period are normally single inhumations placed in pits at the centre of the barrow and they are often accompanied by grave goods which give some indication of the status of the deceased. Among the most significant objects deposited in these graves were pots which belong to the distinctive class of vessels known as beakers. These are distributed throughout western Europe and were introduced to the British Isles from the Continent. They are high quality ceramics which were elaborately decorated in very distinctive styles; this suggests that originally they were used to represent and symbolize ties between certain groups on the Continent and groups in Britain.

The development of contact between Britain

46 One of the large pits which were dug to hold the posts forming the enclosure at Greyhound Yard, Dorchester.

and the Continent may have been used by individuals to control trade and achieve status within the local community. The frequent presence of arrowheads and archers' wristguards in graves which contain beakers suggests that these individuals were a warrior elite. Although Mount Pleasant was constructed by a group using Grooved Ware ceramics – a traditional and very British type of pottery – in its later use the most important ceramics were beakers. This may indicate that the users of beaker pottery took over at least one of the most important ritual monuments in the community and presumably therefore became the dominant group.

The barrows of this period are more widely dispersed than the other monuments. The densest concentration of surviving barrows is on the crest of the Ridgeway between Broadmayne and Long Bredy (**47**). It is likely, however, that the original occurrence was much more wide-spread. The landscape survey around Maiden Castle and rescue excavations in and around Dorchester have revealed that many of the barrows in these low-lying areas have been flattened by cultivation (**48**).

The distribution of barrows indicates that cemeteries were constructed on all the low-lying ridges that cover the area between the Frome and the Ridgeway. Peter Woodward has suggested that they were placed there because cultivation in the Neolithic had eroded the soil cover and made these areas agriculturally impoverished. Settlement was concentrated on the edge of coombs which were infilled with the soil eroded from the ridges and were consequently very fertile.

An exception to this general pattern at this time was the hilltop of Maiden Castle. This prominent ridge has only one or possibly two round barrows (even though there was a significant concentration of barrows on Hog Hill immediately to the west) and there is evidence that it was cleared and cultivated during this period. Beaker sherds have been found in the top of the ditch of the Bank Barrow and the

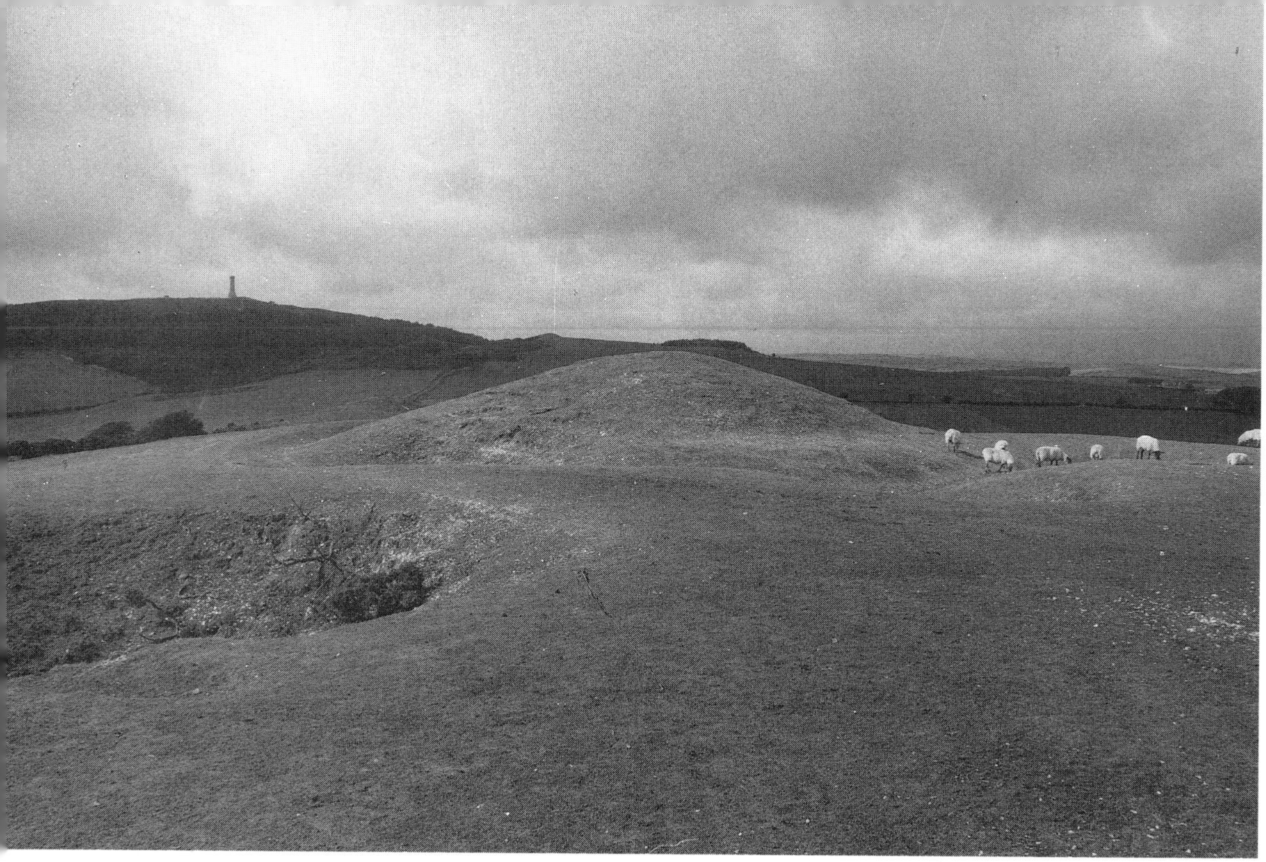

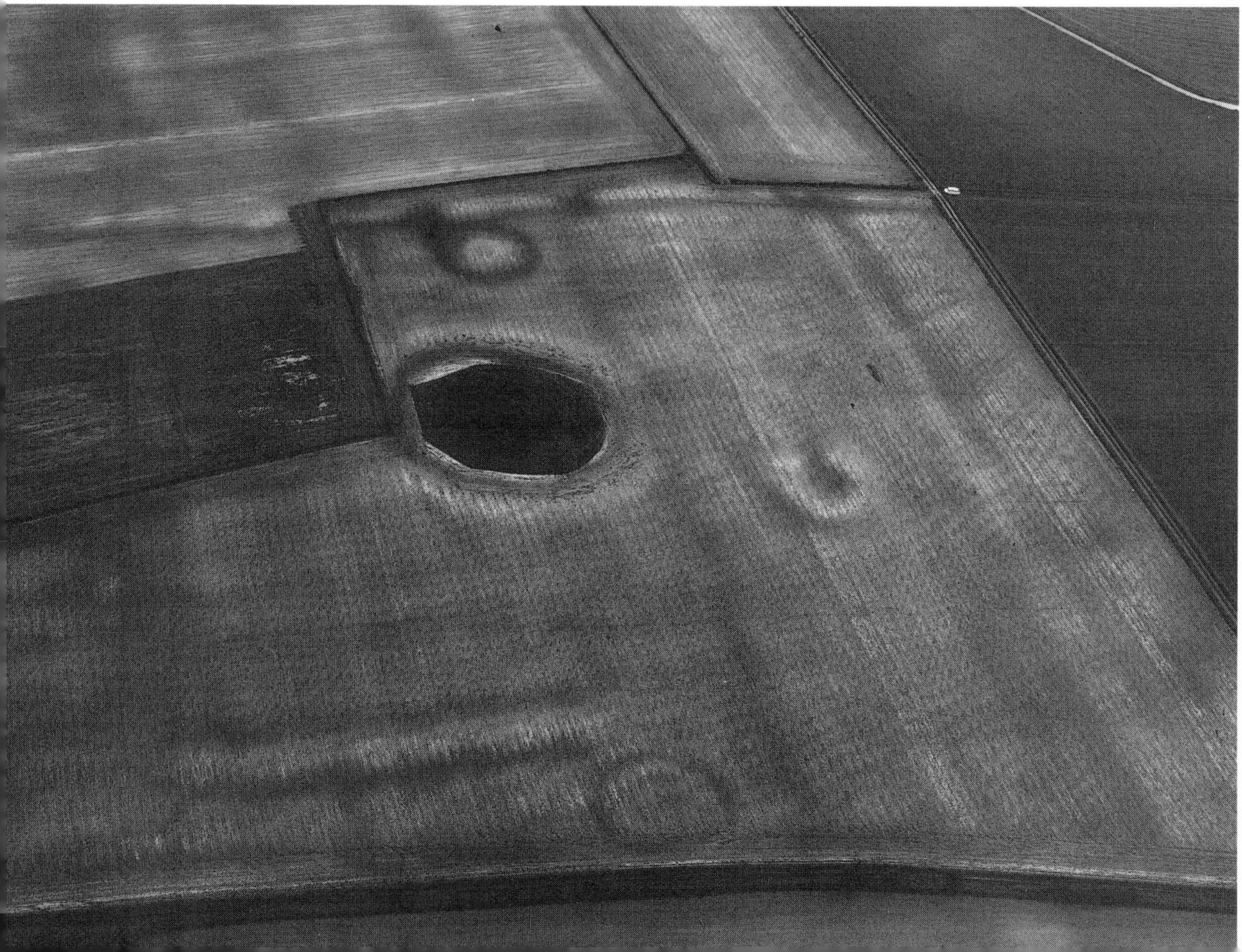

enclosure associated with a layer of chalk rubble which could only have derived from the cultivation of the hilltop.

The beaker pottery from Maiden Castle was of a late type which dates to around 1800 BC (1500 bc). It is of a type more regularly found in domestic contexts and it seems likely that such pottery had by this time lost whatever special significance it had once possessed and was copied for use in more mundane domestic tasks. This change coincides with a move away from inhumation burials to cremations. These were often placed in large urn shaped vessels which

47 *(left) A round barrow at Bronkham Hill on the South Dorset Ridgeway.*

48 *(below left) An aerial view of the ploughed out long barrow, round barrows and small henge at Lanceborough just to the north of Maiden Castle.*

49 *(below) An aerial view of the field systems surrounding Fordington Bottom to the north of Maiden Castle. These have now been completely destroyed.*

also contained grave goods such as daggers, pins and beads. One of the richest graves in Britain dating from this period comes from the barrow at Clandon which lies just over 1.5 km (1 mile) to the west. It contained a bronze dagger, a shale macehead, an amber cup, an accessory vessel and a cinerary urn.

The abandonment of Maiden Castle at the end of the Early Neolithic meant that unlike most of the high ground in the area it retained a relatively well-preserved and nutrient rich soil cover. Consequently when it was cleared in the Early Bronze Age it was a rich agricultural resource and was not set aside for use as a cemetery area. Cultivation, however, quickly exhausted its potential and the hilltop appears to have been used for only a limited period of time. The presence of a thick decalcified turf line which separates the early prehistoric deposits from the later prehistoric would indicate that for many hundreds of years the hilltop was covered by a thick grass sward similar to that present today. During this period it would have been an important grazing resource for the settlements on the low-lying land to the north and south.

The later Bronze Age

It is only when cultivation of Maiden Castle ceased in favour of grass pasturage that we can begin to identify discrete settlements with houses, fields and cemeteries in the surrounding landscape. The period from 1800 to 1000 BC appears to have been a period of major agricultural expansion and reorganization across most of the chalklands of southern Britain, and South Dorset is no exception. The area between the Frome and Maiden Castle was divided into four or five farms which were surrounded by fields (**49**). Similar farmsteads and fields are found along the Ridgeway and extend along the valleys which cut through the chalk uplands of central Dorset. In the latter two areas there are still well-preserved examples of farms and fields but around Dorchester scant traces of these now survive.

Knowledge of farmsteads of this type, however, is fairly good as several have been excavated in south Dorset; Hog Cliff Hill and Shearplace Hill near Sydling St Nicholas, Rowden south of Winterborne Abbas, and Poundbury and Middle Farm on the western outskirts of Dorchester. These settlements all have the same basic components; small circular houses surrounded by small rectangular fields. There are, however, some noticeable differences between the sites. At Rowden houses are dispersed within the fields whereas at Shearplace Hill and Poundbury houses were set beside each other. At Middle Farm the single house was encircled by a ditched enclosure and it is likely that several other enclosed farmsteads of this period exist in the Dorchester area. This variability may be connected with the relative status of the inhabitants or it could be due to small-scale regional and chronological differences.

All these sites were situated on the junction between the rich soils of the valley coombs and the eroded soils of the upland ridges. It is likely that the inhabitants continued to use the barrow cemeteries on the high ground and they did build new barrows, but they were smaller than the originals and many burials were simply inserted into existing barrows or placed beside them. The burials of this period were cremations, often contained in large urns and placed in small pits.

During this period bronze became widely used for the production of a variety of tools and weapons. The implements most commonly found are axes, which were probably general all-purpose tools, but weapons, such as rapiers and spearheads are also numerous. Curiously very few bronze objects are found in the settlements; instead they are found as single, or 'stray', finds – there is a fragment of spearhead from Maiden Castle for example – or in hoards which consist of groups of bronze objects apparently deposited for specific reasons. The particular nature of the deposition of these items gives some indication of their importance, as raw materials for bronze working were difficult to acquire. It is likely that control over the creation and exchange of these implements would have played a significant part in defining status within the community.

Around 1000 BC there seems to have been a major change in the settlement structure in this area. Many of the farmsteads which flourished in the previous period were abandoned. It seems likely that several of the more impoverished areas of the chalk uplands – for example the South Dorset Ridgeway – were depopulated during this period and that arable agriculture returned to the richer areas of the river valleys. This abandonment partially explains the preservation of these archaeological landscapes down to the present day. It is likely, however, that the areas were still a valuable grazing resource and it is noticeable that at this point sheep become much more important in the archaeological record.

The increasing importance of livestock might explain the appearance of major linear earthworks in the area around Maiden Castle. Deep ditches have been discovered cutting across the original Bronze Age field systems and dividing the landscape into large units. The hillfort of Maiden Castle was built on the junction of several of these boundaries and it is possible that the original outline of the fort is partly defined by earlier earthworks.

Unfortunately little is known about the settlements of this period, since most of the sites occupied before 1000 BC were abandoned. It is possible that some of the enclosures identified from cropmarks continued to be occupied and may even have expanded but recent excavations suggest that it is more likely that the settlements were dispersed across the landscape with no distinguishing features to identify them. Excavations at Coburg Road on the western edge of Dorchester revealed a settlement with several post-built houses and storage pits. The presence of storage pits is a feature which became increasingly important in the Iron Age. Their occurrence, taken together with the construction of the linear earthworks, indicates that control of the agricultural resources of the community was becoming increasingly significant in the period immediately before the construction of the hillfort.

Conclusion

The years between the abandonment of the Early Neolithic enclosure and the construction of the Iron Age hillfort were characterized by a major transformation of the archaeological record of human settlement. For early prehistoric communities our knowledge of human activity is dominated by elaborate and frequently enormous religious sites which are typified by the henge at Mount Pleasant. For settlement after about 2000 BC (1650 bc) our information is based on the apparently more straightforward evidence of settlements, both houses and fields systems. This development is not fully represented at Maiden Castle as the hilltop appears to be on the edge of the major areas of activity in the Frome valley and the South Dorset Ridgeway. However, the situation changes dramatically around 500 BC when Maiden Castle once again became an important centre for surrounding communities.

6

The first hillfort

Several important changes mark the transition from Bronze Age society, described at the end of the last chapter, to that of the Iron Age. The most obvious was a decrease in the importance of bronze and an increase in the availability of iron. There was also a significant change in the nature of settlement; the small homesteads of the Bronze Age were replaced by larger communal settlements in hillforts.

These changes were not absolute. Iron was known during the Late Bronze Age but its use was normally restricted to small objects such as pins. Several large hilltop enclosures too, were constructed in the Late Bronze Age but they do not appear to have been permanently occupied. Nor were all areas, even within Wessex, transformed to the same degree. Many small settlements in Purbeck (such as Eldon's Seat) were continuously occupied across this transitional period. It is also clear that much of the population in the early Iron Age did not live in hillforts as open settlements were fairly common and in many areas, such as Cranborne Chase where Iron Age settlements are frequent, hillforts were never built.

Nevertheless the importance of the changes taking place cannot be disputed. The appearance of hillforts indicates a transformation in the organization of society. The scale of their defences was considerably greater than anything constructed in the previous 1000 years and these were the first settlements which could be called villages (**50**). The widespread adoption of iron technology also freed the inhabitants of southern England from their dependence on other regions. Iron, suitable for the production of the simple tools used during this period, was available throughout southern England. Close observation of the cultivated fields on the chalk would have been sufficient to recover large quantities of iron sulphide nodules. In contrast, the copper and tin required for the production of bronze tools was only available in areas such as Cornwall, west Wales and Ireland and analysis suggests that most of the tools in southern England were imported, probably as scrap, from the Continent.

Invasions and the Continent

The two major changes outlined above have been linked in many theories which have tried to explain the transformation that took place at this time. The most common theory, accepted by many archaeologists in the first half of this century, was that hillforts were an unsuccessful response to invasion from the Continent and that the invaders brought in the new technology of iron production.

In the report of the original excavation of Maiden Castle, Wheeler emphasized that the presence of defended settlements probably resulted from increasing population pressure on the rich agricultural land of the chalk downs. He firmly believed, however, that one of the causes of the tension was an influx of immigrants who introduced the changes in the material culture which are clearly present in these forts. Most significant was an apparent change in the type of pottery used and the presence of small numbers of distinctive swords and metal objects such as razors and pins. Other writers argued that the appearance of hillforts was a direct result of an invasion with the incomers constructing a series of forts from which they could dominate a cowed and subservient population.

In the last thirty years these interpretations have been seriously challenged. It was realized

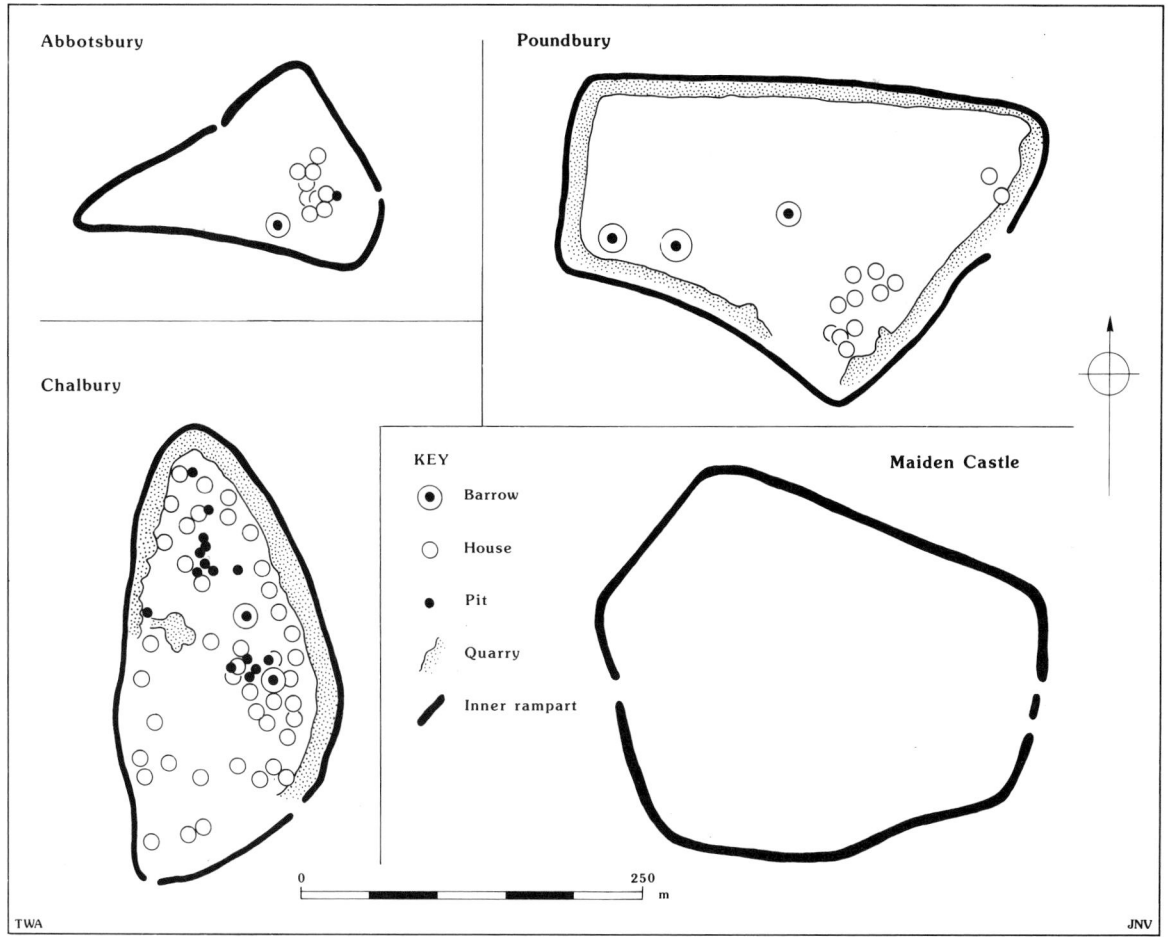

Abbotsbury

Poundbury

Chalbury

KEY

⊙ Barrow

○ House

• Pit

Quarry

Inner rampart

Maiden Castle

0   250
         m

TWA   JNV

50 *Comparative plans of the Early Iron Age hillforts of Abbotsbury, Poundbury, Chalbury and Maiden Castle showing the evidence for settlement in the first three.*

that contact and trade across the Channel were relatively important features of many periods (one of the most visible being the Late Bronze Age), but that the Iron Age does not seem to have been one of these. Continental imports were relatively rare and artistic influence on ceramic and metal types was absent until the very end of the period. Perhaps more important, however, was a refinement in our perception of how social change takes place. Throughout the period when the 'invasion hypothesis' was prevalent the underlying assumption was that the societies or cultures which could be recognized in the archaeological record were relatively static. Once they started using a particular style of pottery or tool or became dependant on a certain species of animal or crop, there would be no reason for them to change. Consequently the changes visible in their material culture could only be due to

outside influence. These outside influences could be natural events, such as a change in the climate, but population movements were thought to be the principal catalyst for change. Ultimately most developments were thought to have diffused slowly from the major centres of civilization in the Middle East or the Mediterranean.

Recent work in anthropology and sociology has shown that this is a rather simplistic explanation. Societies are much more complex and it is unlikely they ever achieved a stability which would allow this kind of adherence to a single set of lifestyles over a long period of time.

71

There are always elements within society that desire change. Often this results from an unequal distribution of power among its constituent members. Those who are relatively weak will always seek ways of undermining the status of the people with power; they, in turn, have to think of new ways of dominating the mass of the population. This continual struggle for power will have a direct effect not only on the more obvious emblems of status such as weapons and ornaments but on all aspects of the material culture. The manner in which relationships between individuals are organized can be subject to radical change as a result of the internal power struggles of that society. Every part of the material culture in use symbolizes the owner's status and his relationship to others. Consequently changes in objects – the expression of material wealth or possessions – will reflect changes in social relationships.

Theoretical approaches such as these have helped to increase our awareness of the complexities of past societies. Recent work on this period has therefore concentrated on explaining change as a result of social and economic dynamics within a community. The widespread introduction of iron can be seen as the key factor largely because of the crucial importance bronze appears to have played in the preceding record.

In the Late Bronze Age, extensive trade networks were created to obtain access to regular sources of copper and tin which linked southern England to Brittany and through this to areas such as northern Spain and central Europe. These trading relationships also facilitated the movement of other trade goods as well as ideas and people between these areas and it would be no exaggeration to say that certain communities in southern England had more in common with communities across the Channel than their neighbours in England. Within southern England a number of regions can be defined by the distribution of different types of objects. There were particularly important regional styles of pottery and bronze axes, but the quality of certain weapons and their widespread distribution suggests that these were used to define a hierarchy. For instance, certain objects, such as shields and enormous spears, could only conceivably have been used as parade equipment, primarily designed to symbolize the importance of the person wearing them.

Bronze was therefore crucial not only as a mechanism through which important economic relationships were organized but also as a means of expressing the status and regional allegiance of an individual. Consequently the availability of iron allowed communities which had hitherto been dependent on established trading relationships to break free and to begin to undermine the competitive structures of Late Bronze Age society.

The hillfort

It is with this context in mind that we need to examine the evidence for the first hillfort at Maiden Castle. This was a 6.4 ha (16 acre) enclosure defined by a single rampart and V-shaped ditch (**51, 52, 53**) which provided a boundary over 8.4 m (28 ft) in height (from the base of the rampart to crest of the bank). Access was by a single entrance on the north-west side and by a double entrance in the centre of the east side. The latter is a very unusual feature which cannot be paralleled at other hillforts in the British Isles. It is possible that it was created because the hillfort sat astride a number of previously separate territorial units as it is clear that the fort lay at the focus of several major linear boundaries. One of these ran east to west along the ridge of the hill and would have passed between the two gateways if it continued as far as the entrance. It seems that separate farming communities had come together to live in the fort and it was desirable to provide separate access to the different land units.

The most substantial feature of the hillfort at Maiden Castle was its defences and these have been thoroughly examined in Wheeler's work and in the recent excavations. It is rather surprising given the area excavated by Wheeler, that the recent excavations were able to produce new information which resulted in quite a radical re-interpretation of the defences. The picture Wheeler presented was of a vertical wall with massive timber uprights joined by horizontal wooden planks. Evidence of this impressive wall clearly survived at the eastern entrance to the fort (**54**) where lines of post-holes containing timbers at least 25 cm (10 in.) in diameter were found at the front and back of the bank, but when the recent excavations

51 *The ditch of the Early Iron Age hillfort in 1936. (The Society of Antiquaries.)*

52 *The ditch of the Early Iron Age hillfort during excavation in 1985.*

53 *The rampart of the Early Iron Age hillfort revealed by the 1985 excavations.*

opened up a large area on the west side of the fort there was no evidence for this elaborate wall. The rampart consisted simply of a dump of chalk which was fronted by a small turf stack which could only have acted as a marker, not as a significant revetment.

The implication is therefore that the elaborate timber-faced rampart was restricted to the area around the entrance and was largely designed to impress visitors to the settlement. It is possible that the rampart was originally planned to be timber-faced all the way round, but the enormous amount of labour required to construct the entire circuit in this manner would have soon forced the abandonment of this ideal. Another factor may have been that the quantity of timber required was not available in the immediate vicinity of the site. The landscape survey indicated that most of the area

around Maiden Castle lost its tree cover in the Late Neolithic or Early Bronze Age.

These conclusions should be borne in mind when examining the excavations of other hillforts. Many of the hillforts of southern England are thought to have had timber ramparts but though it is clear that this was the case at extensively excavated sites such as South Cadbury in Somerset and Danebury in Hampshire, there may be other examples similar to Maiden Castle. Excavation of the defences of a hillfort on a large scale is an expensive and time-consuming business. The structure and history of most ramparts are known only from a few narrow slit trenches and these are often placed next to the entrances.

Another discovery from the recent excavations was that the original defences had been rebuilt at least once. The ditch was re-excavated

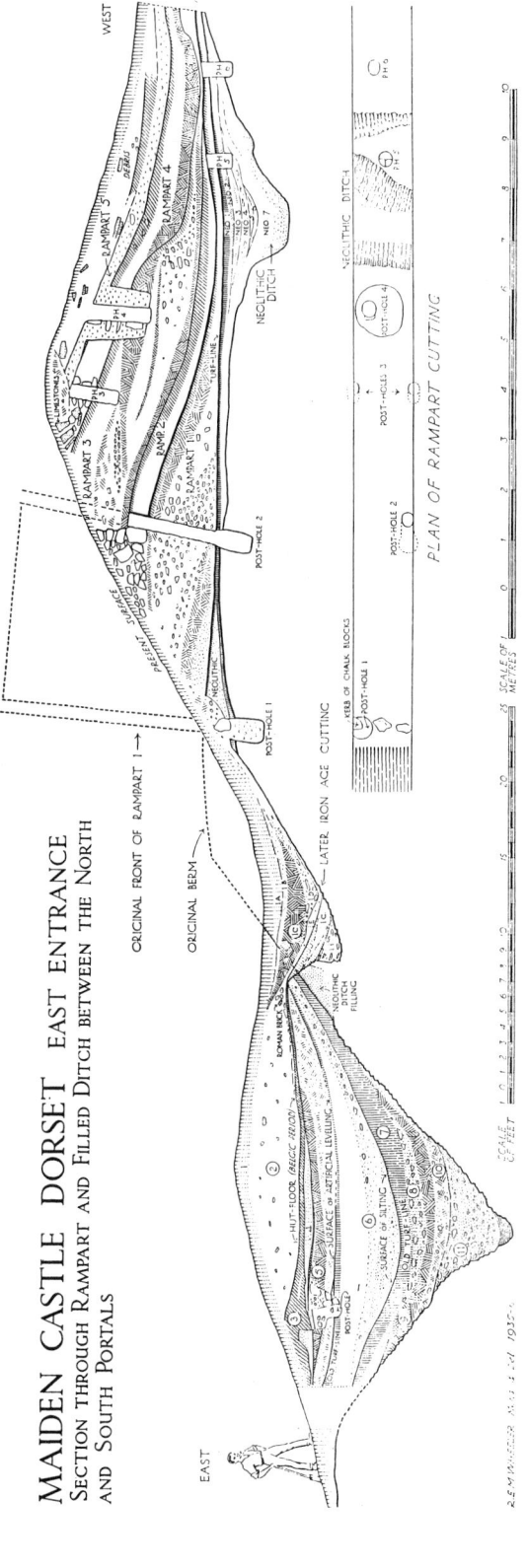

54 *Wheeler's illustration of the deposits that form the inner defences of the hillfort at the eastern entrance.*

on a slightly different line and had been deepened by about 1.5 m (5 ft) to make it 7 m (23 ft) deep, though it remained a steep-sided V-shaped ditch. The soil from this ditch was deposited at the back of the original rampart where it clearly stands out as a dump of mixed soil and chalk lying on the top of the clean chalk of the original rampart.

The refurbishment of the defences coincides with an elaboration of the original eastern entrance (see **colour plate** 4). An outer bank and ditch were built from the corners of the original fort and in front of the two gateways these turned back to form banks flanking the side of the roads leading to the gate. A central bank between the two entrance roads was formed by emphasizing the original field boundary. This extension, like the original rampart in this area, was fronted by a vertical wall supported by large timbers, but unlike the original wall the panels between the verticals were infilled by carefully built stone walls (**55**). The stone was limestone and had to be quarried from the other side of the South Dorset Ridgeway, at least 3.2 km (2 miles) away. The reconstruction would have created a very impressive front door for the community and already, at this early stage, marks Maiden Castle as the settlement of an important group.

Hillforts in Dorset

There are about 31 hillforts known in Dorset (**56**), ranging from the small fort at Woolsbarrow near Wool, which encloses an area of 0.9 ha (2.25 acres), to Hod Hill near Blandford, which encloses an area of 21.6 ha (54 acres). The average size of a Dorset hillfort is 6 ha (14.8 acres). Neither of the above two hillforts, however, is likely to be contemporary with the first phase at Maiden Castle. This belongs to a group of large hillforts which lies just above the average, ranging from the 6 ha (15 acre) fort at Nettlecombe Tout to the 8 ha (20 acre) fort of the second phase at Hambledon Hill. Most of the forts in Dorset lie below the average size and can be divided into two groups – small forts, including Woolsbarrow and Abbotsbury Castle (**colour plate 7**) at 1.8 ha (4.5 acres); and medium-sized forts, ranging from Pilsdon Pen at 3.1 ha (7.75 acres) to Poundbury at 5.5 ha (13.5 acres). Only three hillforts are significantly larger than the three groups, the very large later forts of Hambledon Hill, Maiden Castle and Hod Hill.

Excavation of these hillforts has not been as

55 *The limestone revetment of the Early Iron Age outworks of the eastern entrance, exposed in 1936. (The Society of Antiquaries.)*

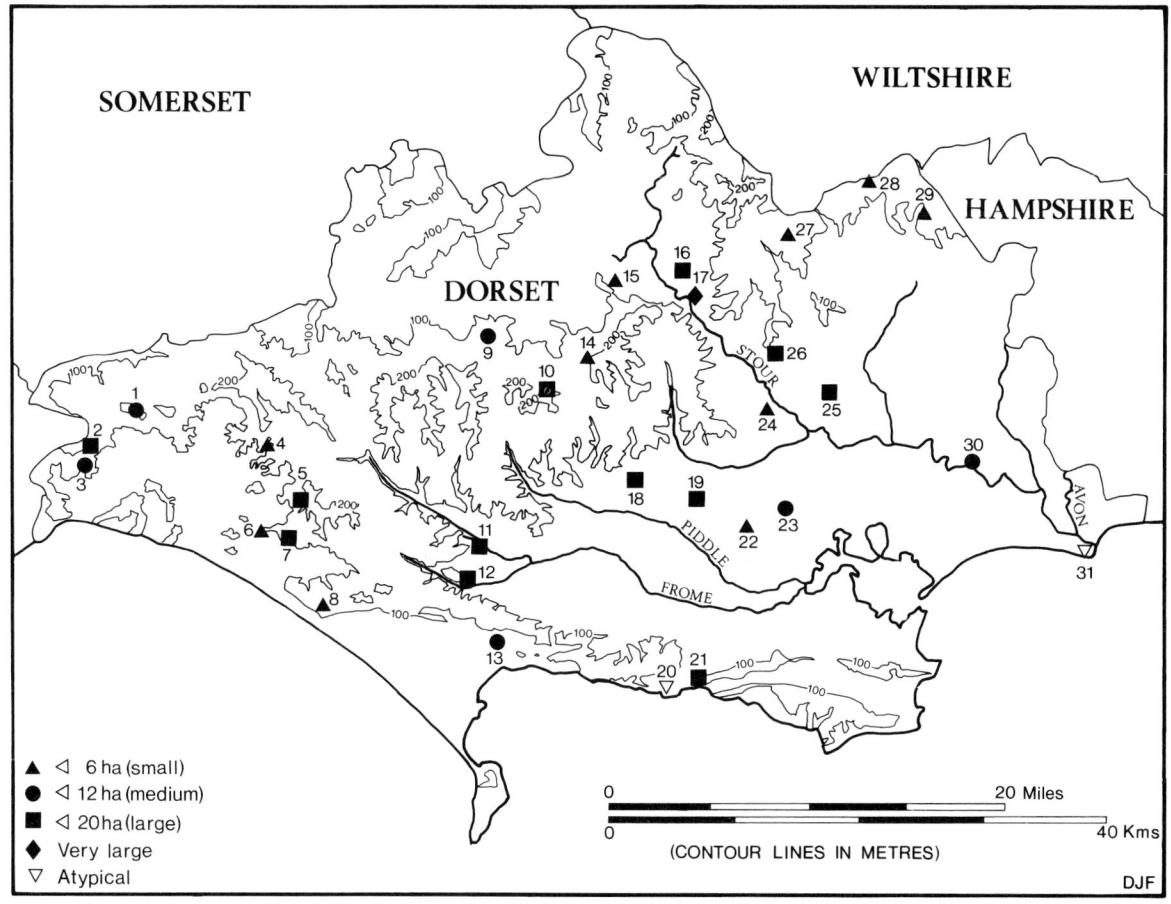

56 *Hillforts and related enclosures in Dorset.*
(1) Pilsdon Pen; (2) Lambert's Castle;
(3) Coney's Castle; (4) North Poorton;
(5) Eggardon; (6) Shipton Hill; (7) Chilcombe;
(8) Abbotsbury Castle; (9) Dungeon Hill;
(10) Nettlecombe Tout; (11) Poundbury;
(12) Maiden Castle; (13) Chalbury;
(14) Rawlsbury; (15) Banbury; (16) Hambledon
Hill; (17) Hod Hill; (18) Weatherby Castle;
(19) Woodbury; (20) Bindon Hill; (21) Flower's
barrow; (22) Woolsbarrow; (23) Bulbury
Camp; (24) Spetisbury; (25) Badbury Rings;
(26) Buzbury; (27) Bussey Stool Park;
(28) Mistlebury Wood; (29) Penbury Knoll;
(30) Dudsbury; (31) Hengistbury Head. (After
Dorset Archaeological Committee Hillforts
leaflet.)

extensive as in some areas of Wessex and it is only possible to date a few of the forts. Nevertheless the results do provide a pattern which confirms the generalizations made at the beginning of this chapter; four out of six excavated medium- to large-sized hillforts – Poundbury, Chalbury, Hambledon Hill and Maiden Castle – were first constructed in the Early Iron Age. Of the other two, Pilsdon Pen and Eggardon, only the former has been extensively excavated. The earliest phase in all of these hillforts was an enclosure defined by a single bank and ditch, entered through a simple entrance. Only later were the elaborate entrances and multiple ramparts created.

The defences of both Poundbury and Chalbury were sectioned in the process of the excavation. Poundbury **(57)** lies next to the River Frome 3 km (1.8 miles) to the north of Maiden Castle and was very similar to it. It had a V-shaped ditch 8.8 m (29 ft) wide and 4.2 m (14 ft) deep and a chalk bank 9.7 m (32 ft) wide and

2.74 m (9 ft) high, with vertical timbers similar to those around the entrance. This timbering was found at the back of the hillfort and must indicate, in contrast to Maiden Castle, that the circuit was completely timbered. The rampart had been rebuilt at least once as at Maiden Castle. The defences at Chalbury were completely different (**58**). It was built on the south side of the South Dorset Ridgeway overlooking Weymouth Bay and unlike Poundbury and Maiden Castle which were built on chalk it was built on an outcrop of limestone. Consequently the rampart was largely built with limestone slabs, quarried from the surrounding small flat-bottomed ditch. Its rampart too had been rebuilt at least once.

The close similarity in date and size between the hillforts at Poundbury, Maiden Castle and Chalbury (see **50**), and their geographical proximity is useful as it is only by comparing the evidence from all the sites that we can understand what the occupation inside Maiden Castle might have been like. At Maiden Castle the extensive destruction caused by later occupation makes it difficult to identify features from the Early Iron Age occupation. The other two sites are, however, very well preserved (Chalbury is probably one of the best preserved forts in England) and appear to have had a chronologically restricted period of occupation.

Three types of features are still visible in the interior of Chalbury. There are circular depressions, which can be divided into categories large and small, and large amorphous depressions. Excavation has shown that the first two features are respectively houses and grain storage pits, but the function of the latter is less clear and they may be more recent quarries. The pits are clustered in two concentrations – one in a line running north to south from the rampart and the other around the Bronze Age barrow in the centre of the hillfort. There are over 40 houses spread out across the hilltop with what appears to be a concentration inside the rampart. Only one house was completely excavated and this was 10 m (33 ft) in

diameter and was defined by a circular stone wall. Strangely no hearth and no structural post-holes were uncovered.

If the density and the arrangement of houses and pits at Chalbury is considered to be typical of hillforts of this period it would suggest that they were all intensively occupied and relatively well-ordered settlements. This pattern, however, is not repeated at the hillfort of Poundbury. It is not as well preserved as Chalbury for cultivation has obscured the occupation. During the very hot summer of 1976, however, a number of features in the interior showed up as parchmarks. These indicated that a cluster of up to twelve houses was located in the south-east corner of the hillfort but that most of the rest of the interior of the hilltop was empty. This explained the results of the 1938 excavations which extensively sampled the interior but found no trace of any occupation.

A parallel for the occupation at Poundbury can be found in another nearby hillfort, Abotsbury Castle (**colour plate 7** and see **50**). Like Chalbury this hillfort is built on limestone and most of the interior has not been cultivated. It is one of the smaller forts and as it has never been excavated it cannot be dated and we cannot therefore be certain that it is directly comparable. In the interior of this fort a cluster of up to nine stone-walled houses is clearly visible in the sheltered north-east corner of the site; the rest of the interior is apparently empty. The houses are 6 m (20 ft) in diameter and appear to be similar to those at Chalbury.

It is unclear which of these sites forms the most appropriate parallel for the occupation at Maiden Castle. The continuity of activity into the Middle and Late Iron Age and the complex development of the eastern gate might suggest that it was a densely occupied site similar to Chalbury but this was not entirely borne out by the results of Wheeler's excavations. He excavated a very large area in the interior of the hillfort and discovered about 27 pits, a couple of hearths and a cluster of post-holes which could date to the Early Iron Age (**59**). The arrangement and size of the post-holes suggests that they represented a number of small rectangular structures which are normally interpreted as granaries. This evidence would suggest that Wheeler excavated an area of the hillfort that had been set aside for the storage of the community's crops and that the houses were concentrated elsewhere.

57 *A view of the hillfort of Poundbury from the north side of the River Frome. Dorchester lies to the left.*

58 *A view of the hillfort at Chalbury overlooking Weymouth Bay.*

59 *The large area of the interior of the hillfort*
excavated by Wheeler.

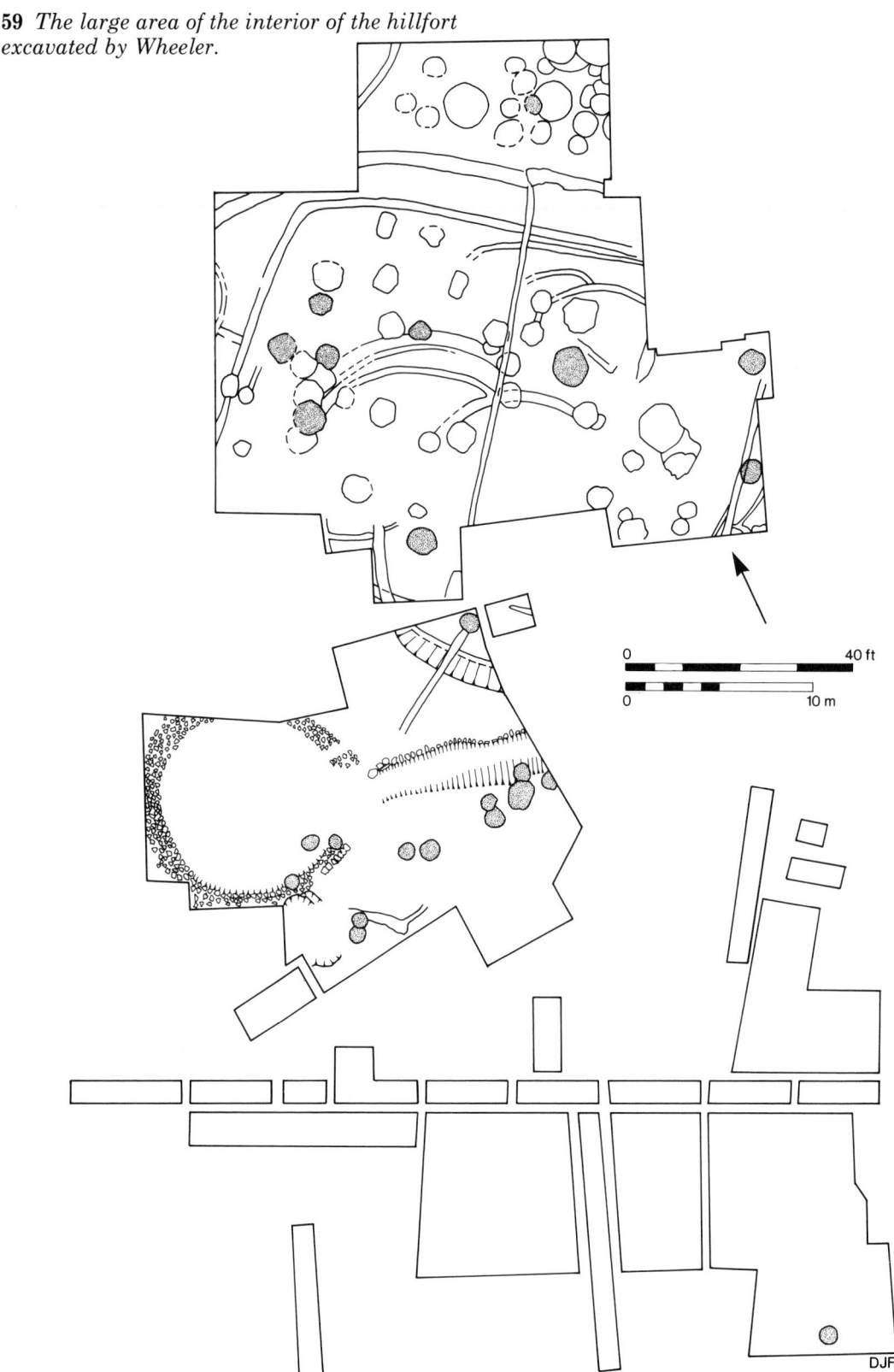

(above)
1 An artist's impression of the creation of the Causewayed Camp.

(right)
2 An aerial view of Maiden Castle from the south-west. In the foreground is the South Winterborne valley, in the background Dorchester (University of Cambridge, copyright reserved).

3 The southern ramparts of Maiden Castle.

4 The eastern gateway to the hillfort. In the background is Dorchester.

5 An aerial view of the eastern entrance to the hillfort (Royal Commission on Ancient Historical Monuments, England).

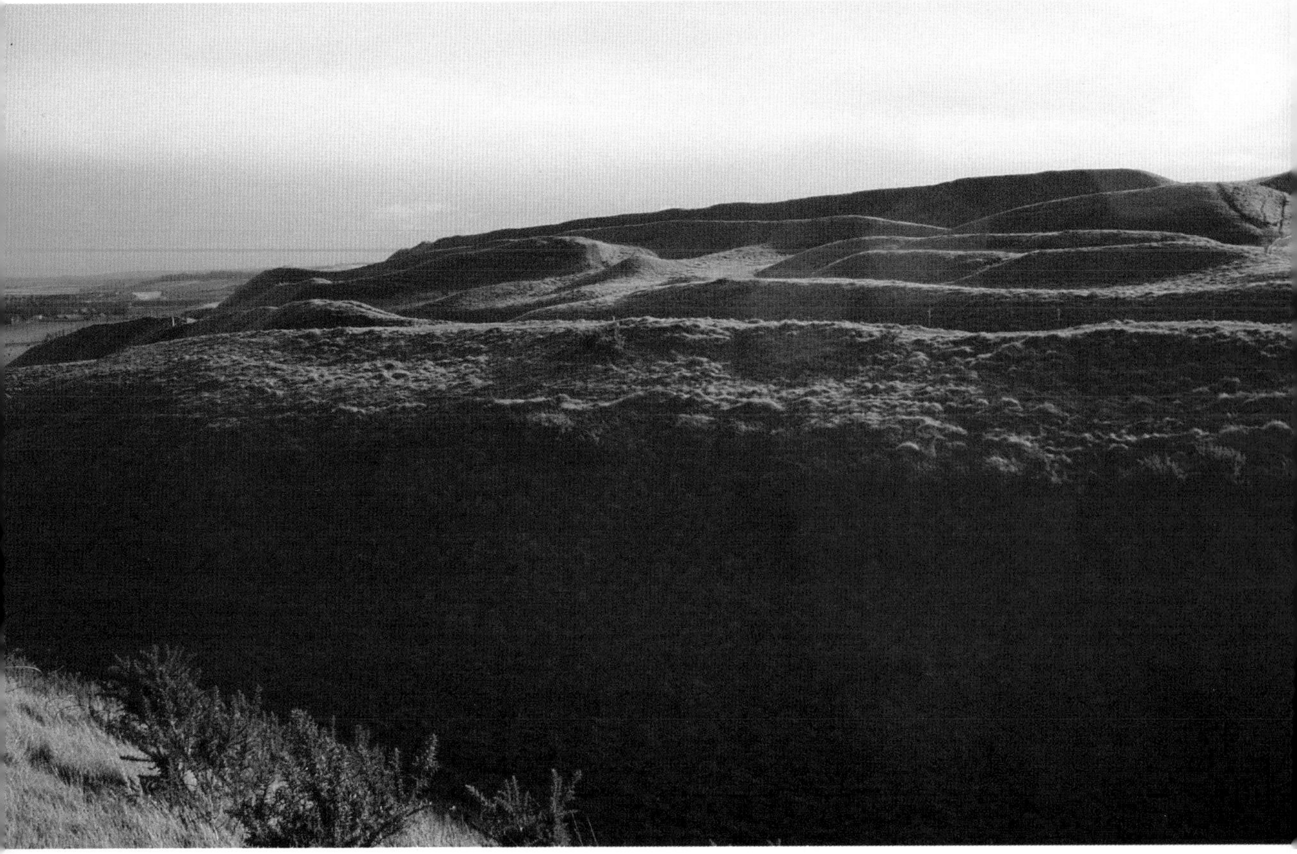

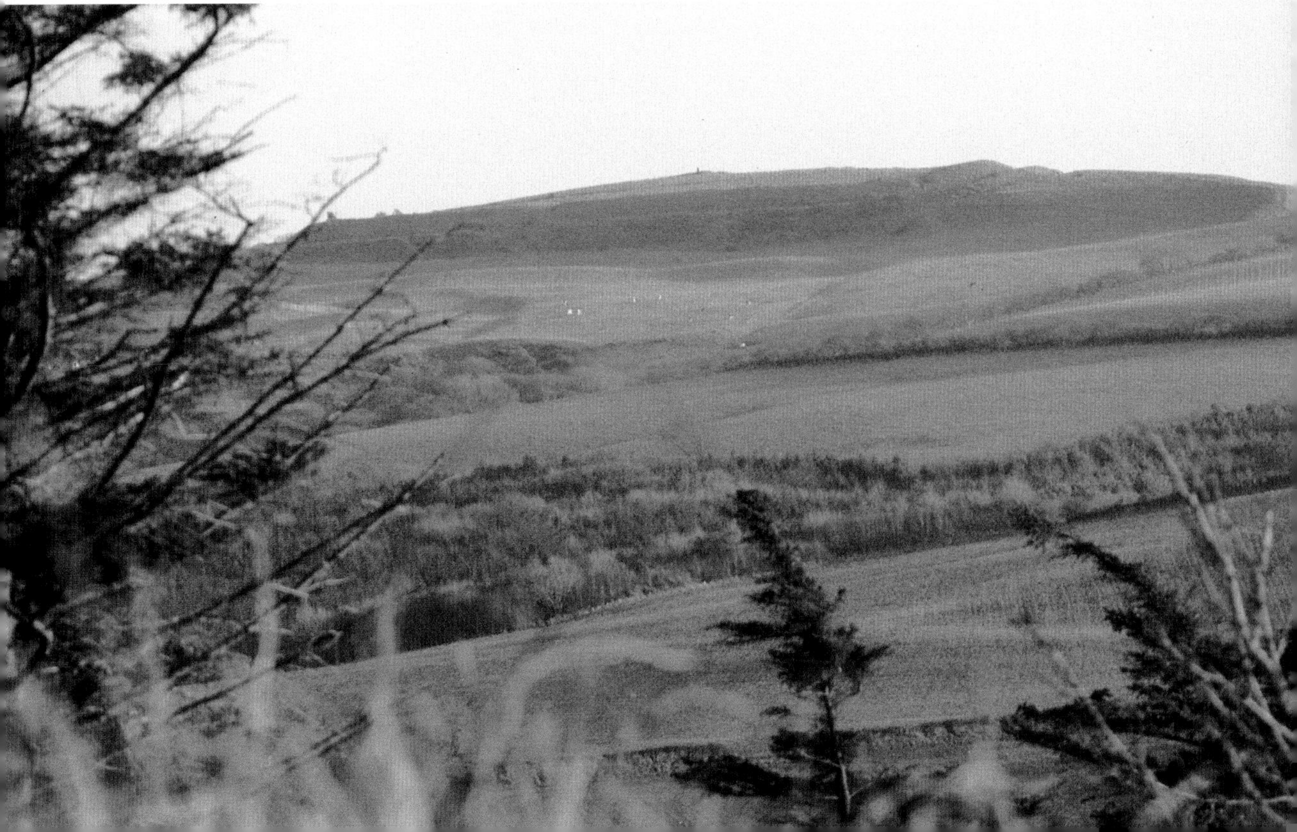

(top left)
6 The western entrance to Maiden Castle showing the complexity of the overlapping earthworks that form the defences in this area.

(bottom left)
7 The hillfort of Abbotsbury Castle which lies 12km (7 miles) west of Maiden Castle.

(above)
8 Recent excavations in the south-west corner of the hillfort. In the foreground are some of the large grain storage pits which are such an important feature of the occupation of the hillfort.

9 A highly polished and finely decorated bone 'weaving comb' found during the 1985 excavations. These are probably not used in the weaving process but may be for plucking wool from the sheep (Ancient Monuments Laboratory).

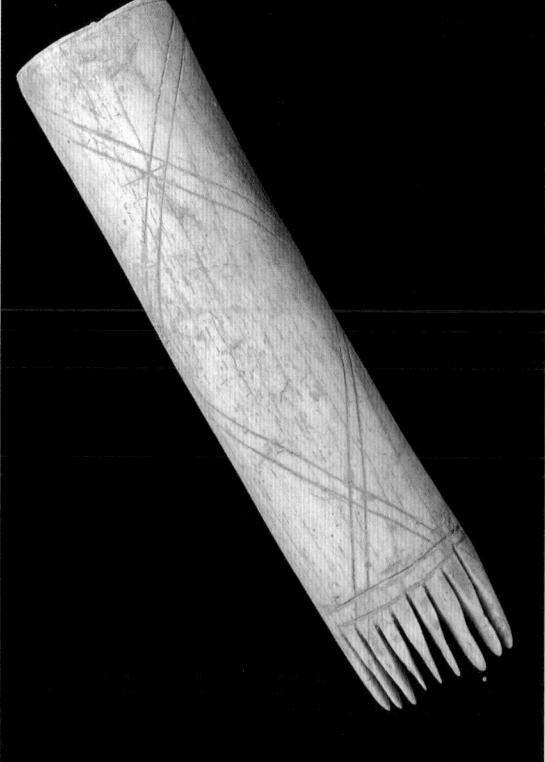

(below)
10 The excavation of a large grain storage pit dating to the Iron Age occupation of the hillfort.

11 Reconstruction of the second phase of occupation in the south-west corner of the hillfort. Houses during this period appear to be grouped in clusters scattered across the interior.

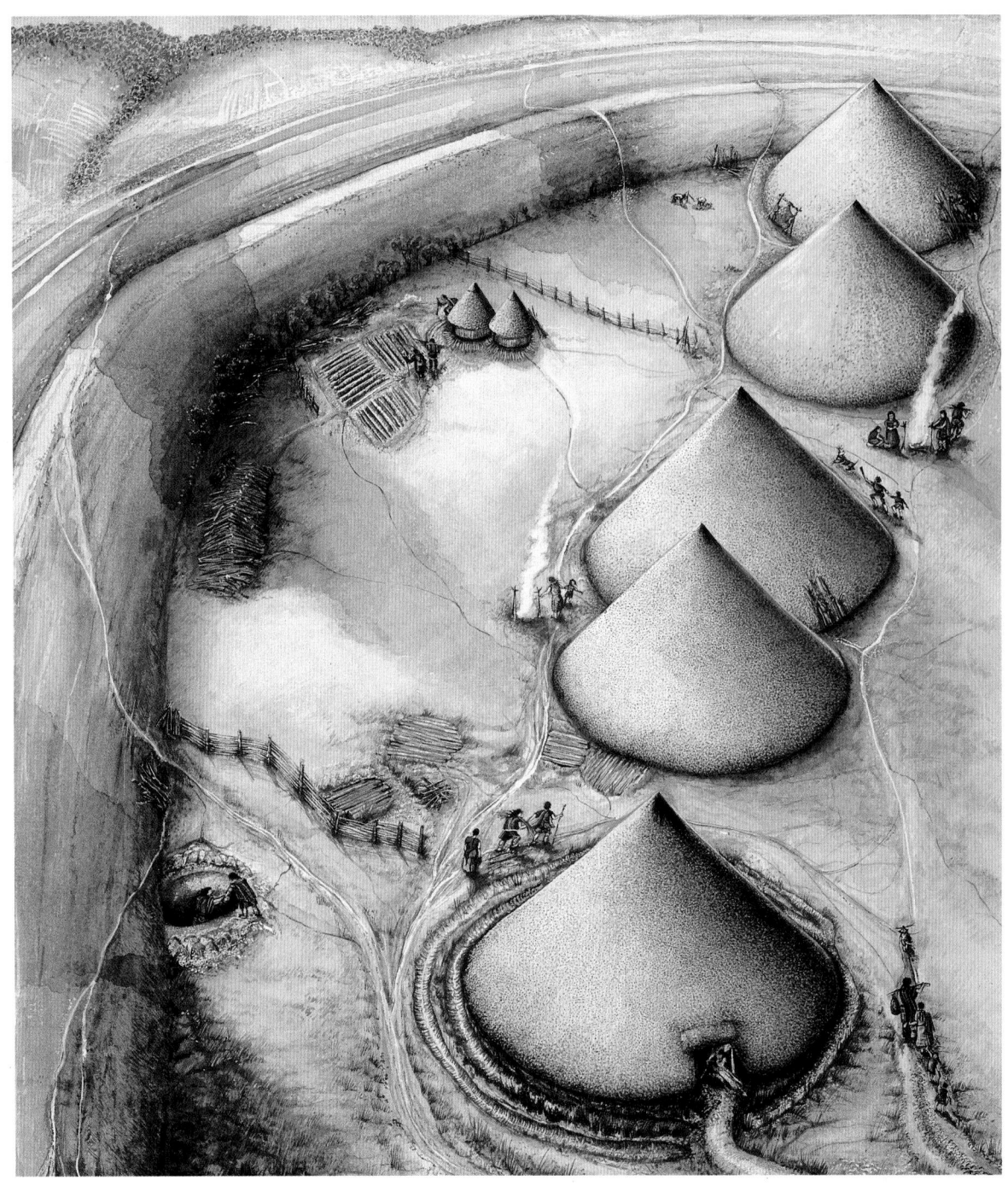

12 Reconstruction of the third phase of occupation in the south-west corner of the hillfort. This period marks a major reorganization of the hilltop with rows of houses aligned along major routes across the interior of the fort.

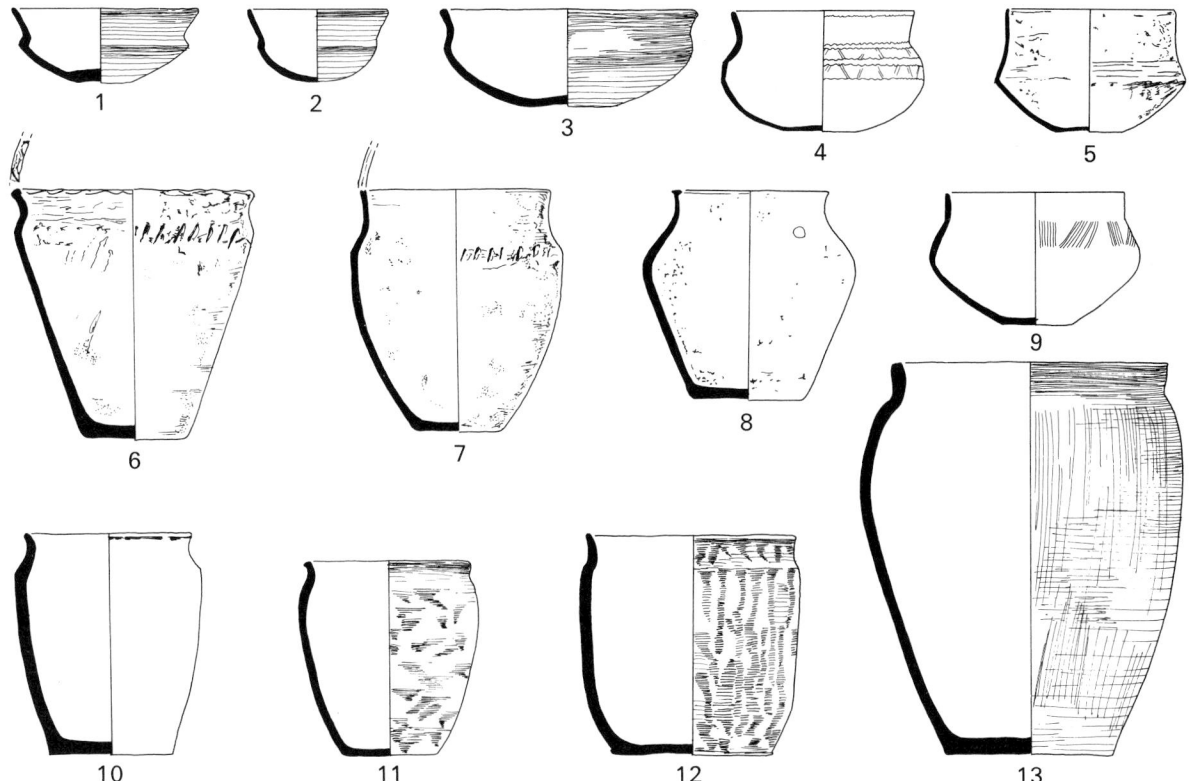

60 *Early Iron Age ceramics. Winnal Down, Hampshire (4–9), Maiden Castle (1–3, 10–13). The large jars throughout Wessex are very similar but there are major differences in the fine wares (after Fasham 1985 and Wheeler 1943).*

The finds

The quantity of finds belonging to the Early Iron Age period from Maiden Castle was disappointingly sparse. There was a collection of pottery which could be divided into large crude jars, distinguished by a pronounced shoulder just below the rim, and fine open bowls (**60**). The latter are also carinated but the carination is low on the body and above it the walls of the pot flare out. The most distinctive feature of these vessels is the effort that has gone into their production. Most have a bright red surface which is produced by a complex process of controlled firing and burnishing (polishing). The best examples were originally fired to a leather hard finish, and were then covered by a thin layer of clay slip which was rich in iron oxides to give it the red colour, then refired and finally burnished to make a smooth and shiny surface.

An assemblage of similar pottery was recovered in the excavations at Chalbury but the largest collection of similar material from Dorset comes from two undefended settlements on the Purbeck coast: Rope Lake Hole and Eldon's Seat. Here the variety in the large storage jars and cooking pots is much greater but the complete contrast between these vessels and the fine bowls was still striking. This contrast can be seen throughout Wessex in the Early Iron Age. Further north in Hampshire and Wiltshire, however, the fine-ware bowls were slightly different. Here they are decorated with zig-zag lines incised into the surface and have ridges or cordons on the body, hence their name 'scratch cordoned bowls'. This difference between Dorset and the rest of Wessex is one of the few instances of the development of a distinct regional style in this period. The crude jars are the same throughout Wessex and there is no sign of a distinction in any other aspects of material culture or economy.

Our knowledge of the material culture and the economy of this period is limited. The numbers of finds recovered from the sites at Maiden Castle, Chalbury and Eldon's Seat were minimal and are very similar to later Iron Age material which will be described below (p. 97). The only site where information on the economy of this period has been obtained is the open settlement at Eldon's Seat; even this, however, does not include evidence for the crops, only the animals. The main feature of the assemblage was the increased importance of sheep. Cattle had been the dominant animal throughout the Neolithic and Bronze Age but by the end of that period they were diminishing rapidly in importance as sheep became more and more common. This change supports the idea that the landscape had changed dramatically as sheep only flourish on open grasslands.

Conclusion

Several important points emerge from a comparison between Maiden Castle and the other Early Iron Age hillforts of Dorset. It is clear that the small, economically interlinked settlements of the Late Bronze Age amalgamated into large self-sufficient communities. These communities often had a sizeable grain-storage capacity which suggests that they had to rely on their own agricultural production to survive. There is also a marked decline in the quantity and variety of the material culture. Specialized production and exchange of high quality tools were in decline and there were no major distinctions in function or status between separate communities. The agricultural independence of the Iron Age communities may be a direct result of the collapse of what had been extensive Bronze Age reciprocal trading relationships.

In these fragmented societies the primary means of achieving status and power appears to have been through control of land which was capable of supporting a large community. The construction of grand and elaborate defences was one of the few indications that a community had some status and it is noticeable that the Early Iron Age hillforts of Dorset are situated in positions with easy access to extensive areas of rich and diverse agricultural land. The four hillforts already discussed – Maiden Castle, Poundbury, Chalbury and Abbotsbury Castle – all lay close to good areas of chalk upland (which had been heavily cultivated in the Bronze Age) and expanses of low-lying land with access to permanent water sources which are good for grazing. The sites at Maiden Castle and Chalbury which developed as the more important centres were perhaps the best placed to exploit these resources.

The construction of defences around these settlements suggests that the land controlled by these communities was actively fought over. Control of good agricultural land would support a much greater population than was otherwise possible and would give the community a potential advantage in any conflict over resources.

There is evidence for major social change therefore between the Bronze and the Iron Ages. In the Late Bronze Age power and wealth were associated with individuals who controlled trading relationships and acquired rich and prestigious objects. In the Iron Age power was associated with communities and derived from land and agricultural production, and manifested itself in the defence of the community and the storage and control of its produce.

7

The developed hillfort

In the first two or three hundred years of its existence the hillfort of Maiden Castle was closely similar to other hillforts in Dorset. Likewise the situation in Dorset can be paralleled throughout Wessex with probably over a hundred hillforts of comparable form and size constructed at this time. The hillfort we can see today, however, is almost unparalleled in the British Isles and it is during the three hundred years of the Middle Iron Age that it acquired the characteristics which make it so distinctive.

There are two principal features which made Maiden Castle exceptional at this period: the area enclosed by its ramparts was substantially increased and its defences became far larger and more complex. Both of these developments occur in other hillforts scattered across Wessex but the scale of the expansion at Maiden Castle is the factor which distinguishes this hillfort making it a testament to the organizational skills and constructional abilities of the prehistoric communities of southern England.

Expansion

The most dramatic transformation at Maiden Castle occurred about 450 BC when the area enclosed by the hillfort defences was increased from 6.5 ha (16 acres) to 19 ha (47 acres), an increase of 293 per cent (see **2**). The new area was initially enclosed by a relatively simple bank and ditch very similar to the one that had defined the western edge of the original fort and much simpler than the timber and stone revetted bank that had been constructed around the eastern entrance. The bank was a dump of soil and chalk, just over 2.7 m (9 ft) high, excavated from a relatively shallow ditch.

The space enclosed by this extension lay to the west of the original hillfort. The western rampart cut across the ridge along the edge of a dry valley which separates Maiden Castle from Hog Hill. The area within now comprised two areas of high ground split by another dry valley that ran into the South Winterborne. This valley may have been deliberately incorporated within the fort, since a shaft was sunk into it presumably to establish a water source for the inhabitants.

Several hillforts throughout Wessex were enlarged in a fashion similar to this, but there are far fewer enlarged hillforts than there were small hillforts of the Early Iron Age. Although no other hillfort was enlarged to the size of Maiden Castle the fort most closely comparable is Hambledon Hill in central Dorset. This hillfort was originally 4.85 ha (12 acres) in size and lay at the end of one of the spurs leading from a large plateau of chalk. It was expanded twice: the first time the size of the fort increased to 8.1 ha (20 acres), the second to 12.5 ha (31 acres). As at Maiden Castle the expansion occurred along the ridge and stopped just short of the main area of high ground. The ridge at Hambledon Hill, however, is much steeper and narrower than that at Maiden Castle. This considerably restricted the area that could be enclosed and gave this site sizeable natural defences.

A number of Dorset hillforts – Weatherby Castle, Flowers Barrow and Badbury Rings – were also expanded, presumably at the same time, but in all these cases the expansion was minimal and it is unlikely that the extra area enclosed was permanently occupied, though it may have been used for a variety of activities. It is clear that these expanded hillforts (**61**) are relatively widely spaced. Within each region of Dorset one of the hillforts seems to have been

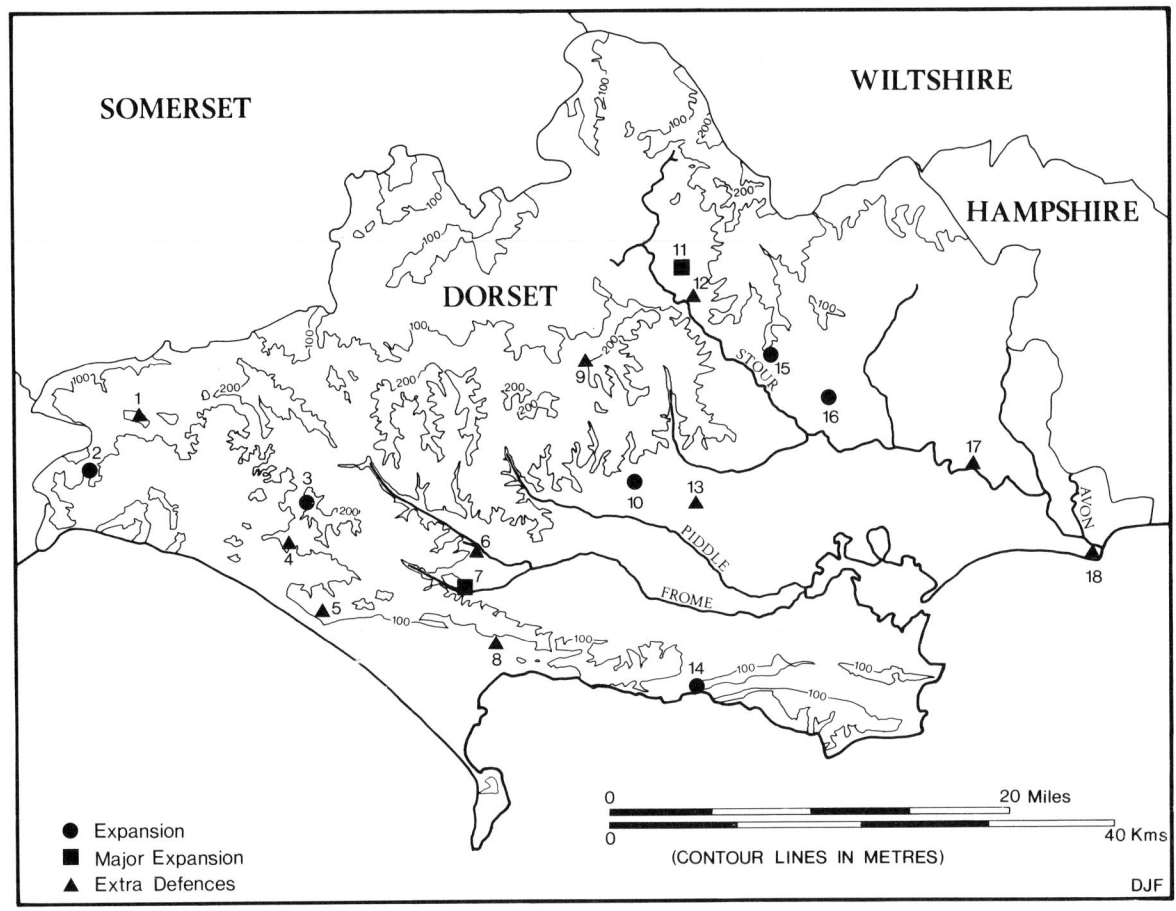

enlarged whilst its neighbours remained unchanged. An examination of the hillforts around Maiden Castle suggest that these unchanged hillforts were actually abandoned at this time. There is no sign of Middle Iron Age occupation in the hillforts of Poundbury and Chalbury. Furthermore, the landscape survey around Maiden Castle and the rescue excavations in and around Dorchester have so far failed to identify any Iron Age settlements which date from this period. It seems therefore that Maiden Castle expanded specifically to absorb the inhabitants of settlements in its immediate vicinity (the area between the South Dorset Ridgeway and the River Frome). In the area immediately to the south, around the hillfort of Chalbury, there is evidence for a basic continuity of settlement. Sites, such as Quarry Lodden, have produced evidence for activity from the Early Iron Age through to the Roman occupation, but the nearby hillforts were abandoned.

61 *The distribution of developed and expanded hillforts in Dorset. (1) Pilsdon Pen; (2) Coney's Castle; (3) Eggardon; (4) Chilcombe; (5) Abbotsbury Castle; (6) Poundbury; (7) Maiden Castle; (8) Chalbury; (9) Rawlsbury; (10) Weatherby Castle; (11) Hambledon Hill; (12) Hod Hill; (13) Woodbury; (14) Flower's Barrow; (15) Buzbury; (16) Badbury Rings; (17) Dudsbury; (18) Hengistbury Head. (After Dorset Archaeological Committee Hillforts leaflet.)*

The expansion of Maiden Castle therefore appears to indicate that this hillfort and its occupants had become the most important community in South Dorset. They absorbed the previously independent community which occupied the hillfort of Poundbury and forced the population of the hillfort of Chalbury to abandon their defended stronghold for unprotected settlements amongst the fields. If they were indeed linked in this way, these changes could

be interpreted as the result of a protracted armed struggle between the different communities. The inhabitants of Maiden Castle would have triumphed because the site commanded very rich agricultural resources that could support a population greater than that concentrated in any of the other hillforts and so gave them an edge in any conflict. There is very little sign, however, of any armed conflict in the archaeological record, nor is there any evidence for the destruction of the defences at either Chalbury or Poundbury, or for the burning down of houses in either settlement.

Defences

Almost immediately after the expansion of Maiden Castle the inhabitants of the hillfort began a programme of massive and almost continual aggrandizement of the defences. This

62 *The inner rampart of the expanded hillfort in 1935. (The Society of Antiquaries.)*

63 *The ramparts of Maiden Castle looking east, in 1935. (The Society of Antiquaries.)*

started with a relatively insignificant heightening of the rampart, followed by a further heightening to about 3.5 m (11 ft) (**62**). Probably contemporary with this refurbishment was the construction of extra ramparts in front of the original bank. Four ramparts were built on the south side of the ditch and they were separated by three ditches which provided the source of the chalk for their construction. The distance between the inner ditch and the second bank is quite substantial and because the valley side was relatively shallow this has created large flat areas of ground (known as berms) amongst the ramparts (**63**). On the north side of the hillfort the ground was much steeper. Only three banks were necessary and they were placed close together. At the eastern entrance to the hillfort these ramparts enveloped the original hornwork and access to the hillfort was diverted from the straight entrance by extensions to the original axial ditch which separated the two entrance passageways (**64**).

These additions to the original single rampart were soon followed by a much more substantial rebuilding of the defences with a complete redesign of the entrances. The inner rampart was heightened to over 5.5 m (18 ft) and to obtain the rubble and soil for this rampart a large but relatively shallow quarry was excavated on the inside of the rampart. This quarry is not visible as a prominent feature today but excavation and detailed field survey indicate that it exists all the way round the inside of the fort. To achieve a relatively tall and narrow rampart the builders had to revet the loose stone and chalk rubble with carefully built internal stone walls. These revetments were covered by a layer of soil to create the smooth profile that characterized all the earlier ramparts.

Contemporary with this was a further major reconstruction and redesign of the entrances to the hillfort (see **64**). The eastern entrance was radically altered again with the existing more

64 *The development of the eastern entrance. Phases 1 and 2 are Early Iron Age, phases 3 and 4 Middle Iron Age.*

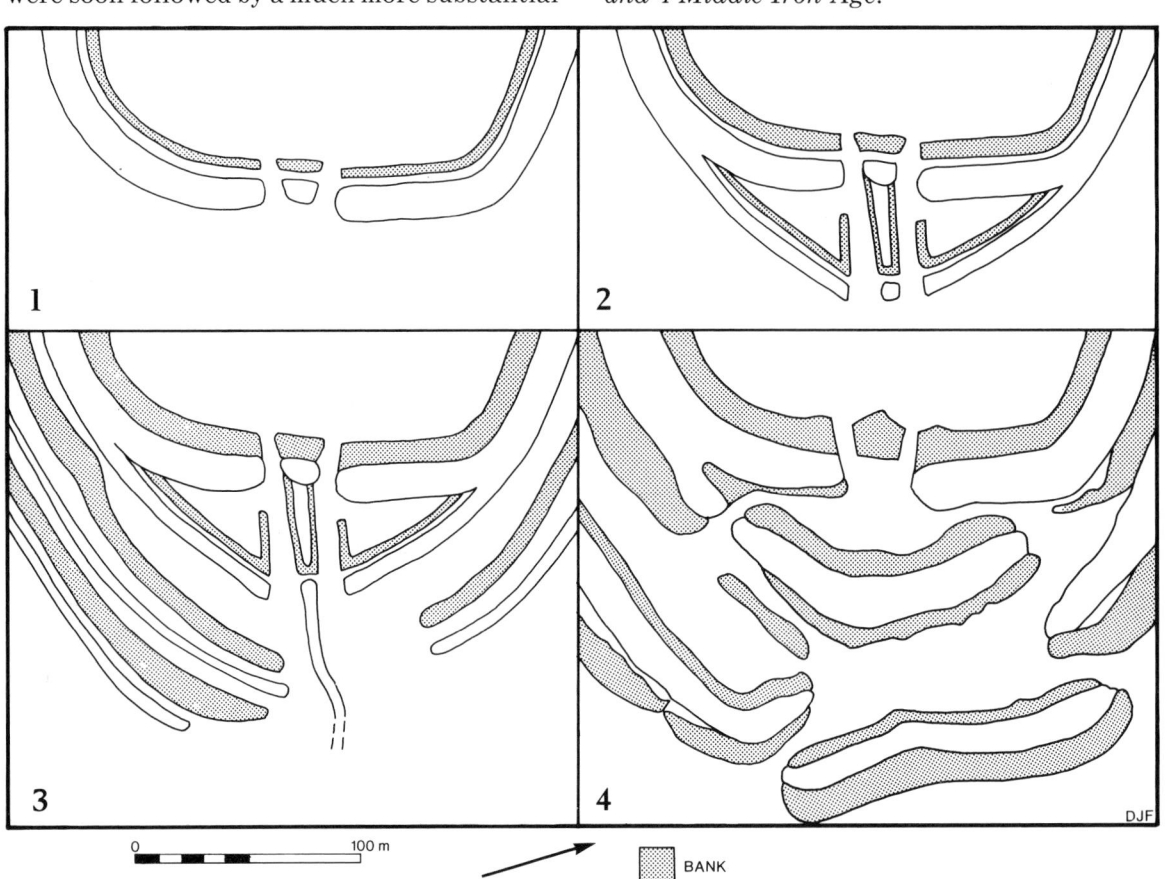

0   100 m

BANK

or less straight access to the interior blocked by a complete rebuilding of the central hornwork. Access was by a roadway which wound in through overlapping earthworks which forced visitors to walk along narrow passages flanked by ramparts. On the ramparts were stone platforms presumably occupied by armed guards. A similar but more complex effect was created at the western entrance (**colour plate 6**).

Changes to the defences of hillforts occurred throughout Wessex. In Dorset the hillforts that were expanded also tended to be more elaborately defended with either multiple banks and ditches or heightened inner banks. Badbury Rings is probably the best example of a multivallate hillfort but the banks are relatively insignificant compared to those at Maiden Castle. At Hambledon Hill the steep sides of the surrounding coombs meant that most of the circuit of the defences had relatively insignificant defences. Where the ridge joins the main hill, however, the banks were much higher. Similar modifica-

tions to the ridge side occur at the hillforts of Abbotsbury Castle and Coney's Castle.

Occupation

Traces of occupation contemporary with this period of rampart construction are surprisingly scarce at Maiden Castle. To a certain extent this must be because in the area examined by the recent excavations the quarry would have removed much of the evidence for earlier occupation (**65**). However, quite a large area was examined between the quarry and the rampart and behind the quarry. The only features which appear to date to this period were roughly square structures defined by four large postholes (**66**), and known as '4-posters'. There were four of these in the trench; two apparently in a line behind the rampart and two more in the interior (see **67**).

These '4-posters' are a regular feature of hillforts and other Iron Age settlements throughout England. They are perhaps most common in the hillforts of the border country between Wales and England where the interiors of some forts appear to be completely covered by these small rectangular buildings. There has

65 *An aerial view of the 1986 excavations in the south-west corner of the hillfort.*

66 A '4-post' granary under excavation.

been much debate about the possible function of these structures and many who have excavated at these hillforts have argued that they are the remains of houses, since otherwise there is very little evidence for housing. This interpretation seems unlikely, however, as the average size of these structures would only be just over 2 m (6.5 ft) square, too small to be a comfortable dwelling. It is likely that the actual houses await discovery by more extensive excavations.

Alternative suggested functions for these structures include watch-towers and exposure platforms for the dead since the '4-posters' are often observed to be concentrated around the edge of the forts. However, their occurrence in large numbers – on many sites there are several rows – makes both of these interpretations unlikely. The current consensus of opinion among archaeologists is that '4-posters' were granaries; the concentration of such structures in hillforts indicating that the inhabitants controlled the distribution of basic food supplies to a large number of people. There is some suggestion that an earlier preference for granaries above ground ('4-posters') was replaced by one for pit silos in the Middle Iron Age. It

should be emphasized, however, that not all post-built structures need be granaries, for many other structures are likely to be present in a settlement.

Since the importance of Maiden Castle derives partly from its position and relationship to an exceptionally rich area of agricultural land it is only logical that the next step taken by the inhabitants should be to achieve direct control over the food produced on the surrounding land by bulk storage inside the hillfort. The ability to store large quantities of food on the hilltop would also be essential for the construction of the defences. The scale of these earthworks implies that they were built not only by the inhabitants of the fort alone and it seems reasonable to envisage a period during the year when large numbers of labourers came into the hillfort from the surrounding communities to work on the ramparts. This would both explain the position of the granaries around the edge of the fort and would also provide another mechanism which enabled the community at Maiden

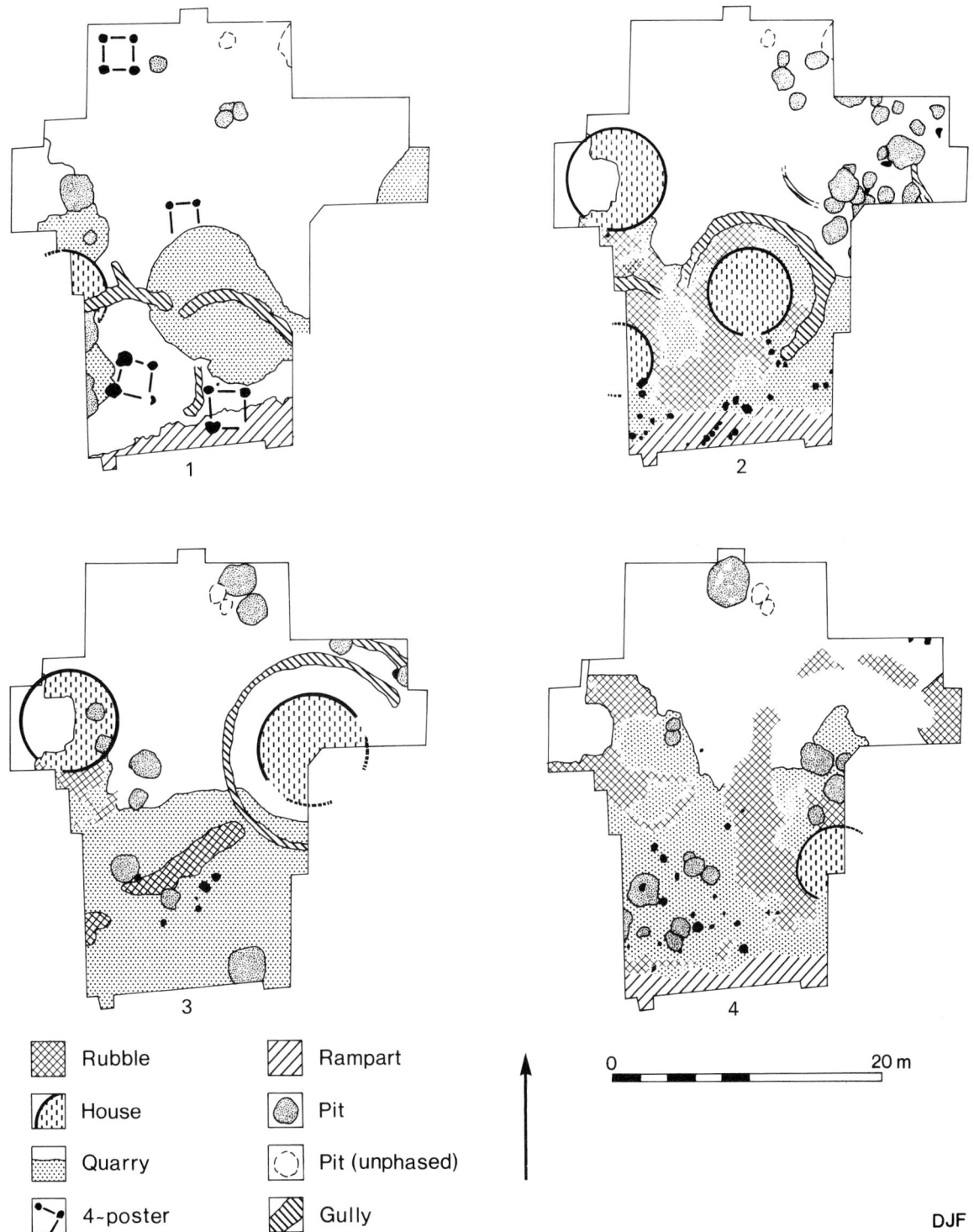

Rubble
Rampart
House
Pit
Quarry
Pit (unphased)
4-poster
Gully

DJF

0   20 m

67 *The four phases of occupation exposed by the recent excavations in the south-west corner of the hillfort.*

Castle to control the life and actions of the surrounding communities. It is thus not surprising that the first structures built inside the extension to Maiden Castle were these granaries. It is even possible that they were built before the construction of the rampart. It would after all only be possible to use a large labour force if food was already available on site. The removal of basic food supplies from the surrounding communities would also be a very effective means of forcing these communities to move into Maiden Castle.

In the initial stages of the occupation of the extended fort, settlement was probably concentrated in the interior, leaving plenty of space for the people building the ramparts to carry out their work. Only after the massive refurbishment of phase 4 (see below) is there any evidence that the area behind the rampart was occupied and it is likely to have occurred some time after the quarry was excavated as the occupation sits on about 0.5 m (1.5 ft) of silt which had accumulated in the abandoned quarry. It must indicate that the phase of defensive construction had more or less come to an end as with the building of houses close to the bank it would have become very difficult to accomplish a major rebuilding on the scale of the previous periods. Nevertheless minor refurbishments and heightening did take place in the succeeding periods.

The occupation in the area can be divided into four phases (**67**). The earliest traces, phase 1, are not very substantial; they amount only to gullies, post-holes and pits and an increase in the amount of rubbish deposited. The only building which may have been a house lay on the western edge of the excavated trench and had been badly mutilated by later activity. This evidence all suggests that the excavations uncovered the edge of an area of occupation. The principal focus for activity appears to have been immediately west of the area examined, in the south-west corner of the fort.

The next phase of activity, phase 2, was completely different. The area excavated seems to be the focus for a small family group, with three houses identified, one in the centre of the trench, and the other two on its western edge. The area between the houses was roughly cobbled over with chalk, flint and limestone rubble, in some areas several times. The presence of a number of post-holes of various dimensions suggests that the area was divided by fences and also contained other small temporary structures. Immediately in front of the central house was a group of post-holes which must be the remains of a set of steps on to the rampart. Behind the houses was a cluster of pits (**colour plate 11**).

The central house is one of the best preserved houses discovered at Maiden Castle and it has features typical of Iron Age houses throughout the British Isles (**68** and **69**). It was circular, about 6 m (19 ft) in diameter, and surrounded by a slight bank thrown up from a ditch which encircled it. The position of the wall was defined by the inner edge of the bank and the spread of a charcoal-rich occupation layer in the interior of the house. There was no evidence for the remains of the wall itself. It is likely to have been a wattle wall based on vertical stakes which have left no obvious trace in the soft silt on which the house was built. The main structural timbers of the house were a ring of posts. At the top, these would have been tied to a horizontal ring which held them rigid and on which the roof beams would have rested. These posts were not set in post-holes, since once the horizontal tie was in position the structure would have been relatively stable. The positions of several of the posts are identifiable because they were placed on small pads of stone to stop them sinking into the underlying silt. The entrance to the house faced south, towards the rampart, and was marked by a fence, which enclosed the terminal of the encircling ditch on the east side, and by a limestone pavement. A post-hole on the west side of the entrance and a threshold of flint blocks suggests that the entrance might have been a substantial wooden door which pivoted on the post.

The interior of the house was dominated by a repeatedly rebuilt central hearth, and spread over the floor around the hearth was a great deal of ash from its use. Three rebuilds were identified; the first two were relatively simple – a shallow scoop was dug and filled with flint pebbles which were sealed with a layer of clay on which the fire was lit – but the final hearth was more complicated and could be described as an oven. It survived as a horseshoe-shaped setting of stones, with its open end facing northeast, which would have been the supports for a clay dome that had almost completely decayed away. There was a scatter of other features inside the house, including post-holes, which may indicate a partition wall, and a hollow

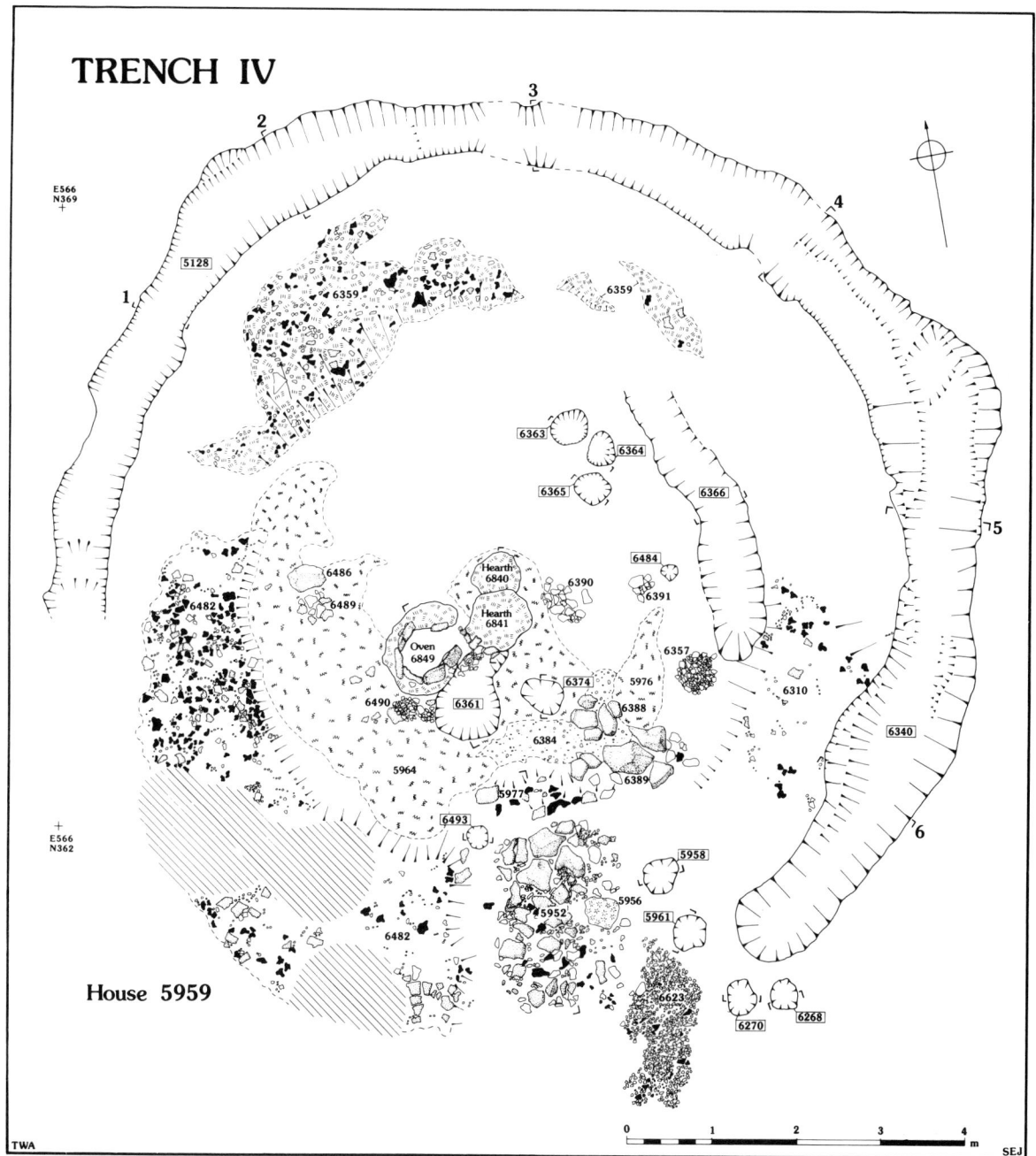

68 *A plan of the house in the centre of the 1986 trench in phase 2.*

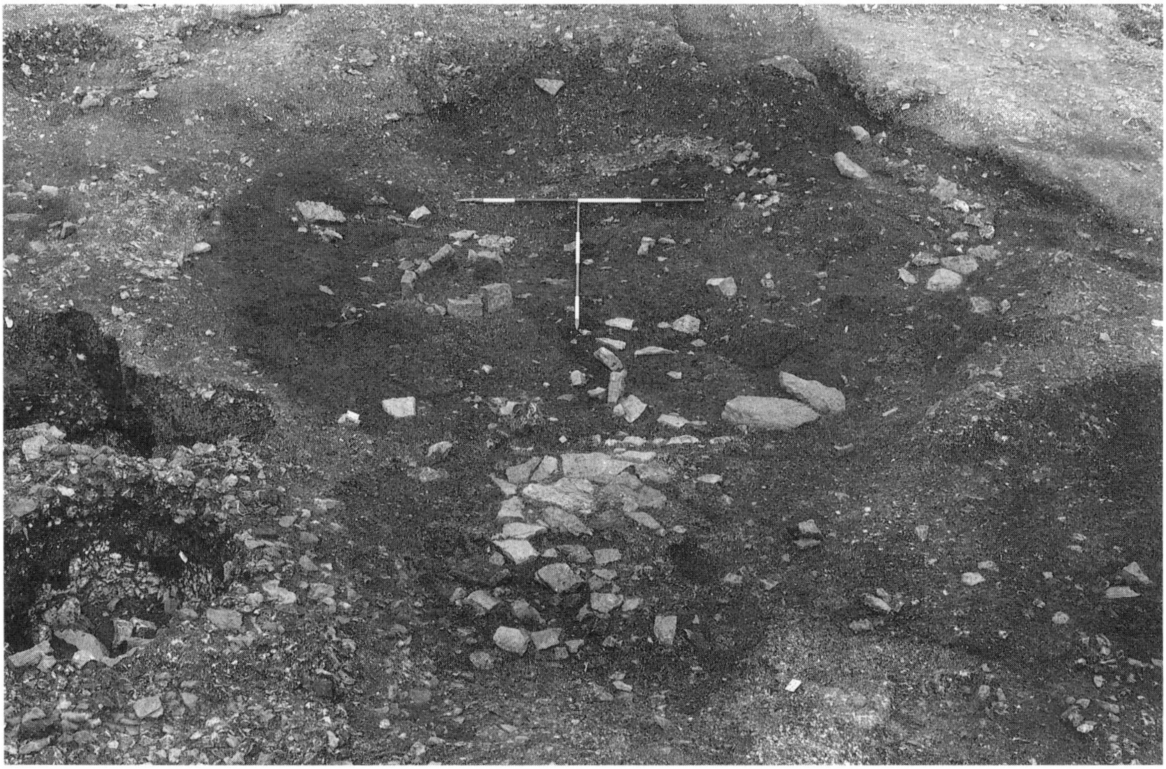

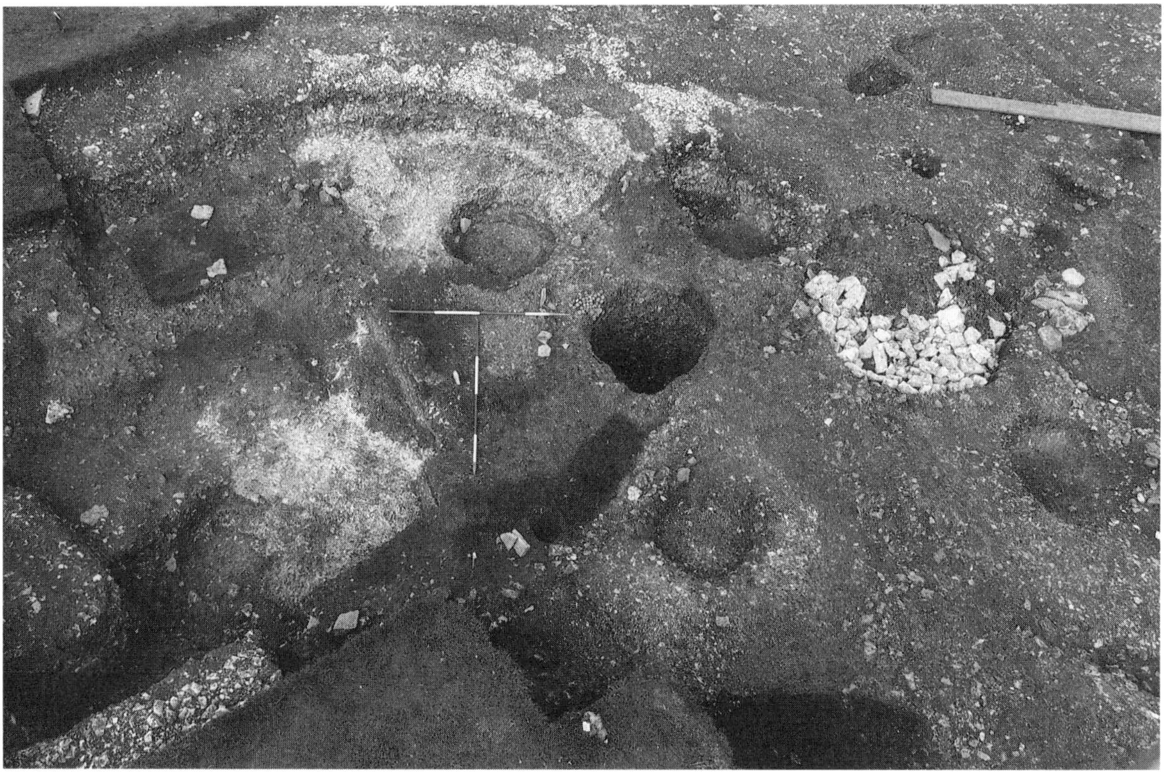

which might have marked the position of a bed. The area of this hollow was noticeably free from ash and other rubbish.

The south-eastern house appears to be very similar to the central house, but only a small area of its interior was exposed. The other house occupied within this phase was only slightly different (**70**). It had been built on a terrace cut into the slope of the hill at the back of the infilled quarry and the floor was part solid chalk, part natural clay and part the silt infilling of the quarry. The structural ring of timbers had been placed in post-holes. Where the floor was of chalk, the line of stakeholes that marked the position of the outside wall was clearly visible. Two hearths were found in the area of the interior excavated in 1986 and an oven had been found in an area excavated in 1935. The entrance faced south and outside it was an area of limestone paving.

It should be stressed that these houses survived because they were sealed by a thick layer of later silt and occupation debris. If the remains of the central house had been exposed to the effects of cultivation after it had been abandoned, most of the important features would have been destroyed. All that would be left would be the surrounding ditch. Similar ditches were found in the interior of Maiden Castle by Wheeler and it is likely that these represent houses whose remains have been badly damaged by later activity, erosion and cultivation of the hilltop.

The presence of hearths or ovens in all three houses and their standardized layout suggests they were dwellings used for cooking, eating and sleeping. This might appear surprising as the houses are quite small, the area enclosed being only 28 sq. m (101 sq. ft). Ethnographic study has suggested that a structure this size could be expected to house about three people. Extensive excavations at the hillfort of Danebury, where 24 houses of two distinct types have been exposed, have shown that the houses in these developed hillforts were remarkably similar.

69 *The house in the centre of the 1986 trench in phase 2.*

70 *The house on the western edge of the 1986 trench in phase 2.*

This occupation was followed by a period of abandonment. The remains of the houses were sealed by a layer of silt up to 20 cm (8 in.) thick, which must derive from the deposition and erosion of middens and the gradual accumulation of soil down the hill side. It is impossible to say how long this period of abandonment lasted, though it may have been around 50 years, nor is it clear how extensive the area of abandonment was. It is possible that the whole hillfort was left vacant but it is perhaps more reasonable to think of this as an area of urban decay inside an otherwise densely occupied hillfort.

The next phase, phase 3, involved the construction of a row of at least three houses. These were all roughly the same size but all had features which made them unique. The western one was built of stone (**71**); the central one was terraced into the hillslope (and was built on top of an earlier house) (**72**); and the eastern one was surrounded by a gully (**73**). They appear to have been occupied for some considerable time as all three were completely rebuilt at least once. The close relationship of the two western houses suggests that they belonged together. The stone walled house was probably the more important of the two as it alone had a hearth. The area between these two and the eastern house was divided by a low chalk bank and the remains of a fence which presumably acted as a property boundary. There was a scatter of pits in and around the houses but there was very little sign of activity compared to the preceding phase. The only outside hearth and cobbled area lay immediately in front of the house terraced into the hillslope.

The reorganization of the houses into rows seems to mark a major event in the occupation of the hillfort. It suggests that those who controlled the hillfort had increasing power over the fundamental structure of social life. The construction of regimented rows of houses may have been an attempt to break down the extended kinship ties of individual families and strengthen the importance of the larger urban community. The variation in house design, however, suggests that the identity of individuals had not been totally absorbed by whatever collective ideals were in force and is in marked contrast to the situation in some other hillforts. At Danebury there was a similar reorganization of the settlement late in the life of the hillfort which created a row of practically

identical houses in a quarry hollow behind the rampart.

Our understanding of the occupation in the centre of the hillfort at this time is not clear as there was no sizeable excavation of the interior during the recent work. Wheeler did excavate a large area in the interior of the earlier hillfort (see **59**) but it has not been possible to work out the chronological phasing of the area in any great detail and the Iron Age occupation was also considerably disturbed by later Roman activity. Despite these disadvantages, a number of observations can be made. The area is divided up by several featureless strips which are best interpreted as routes guiding traffic through the interior. These appear to divide the area into a zone of houses, which survive only as ring ditches, and a zone of pits. The Bank Barrow which would have survived as a low mound in this period was also left undisturbed by new refurbishments and was either another route or

71 *(above) The excavation of a stone-walled house in 1935. This house was part of a row of houses behind the rampart. (The Society of Antiquaries.)*

72 *(top right) The house on the western edge of the 1986 trench in phase 3.*

73 *(right) The house on the eastern edge of the 1986 trench in phase 3.*

was deliberately avoided as a mark of respect for its age and ritual significance.

This basic pattern is confirmed by the magnetometer survey of the interior of the hillfort (**74**). Such a survey is a measurement of the magnetic enhancement of the soil, recorded in a series of readings taken on a grid of points across the site. Any burning converts the weakly magnetic iron oxides present in the subsoil into strongly magnetic iron oxide and thus produces areas of

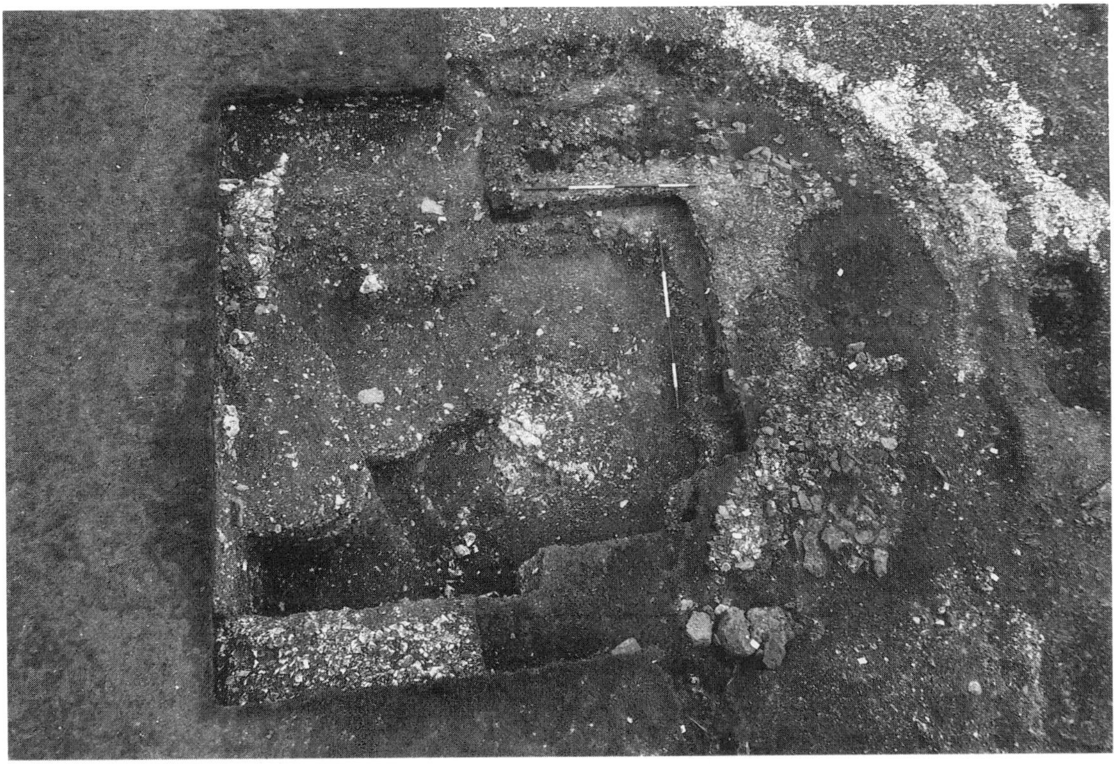

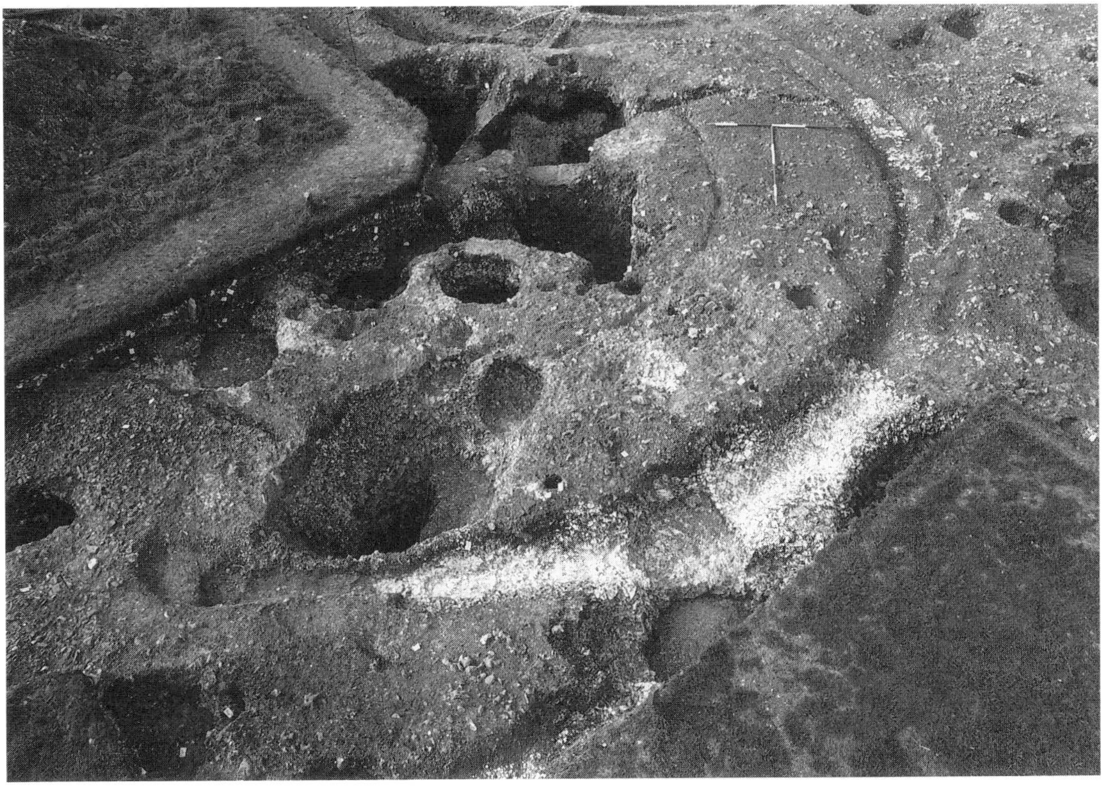

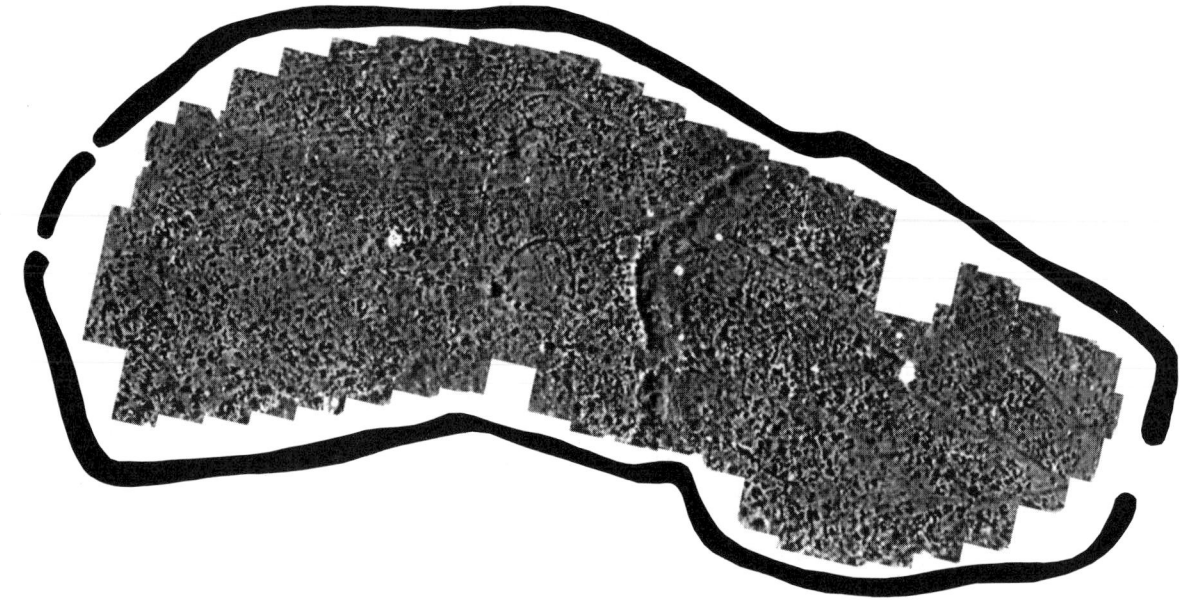

enhancement which can be measured. On a densely occupied site such as Maiden Castle the disturbed soil has often been considerably enhanced by fires and the dumping of ash from them. Consequently when a reading is taken above a deep feature such as a pit or a ditch the volume of magnetically enhanced soil will give a higher than average reading, whereas readings taken over walls or cairns will be lower than average because of the reduction of the volume of disturbed soil above them. Interpretation of the findings of such readings is always problematical for many factors can disrupt them and it is not often that a survey produces an undisputed picture of the features that survive. The quality of the Maiden Castle survey and the clarity of the features visible is exceptional.

The most obvious feature the survey revealed is the density of occupation that covers the entire hillfort. Most of the features that are visible on this plan are likely to be grain storage pits (**75**) and this survey gives us some idea of the huge quantities of grain that could be stored in the hillfort (**colour plate 10**). Also clearly visible is the bank and ditch of the Early Iron Age defences and a small enclosure in the centre of the hillfort. Slightly less obvious are a number of linear features which cut across the hilltop from east to west. The clearest and most regular

74 *The magnetometer survey of the hilltop.*

is the Bank Barrow which excavation has shown was avoided during the Iron Age. Radiating from the eastern entrance are other lines which are probably a series of routes which provide the main access across the hillfort and were discovered by Wheeler in the centre of the fort. A very similar pattern was discovered during the excavation of Danebury where the routes also acted as boundaries partitioning the interior of the hillfort into storage and occupation areas. It is possible that this is comparable to the situation at Maiden Castle but the information from the magnetometer survey is not susceptible to sufficient analysis to be able to distinguish the different types of use.

The presence of very large numbers of pits in the developed hillforts of the Middle Iron Age marks them as quite different from the Early Iron Age hillforts. Early forts were only provided with a relatively limited storage capacity which on the face of it appears to be appropriate for the size of the community inhabiting the fort. The storage capacity of the numerous pits at Maiden Castle and at hillforts such as Danebury, however, was apparently well in excess of what would be required by its inhabitants. In the initial stages of expansion of

75 *Grain storage pits excavated in 1935. (The Society of Antiquaries.)*

the hillfort, this increased capacity may well have been necessary to support the workforce engaged in the construction programme on the defences but the immediate requirements of this labour force seem to have been catered for by the construction of four-post granaries above ground. Most of the pit silos were created in the later Middle Iron Age when the occupation was expanding and rampart construction was less important. At this stage the grain stored in the hillfort must have become increasingly more significant as a commodity which could be used to stimulate exchange and the development of specialized economies. This will be discussed more fully in the next chapter where the material culture and the economy of the hillfort is examined.

The final phase of activity, phase 4 (see **67**), in the south-west corner of the fort was very different. The highly structured settlement of the previous phase was replaced by a disorganized spread of occupation which included hearths, pits and post-holes, among which the remains of only a single house could be tentatively identified. The density of features and the quantity and quality of the finds from this phase, however, indicate that a considerable amount of activity took place. This may not necessarily have been continuous but it lasted some time as in several places there was a sequence of overlapping features. The latest finds date from the beginning of the first century AD but it appears as if this part of the hillfort was abandoned before the Roman conquest. This final phase immediately preceding the Roman conquest will be discussed in detail in chapter 9. It is important to note, however, that there was a major change in the nature of occupation of the hillfort in the first century BC involving a breakdown in the basic structure of the hillfort occupation and gradual abandonment of its western part.

The sequence of structural phases encountered in the south-west corner of the hillfort cannot be proved to be directly representative of the occupation of the whole hillfort. It can, however, be paralleled at other sites, which suggests that there is a general pattern of occupation in developed hillforts such as these. The sequence at Maiden Castle begins with a period when much of the interior of the extended hillfort is unoccupied but provision for grain storage in above-ground granaries is extensive. This coincides with a concentration

of effort on the defences, when multiple banks and ditches and very complex entrances are created. There is then evidence for a gradual increase in the occupation of the interior: small clusters of houses, possibly representing extended family groups, are now scattered across the interior. This relatively unstructured occupation is reorganized in the next phase; the houses are constructed in rows parallel to routes running east to west across

76 *Four of the largest hillforts in the territory defined by pottery similar in style to that found at Maiden Castle in the Middle Iron Age.*

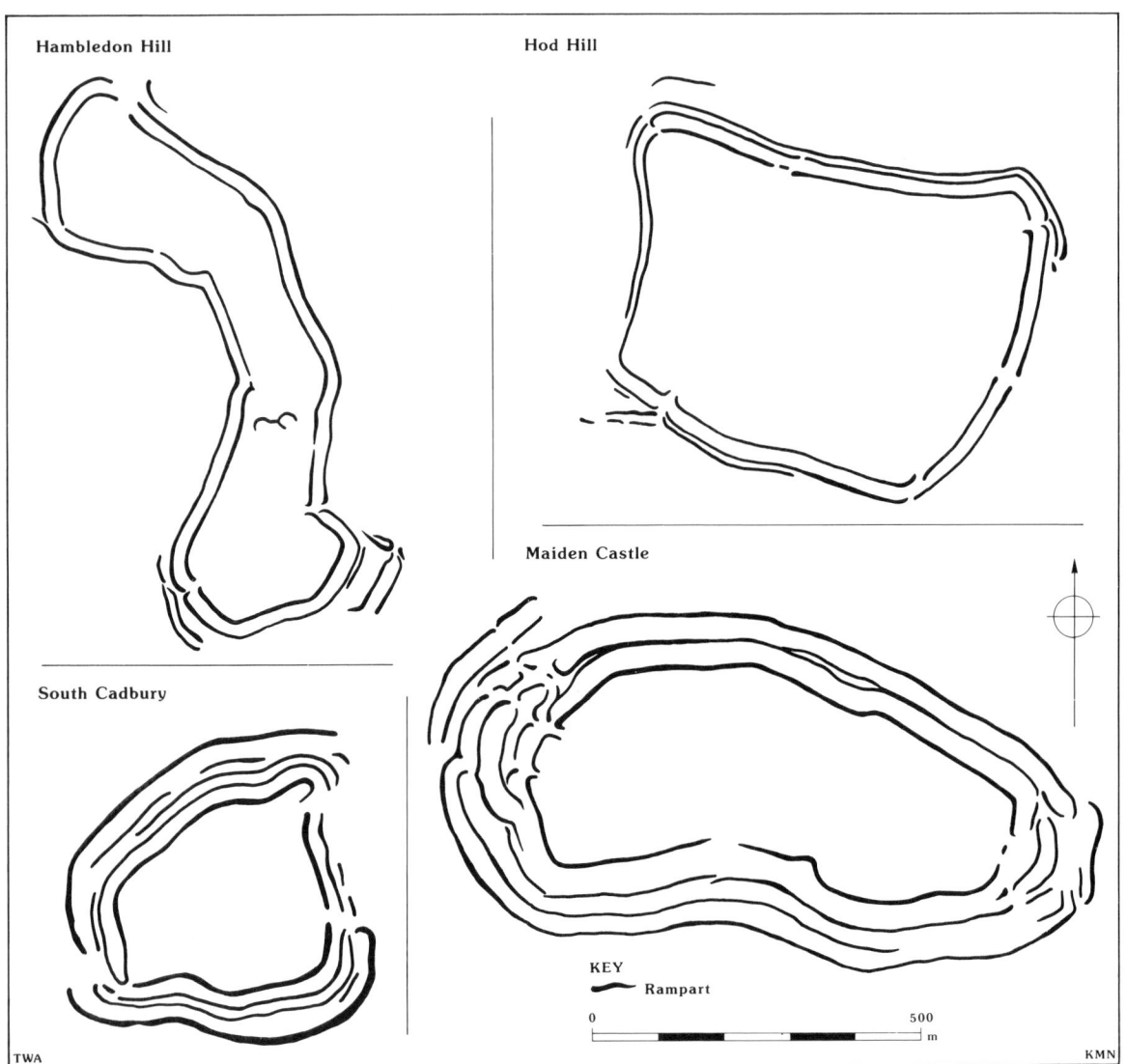

Hambledon Hill

Hod Hill

Maiden Castle

South Cadbury

KEY
— Rampart

0　　　　　　　　500
m

TWA

KMN

the hilltop, possibly dividing it into storage and occupation areas. In the later periods the importance of the defences appears to have substantially diminished and there is little evidence that the ramparts received more than cursory maintenance. The final phase of occupation involved a complete breakdown in the structure of the hillfort occupation with gradually decreasing evidence for activity in the western half of the fort.

The landscape around the hillfort

Contemporary with this sequence of activity inside Maiden Castle was a number of important changes in the settlements in the surrounding area. The initial expansion of the hillfort coincided with the abandonment of the settlements and hillforts in the immediate vicinity and presumably the movement of their inhabitants into the fort. Only when the hillfort occupation was at its densest, at the end of the Middle Iron Age, did settlements reappear in the landscape.

The earliest settlement lies immediately east of the hillfort of Poundbury and dates to the very end of the Middle Iron Age. Here there were a number of circular houses which initially sat inside a small enclosure on the valley side overlooking the River Frome. The enclosure was soon abandoned and the houses spread out along the edge of the valley across the enclosure ditch. They were similar in size and construction to those at Maiden Castle and were accompanied by a scatter of grain storage pits. Other settlements, contemporary with the later phase of the Middle Iron Age at Maiden Castle, were discovered during the excavations of the early prehistoric monuments at Mount Pleasant and Flagstones. Evidence for these settlements, precursors to important Late Iron Age settlements, largely comprises isolated pits but there was also a circular house in the centre of the Mount Pleasant enclosure.

Further afield in Dorset there was a rationalization of the dense scatter of hillforts left over from the Early Iron Age. Many hillforts appear to achieve a local pre-eminence by the heightening and multiplication of their defences and an expansion of the area they enclosed. Badbury Rings in the east and Eggardon and Pilsdon Pen in the west are the best examples. Only one hillfort, however, appears to acquire a status comparable to that achieved by Maiden Castle: Hambledon Hill (**76**), which was densely occupied and expanded to enclose an area of about 12.5 ha (31 acres). During the Middle Iron Age the settlement inside this hillfort appears to have moved en masse to the adjacent hilltop of Hod Hill. This had been enclosed in the Late Bronze Age but was abandoned when Hambledon Hill was occupied. It is likely that the settlement moved away from this site initially because the open flat top was too large an area to defend adequately with the small scale resources available to the original hillfort builders. As Hambledon Hill began to expand and the inhabitants became more powerful, it became more and more awkward to occupy the narrow ridge on which the fort was built. Consequently, at about the time that Maiden Castle was reorganized, the inhabitants moved back to the original large flat hilltop where there was scope to lay out a grid of streets which is still faintly visible in the uncultivated southeast corner.

The exact relationship between the small developed hillforts and the two larger hillforts is impossible to determine. It is clear, however, that after an initial period of rapid growth and apparently competitive building in the early part of the Middle Iron Age, the existence of defences appears to have become less important. These changes coincided with changes in the material culture which suggest that these centres acted in co-operation and that alliances had now been negotiated which deflected competition away from internal aggression within Dorset towards external aggression against other territories.

8

Social relationships and economic activity

The previous chapter examined the chronological sequence of events involved in the creation of the extended and elaborately defended hillfort of the Middle Iron Age. The discussion concentrated on the basic structural features of the hillfort and the nature of its occupation. This chapter will examine the finds from this occupation to show what sort of lifestyle was led by the inhabitants.

Food production

One of the prime necessities for any community is to ensure a good supply of food. Food production, therefore, is the first aspect of the economy that requires examination. Evidence for food production is of three main types: the remains of food itself, normally animal bones and carbonized plant remains; the tools used in food production; and the management of the land used for production.

The evidence from the agricultural tools found on the site at Maiden Castle does not give a very clear picture of farming practices. The only tools which could be associated with agriculture were the iron tip of a wooden ard and an iron sickle or reaping hook. Examples of both of these are found on other Iron Age sites and sickles are very common. The most important agricultural tools, however, for instance spades and ards, were largely, if not completely, wooden and these only survive in waterlogged conditions. The few that have survived come from the bogs of Scotland and Ireland and it is not clear how relevant these are to the agricultural process in southern England.

An examination of traces of Iron Age management of the landscape surrounding Maiden Castle is also less than informative. Until recently it has been assumed that the small rectangular fields which can be seen to surround Maiden Castle were contemporary with the Iron Age hillforts. In recent years, however, it has been discovered that they date from the second millennium BC. Even the larger linear boundaries which cut across these field systems precede the construction of many of the hillforts, including Maiden Castle. There were in fact no landscape boundaries constructed in this area in the Early or Middle Iron Age; only in the very last centuries of the Iron Age were new field boundaries and systems created. It is clear therefore that during the occupation of the hillfort the inhabitants were content to use ancient field systems that had been laid out several hundred years earlier.

As a consequence of this, the only possible method of examining the agricultural practices of the inhabitants of Maiden Castle in detail is to analyse the waste they produced in the preparation and consumption of food. It should be emphasized that this does not provide direct access either to what was planted (or grazed) in the fields or what was eaten by the inhabitants of the hillfort. The carbonized plant remains found on the site are largely derived from the accidental combustion of cereals which were being processed for consumption or the debris (husks and stalks) from this process (**77**). Only rarely are cleaned deposits ready for food preparation ever found. Similarly the animal bones are the debris deliberately discarded during the butchering of a carcass (**78**). There is no means of comparing either the importance of animals and crops in the diet of the inhabitants or the amount of effort that was put into their production. Nevertheless, the information still provides a valuable picture of the animal and crop husbandry practices of the community.

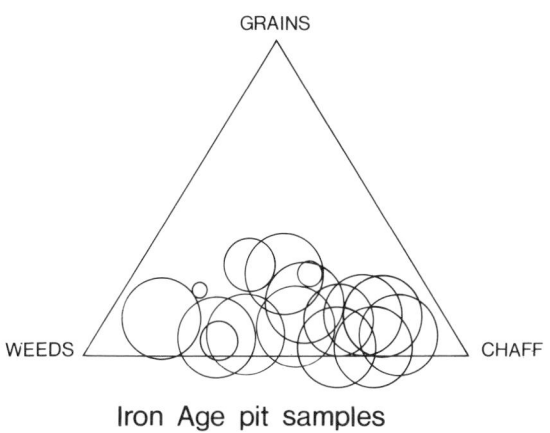

Iron Age pit samples

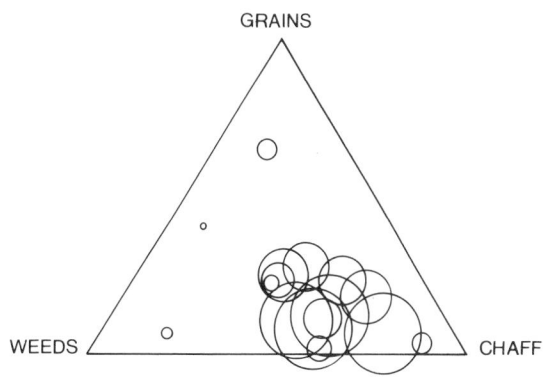

Iron Age samples excluding pits

77 *A diagram showing the different constituents of the carbonized plant material found during the Middle Iron Age occupation of the hillfort.*

78 *The discarded carcass of a sheep found in front of the eastern entrance to the fort.*

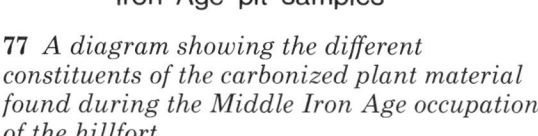

(The following discussion is a summary of the reports on the plant remains by C. Palmer and M. Jones and the animal bones by M. Armour Chelu.)

The most obvious feature of the assemblage of carbonized plant remains is the quantity of material that was recovered. From only 56 samples looked at over 340 identifiable cereal grains were recovered, even though only a quarter of each sample was examined. This is in marked contrast to the Neolithic assemblage where all plant remains were very scarce. As a rough comparison, 10 litres (2.2 gallons) of soil from an Iron Age feature on average contains 33.3 cereal grains but in the Neolithic the same amount would only contain 1.34 cereal grains. This immediately suggests that cereal production has become much more important.

The principal cereal species cultivated by the inhabitants were wheat and barley. In most contexts wheat was dominant but one sample from a grain storage pit contained large quantities of barley. The predominant wheat variety was Triticum spelta, a primitive species marked by its ability to both withstand temperature extremes and grow on a wide variety of soils. Both naked and hulled 6-row barley were found in the Iron Age deposits. This is also a crop renowned for its adaptability and it can be sown in winter or spring. Other cereals present in small quantities were oats and *Bromus*. Though the latter is normally regarded as a weed it was present in sufficiently large amounts at Maiden Castle to indicate that it was used as a food source.

A range of leguminous plants, including beans, peas, lentils and vetches, were present although only in small quantities. It is possible that these plants were more important than they appear but that they were not so often burnt and so do not survive. Other potential crops include *Chenopodium album* (fat hen), corn spurry and *Brassicas*. The latter includes a wide range of possible crops ranging from seed crops such as mustard, leaf crops such as cabbage and brussel sprouts, flowering crops such as broccoli and cauliflower, through to root crops such as turnips. But the surviving seeds, which occur in large concentrations, do not allow any specific identifications.

Until the advent of modern cultivation methods and the widespread availability of chemical fertilizers arable farms were invaded by weeds of a variety of species. Unlike the cultivated crops, which had been chosen to have a wide tolerance of environmental and soil conditions, these weeds are often quite particular to the soils, the climate or the cultivation techniques used. Consequently the weed species present at Maiden Castle give an indication of the areas exploited by the occupants of Maiden Castle and the methods they used.

One very important feature of the weed assemblage is the absence of evidence for nutrient depletion of the soils cultivated. Species such as Chenopodiaceae and *Stellarietea media* which need soils rich in nitrogen are abundant. The weeds indicate, too, that crops were, not surprisingly, grown on the chalk downland and the sandy areas which cap the chalk but they give no sign of exploitation of the heavier soils of the coastal plain or the river valleys. The presence of large quantities of *Bromus spp.* suggests shallow ard cultivation was the predominant method of preparing the fields.

The animal bone assemblage was similarly rich and contained a great deal of information which can only be summarized here. The principal domestic species were cattle, sheep and pig but horse, dog (**79**) and goat were also present in small numbers. Wild animals were very rare with only three red deer bones, one badger bone and one hare bone found.

The relative importance of sheep, cattle and pig can be calculated by many different means. The most obvious is by comparing the number of bones of each within the total recorded assemblage. Using this method sheep formed the majority species accounting for 66 per cent, as against 21 per cent cattle and 9 per cent pig. This gives some idea of the relative numeric importance of the species in the fields around Maiden Castle but the great difference in size between these animals means that simple numbers alone may give a false picture of the relative significance in the diet of the inhabitants. This can more accurately be assessed by analysing the weight of bones from each species. On this basis cattle were the most important, accounting for 52 per cent of the assemblage whereas sheep accounted for 30 per cent and pigs remained at 9 per cent.

Neither of these sets of figures, however, necessarily indicates the economic role of the different species as the animals need not have been kept primarily as a source of food. Sheep provide wool, cattle provide milk and some traction power, horses provide traction power

79 *The discarded waste parts (heads and feet) of two dogs that had been butchered for their meat.*

and dogs were used for hunting. Only pigs are normally kept solely for meat. There is indeed some evidence that cattle and sheep at least were not kept just for meat. Approximately 50 per cent of the individuals whose age could be determined survived until they were over three years old which is well beyond the optimum age for culling an animal reared solely for its meat. Beyond the first or second year the animals eat more and put on less weight. Most of the young animals in the assemblage appear to have died accidentally during or immediately after their birth; they indicate that pregnant animals were brought onto the site.

The sheep suffered a very high incidence of dental diseases including caries, congenital absence, tooth loss, periodontal disease, late eruption and bone resorption in the jaw. These complaints were particularly common in young animals and may indicate that the sheep were malnourished, either because there was over-grazing or because they were not receiving enough supplementary feeding during the winter months.

Food preparation and consumption

The assemblages of animal bones and carbonized plants also provide information on how and where food was prepared for consumption. The bones show cut marks which indicate in what way the animals were dismembered and a large part of the carbonized plant remains are the debris from the process of cleaning which all cereals require before they become edible.

A clear picture of how the animals were butchered can be provided by quoting Ms Armour Chelu's report on the bones from the recent excavations: 'The butchery data indicates that all the domestic animals were skinned, certain elements were dismembered and the flesh was filleted from the primary meat-bearing bones. Many of the bones from cattle, sheep and pig had been broken to extract marrow but the bones of dog and horse were not as fragmented which suggests that these species were not fully exploited for this purpose. Cattle and large ungulate ribs were chopped to a roughly uniform size suggesting that these were butchered to be of manageable size for the cooking pot.'

Amongst the assemblage of iron blades from the site are a number of thick choppers which would be more than capable of dismembering the animal carcasses.

The bulk of the carbonized plant remains found in the Iron Age were waste materials derived from crop processing (see **77**). Over 4500 fragments of wheat chaff were found in the 56 samples examined and none of the samples contained more grains than waste products. The quantities of debris clearly indicate that the hillfort was an important centre for the processing of grain. Large quantities of cereals must have arrived at the site on the ear to be threshed and winnowed. In the threshing process the ear is beaten until the hard outer casing and stalk are broken free of the grain. The threshed grain is then winnowed by being tossed into the air so that the lighter chaff blows away to leave only the cleaned grains. It is this lighter chaff which was burnt and preserved.

Once this process was completed the cleaned grain would be ready to be ground into flour or stored whole for later use. Large numbers of querns have been found on the site, though they were surprisingly rare in the recent excavations. In the Middle Iron Age the commonest method of producing flour was with a hand-powered rotary quern which consisted of two stones, held together by a spindle, with the joint between the two at an angle. The grain was poured in through an aperture in the centre of the top stone and was forced through the narrow gap between the two stones and in the process was ground into flour. Varying the gap between the two stones allowed the miller to vary the fineness of the flour produced.

Our knowledge of the cooking and consumption of food in the Iron Age is quite limited. It seems likely that a large proportion of the ceramics found on the site were involved in some way in cooking whilst others were vessels used in the serving or consumption of food. Unfortunately there are no fixed criteria for distinguishing these or other functions. The assemblage can be split by form into two basic categories: jars and bowls, but it is clear that some jars were used for cooking and some for storage. Likewise some bowls were used for cooking but others would be used for eating from. It is possible, however, to distinguish certain types that were favoured for cooking by examining the occurrence of residues on the vessels. Certain types of jar and 'saucepan pots' are regularly found with organic residues adhering to the surface and heavily sooted. In contrast other jar and bowl types are seldom found with these residues, the fine bowls appearing in the later Middle Iron Age, and used for serving food, do not seem to have any parallels in the earlier part of the Middle Iron Age (compare **84** and **85**).

The pots could be used in cooking in a number of different ways. They might be filled with water which was then heated by dropping in hot stones to boil the contents, or they might be packed around with ashes to bake the food. It is unlikely that any of the types would be strong enough to withstand direct heat. There are other ceramic objects which may well have been placed over fires: the so-called oven plates, circular clay discs 0.38 m (15 in.) in diameter perforated by holes 2.5 cm (1 in.) in diameter (**80**). These were originally thought to be designed to sit inside domed ovens (**81**) but the diameters of the plates are too large for this. The ovens themselves would have been used for baking and perhaps we should envisage a product similar to nan bread which is cooked by slapping dough onto the sides of a clay oven.

Manufacturing industries

There is archaeological evidence from Maiden Castle for a range of other activities which would have been important to the community. The most obvious are the manufacturing industries required to produce the wide range of goods found during the excavations. For instance there were large quantities of metal – both bronze and iron tools and ornaments (see **82** and **83**). The production of these ultimately depended on the quarrying or collection of ores, the smelting of the ores to transform them into a metal and the casting or smithing of a tool from this metal. Similar processes are involved in glass production

Copper and tin ores are not available in the vicinity of Maiden Castle and analysis suggests that the bulk of the bronze on the site was imported from the south-west, where sources of

INCHES
CMS.

80 Fragments of oven plates used for cooking over open fires in the Middle Iron Age. (The Society of Antiquaries.)

copper and tin had already been exploited for over a millennium. It is not surprising therefore that there is no evidence for the primary production of bronze at Maiden Castle. There is, however, good evidence for the reworking of scrap bronze in the form of melting and casting the metal. In the recent excavations in the south-west corner of the fort, large quantities of small scrap were found in pits along the west side of the trench. This consisted of fragments of sheet bronze which had been cut to fit into crucibles, fragments of crucibles and splashes of melted bronze. The evidence clearly indicates that there was a bronze workshop in the vicinity

and that it probably lay in the area immediately to the west of the trench – an area excavated by Wheeler. Unfortunately since there are no identifiable moulds from the site we cannot be certain what was being produced though a range of objects, all discovered in the excavations, could have been manufactured locally. There are needles and pins, rods and wire, brooches and rings, studs and rivets as well as

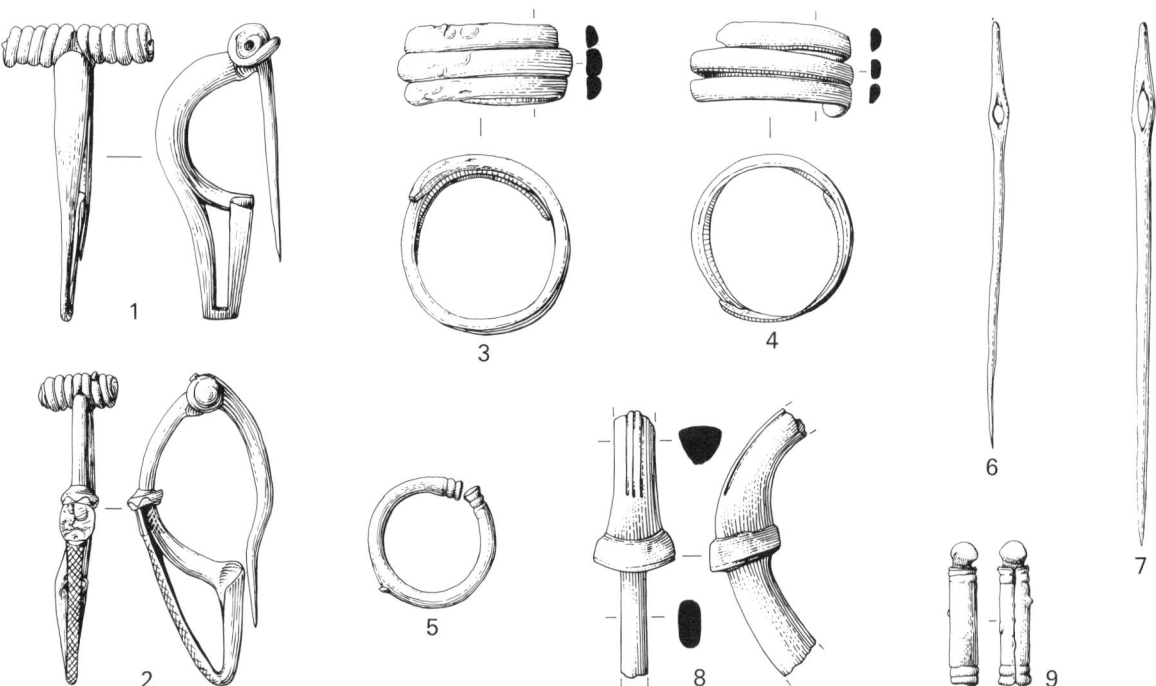

the sheet bronze that was being cut up as scrap (see **82**).

In contrast there are plentiful sources of iron in the vicinity of Maiden Castle. Small iron sulphide (marcasite) nodules can be picked up in the ploughed fields in the surrouding area and these would be a perfectly acceptable source of poor quality iron ore. Better ores are available from the sands and gravels which occur sporadically on Maiden Castle and which form the dominant geology in east Dorset. Consequently one might expect the inhabitants of an important settlement such as Maiden Castle to have played a major role in the primary exploitation of iron ores but this does not seem to be the case. There is a scatter of iron slags from the recent excavations which might have been produced from the initial smelting of the ores but it is equally likely that they result from the production of complex tools from iron blanks imported to the site and that the first smelting was done elsewhere. It is in fact rare to find good evidence for the primary stages of iron production on any Wessex hillfort and it is possible that this activity was restricted to a few specialized centres elsewhere. In contrast, evidence for smithing is relatively common and it is likely that running repairs – a kind of impromptu smithing – was undertaken at the household level to improve the longevity of all basic tools (see **83**).

One of the most important industries during the Iron Age was the production of pottery. Ceramics are the most common finds from sites of this period in Wessex and these industries provide very important information about Iron Age societies. The production of pottery requires only one basic material – clay – and in fact could occur almost anywhere, including on the top of Maiden Castle where clay-filled solution hollows are very common. A plentiful water supply is also important, however, and this would almost certainly exclude Maiden

81 *The remains of an oven found in the centre of a house excavated in 1986.*

82 *Bronze ornaments from the later Middle Iron Age activity at the hillfort. 1, 2 are safety-pin brooches; 3, 4 are rings; 5 is a pennanular brooch which has lot its pin; 6, 7 are needles; 8 is a fragment of horse harness and 9 is part of a larger ornament of unknown form.*

Castle and other hillforts as important production centres. It is possible to make pottery from most clay sources, but production centres are often restricted to sources of high quality clay. Clay from a good source would require little preparation and should be able to withstand the extremes of heat that would be encountered not only in the firing process but in the domestic context in which the pot was later to be used. Sources of this quality are rare.

The evidence from Maiden Castle indicates that there was quite a dramatic change in the manufacturing of pottery during the Middle Iron Age. In the earlier phases pottery appears to have been produced at a number of sources. Some of these were local – pottery was probably being produced at Poxwell, 8 km (5 miles) to the south-east, or around Burton Bradstock and Shipton Gorge, 14 km (8½ miles) to the west. Other sources were more distant: industries in the Poole Harbour area were producing large quantities of pottery. In the later phases of Maiden Castle these industries became an increasingly important source, until in the final phase of occupation in trench IV they made up 95 per cent of the pots in use.

During this period the quality and range of vessels appearing on site changed quite dramatically (**84** and **85**). In the beginning there was a very standardized range of shouldered jars (with rough surfaces showing finger-tip wiping) which seem to have served a range of functions depending on their size. In the later phases there was a varied range of vessels from large storage jars to small bowls. Most of these were very well made with carefully smoothed surfaces which were often decorated.

This pattern of change recurs throughout Dorset. At Gussage All Saints it is clear that the Poole Harbour industries provided all the vessels in the later phases of the occupation and it seems likely that the homogeneity of the ceramics from Dorset in the later periods of the Middle Iron Age occurred because the bulk of the vessels were produced at Poole Harbour. Similar patterns can be seen throughout southern England where there is a general change from the simple and undecorated jars of the earlier phases to a range of well-made jars and bowls which are often elaborately decorated. The shapes of these later bowls and jars and the nature and extent of the decoration seem to define distinct territories which conform to the tribal groupings which appear in the Late Iron

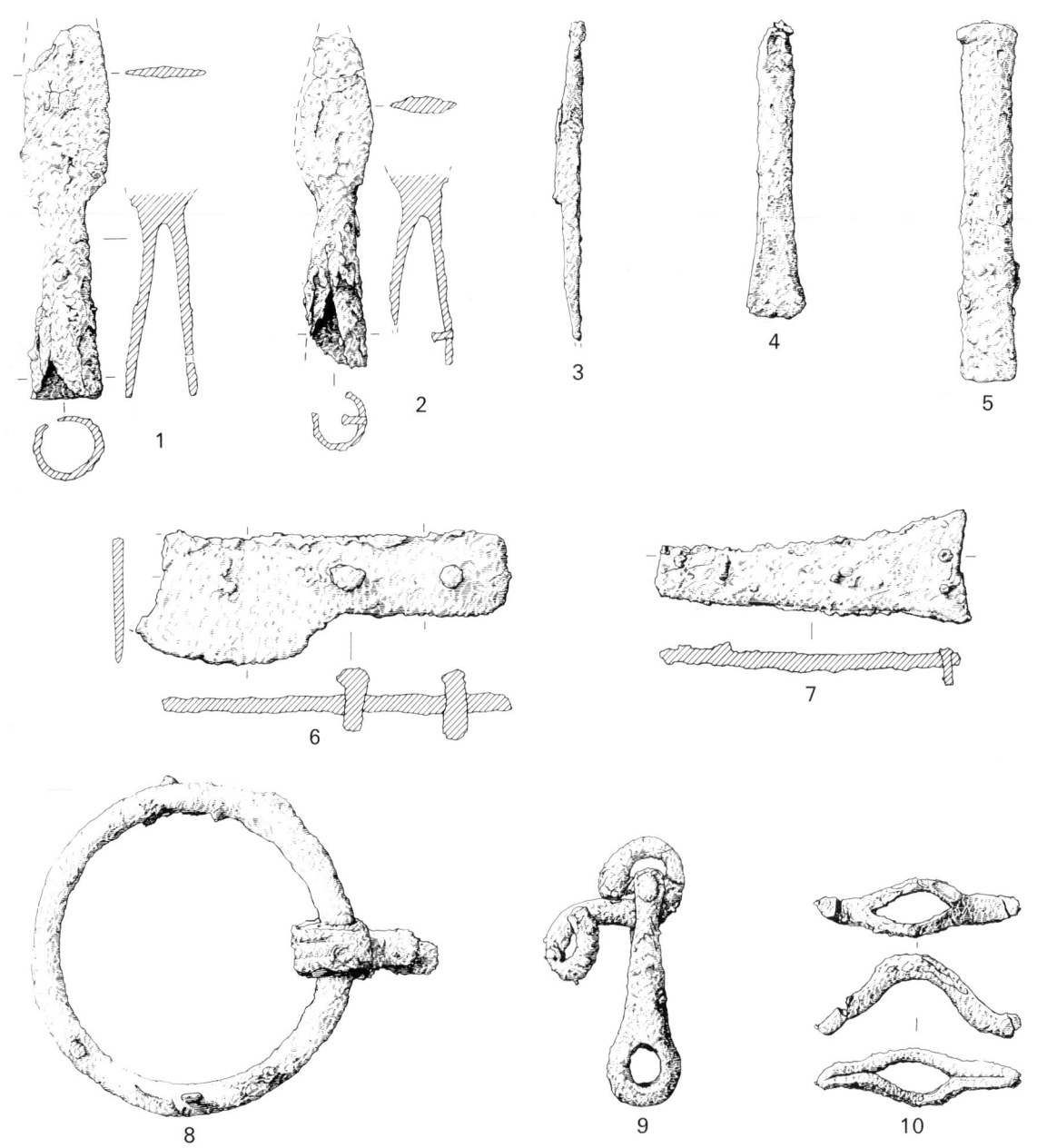

83 *Miscellaneous iron tools and weapons. 1, 2 are spearheads; 3 is an awl; 4, 5 are chisels; 6, 7 are knives, 8 is a suspension ring, 9 is part of a bridle bit, 10 is the hilt guard of a sword.*

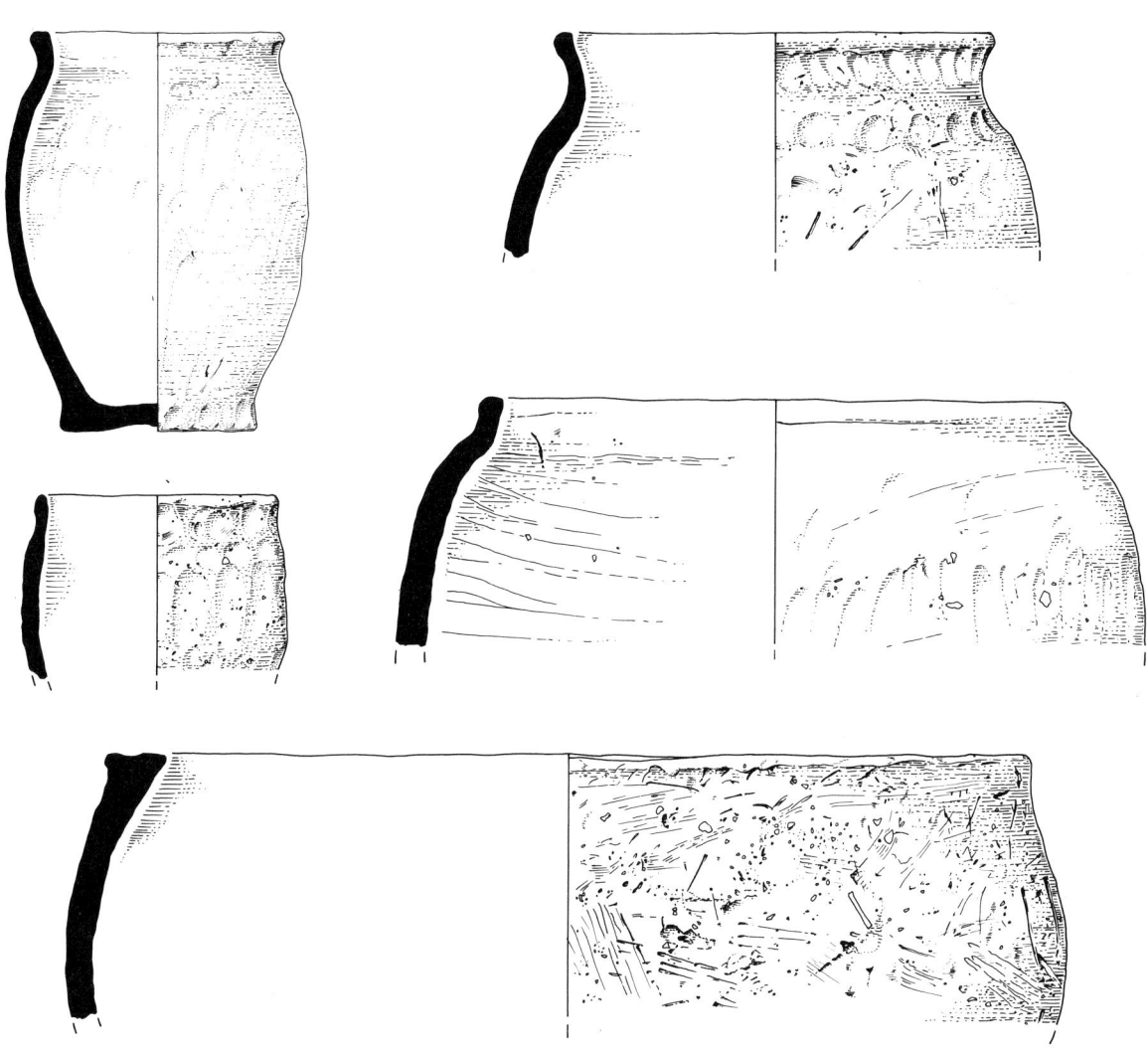

84 *Pottery from the early Middle Iron Age
phases found during the recent excavations.*

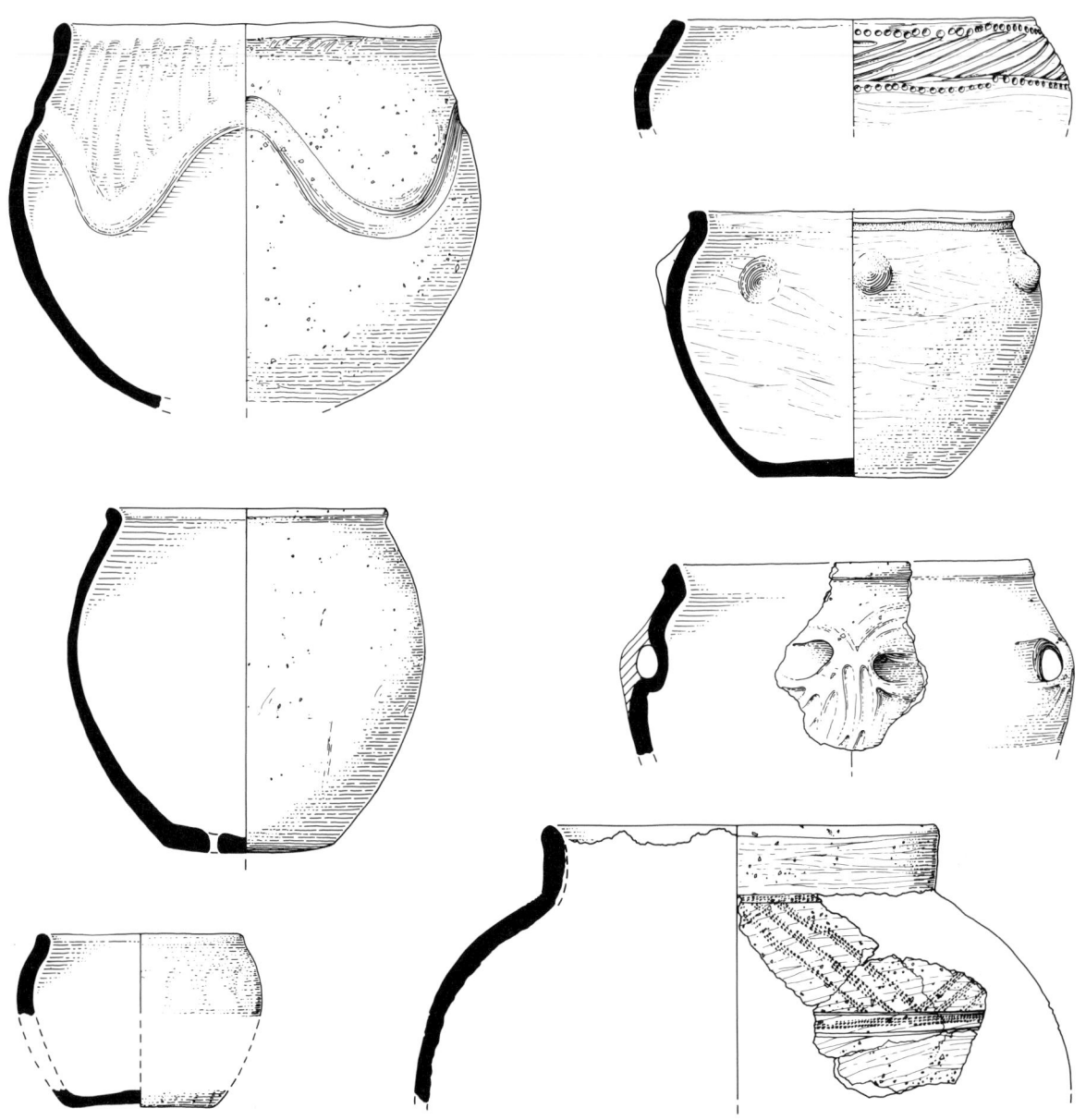

85 *Pottery from the later Middle Iron Age phases found during the recent excavations.*

86 *A hoard of slingstones discovered during the 1986 excavations.*

Age. It is not always clear, however, whether in these other tribal territories the pottery was produced at specialist centres. To the south-west this does seem to be the case but in Hampshire and Wiltshire the clay used was not sufficiently distinctive to be related to a specific source.

Stone tools form another part of the material from Maiden Castle and a variety were found, most of which would have had to be quarried and then imported. The only exceptions were those made from chalk and flint which would have been readily available on the site. Chalk was used to make weights and spindle whorls. Flint was almost insignificant compared to its importance in the Neolithic but a group of hammerstones does appear to date to the Iron Age.

The imported stone objects include slingstones, querns, whetstones and bracelets. The latter were made from Kimmeridge shale, a soft easily-worked stone which can be polished to produce an attractive shiny black surface. The source of this is the sea cliffs at Kimmeridge

Bay in Purbeck. Most of the whetstones also seem to come from a specific location. They are made from Lower Devonian Staddon Grit and it is likely that they come from the area around Plymouth in south-west Devon. The querns come from a variety of sources, some local but some almost certainly from Cornwall and Devon. Slingstones are one of the most ubiquitous stone artefacts on the site and many thousands have been recovered, often in large hoards (86). Though these natural water worn pebbles are present in river valleys close to the hillfort the quantities involved make it more likely that the inhabitants went to Chesil Beach where the right size of pebble is available in abundance. All these stone tools were introduced to the site as finished objects. There is no indication that the occupants of Maiden Castle had an important role in their production or distribution; the inhabitants were thus consumers of material produced elsewhere.

Other industries are indicated not by the final product but by the tools used in their production. Clothing would obviously be important

and even though all trace of this has disappeared we do have evidence for the types of material used and how it was produced. The importance of sheep, and the old age of the slaughtered animals has already been mentioned as evidence that wool production was important. This is emphasized by the number of finds associated with textile production. There are large numbers of spindle whorls which would be used to convert the wool into thread. Chalk weights are the only surviving parts of the looms on which the thread was woven into cloth. There are a range of needles and points, largely of bone (**87**) but including examples in bronze, which could be used for assembling garments. Finally there are the brooches (see **82**), pins and toggles of bronze and bone which were used to fasten the garments. This suggests that the production of cloth and clothes was an

important part of the economy of Maiden Castle.

Another product, now indiscernible in the archaeological record but very important to the inhabitants, was salt, essential for the preservation of meat. Evidence indicates that salt was being produced by evaporating saline water along the Purbeck coast, in Poole Harbour and in the Fleet (behind Chesil Bank). The presence

87 Bone tools found during the recent excavations. 1–4 are called weaving combs but they are more likely to have been used to pluck the wool from sheep; 5, 13 are sheep long bones which have been perforated and appear to have been used as bobbins; 6, 7 are pins; 8–10 are needles (note these are very similar to the bronze needles in 83); 11 is an awl, 12 is a gouge.

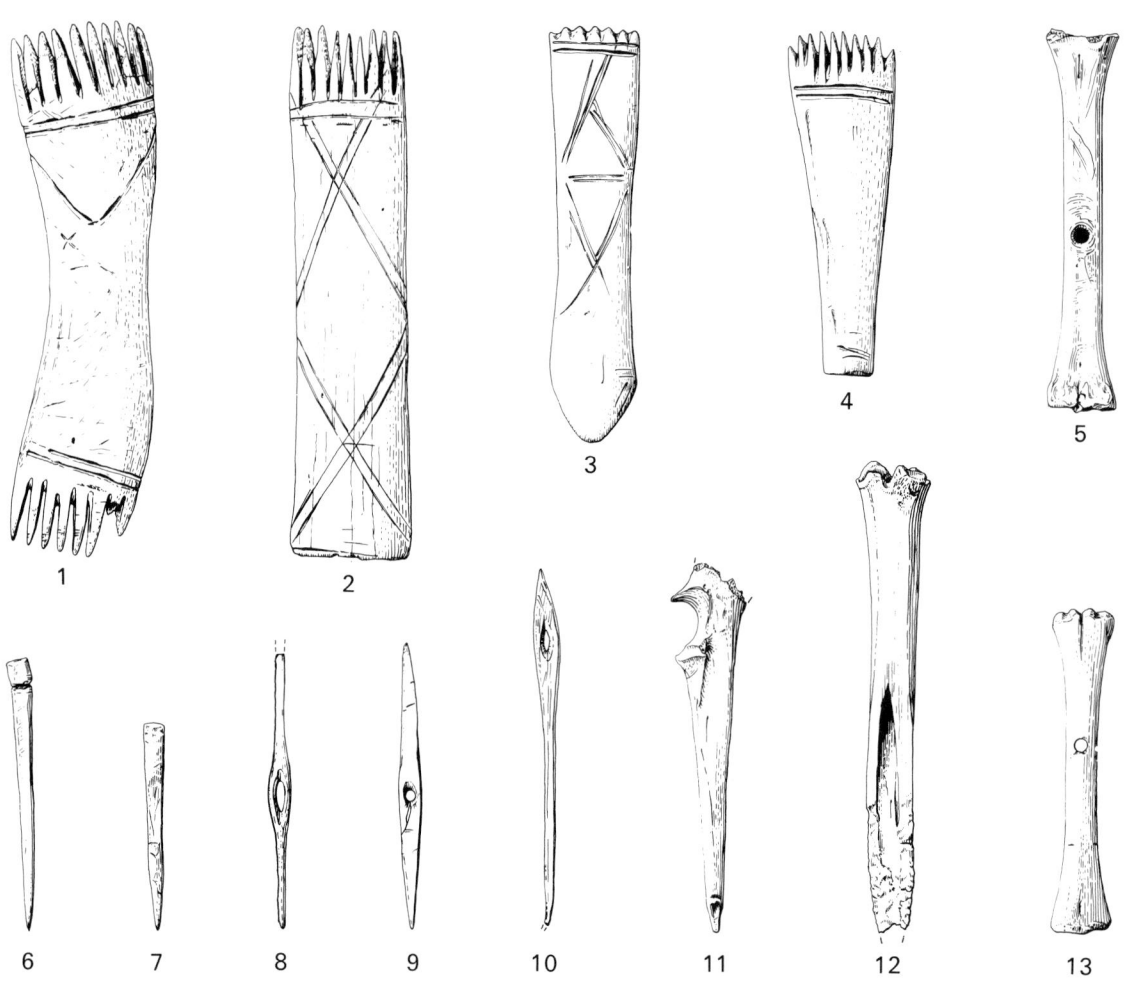

of a distinctive type of crude pottery at Maiden Castle, which acted as a container for the salt, indicates that it was being imported from these production centres.

The hillfort as town

This discussion of the industries involved in producing the material used by the inhabitants of Maiden Castle has shown that the bulk of the objects found on the hillfort must have been brought there from elsewhere. The only processes that have been definitely identified on the settlement, other than those directly associated with food production, are textile production and metalworking. Though the former may be an important regional industry the latter is undertaken on a small scale, probably sufficient only for the production and repair of tools used within the community and not capable of supplying other communities.

This conclusion has considerable implications for the interpretation of the status of the settlement at Maiden Castle. The size of the community inhabiting the hillfort and the organized nature of its occupation would normally define it as an urban settlement but 'towns' are expected to provide services for the larger community. For Maiden Castle to be regarded as a town, one would expect it to be a focus for the major manufacturing industries of the period, in particular pottery and the metallurgical industries. Instead we find that it is a consumer of products made in small settlements on the periphery of the hillfort's territory.

Other characteristic features of an urban settlement might be the presence of a major religious centre; a range of housing which suggests a sharp distinction between different classes of inhabitant; and evidence for a pre-eminent leader. None of these characteristics can be identified at Maiden Castle. The startling homogeneity in the size and shape of most of the domestic buildings has already been noted. The complete absence of a hierarchy in the extensively excavated hillfort of Danebury indicates a culture which places considerable importance on the absence of social differentiation.

It has been claimed that hillforts served as religious centres and the forts of Danebury and South Cadbury, which were similar to Maiden Castle, had small rectangular buildings at their centre which appear to have had a religious function. It is quite likely that a similar shrine exists in the unexplored areas of Maiden Castle. These shrines, however, were small and comparatively insignificant structures and it is difficult to imagine them functioning as anything more than a focus for the immediate community living in the hillfort. The more elaborate shrines or temples of this period appear to be constructed outside settlements – those identified at Hayling Island and Heathrow being good examples.

It is clear therefore that Maiden Castle cannot be described as a town in its full socio-economic sense. To do so would give a misleading impression of the range of activities that took place inside the defences. It is important, however, to emphasize that the size and density of occupation (relative to the surrouding countryside and other settlements) preclude most of the other labels that are normally applied to settlements; it is clearly not a homestead, nor is it merely a village. It is in fact a form of settlement which is unparalleled in the historical records of western society and which therefore has no obvious name – a large settlement dominated by agricultural production and storage. Sites such as these have been described as proto-urban, but this is also misleading as it implies that there is an evolutionary process which links these settlements with towns. This is clearly not the case in southern England where the only truly urban settlements originated in the south-east – an area practically devoid of hillfort settlement. It was only after the deliberate implantation of Roman towns in the second century AD that truly urban settlement was introduced in Dorset.

The chronology of the settlement

This examination of the material from Maiden Castle has not yet fully discussed the chronology of the occupation. To a certain extent this discussion should encompass not only the four hundred years or so of the Middle Iron Age but also the Early and Late Iron Age. During this period sheep gradually increased in importance but not enough to indicate any fundamental change in the economy. Similarly most of the classic finds are present in all the different phases of the occupation that were exposed in trench IV. Nevertheless there are significant developments in the nature of activity in the hillfort during the Middle Iron Age that correspond to the important changes in the ceramic assemblages already mentioned, and coincide

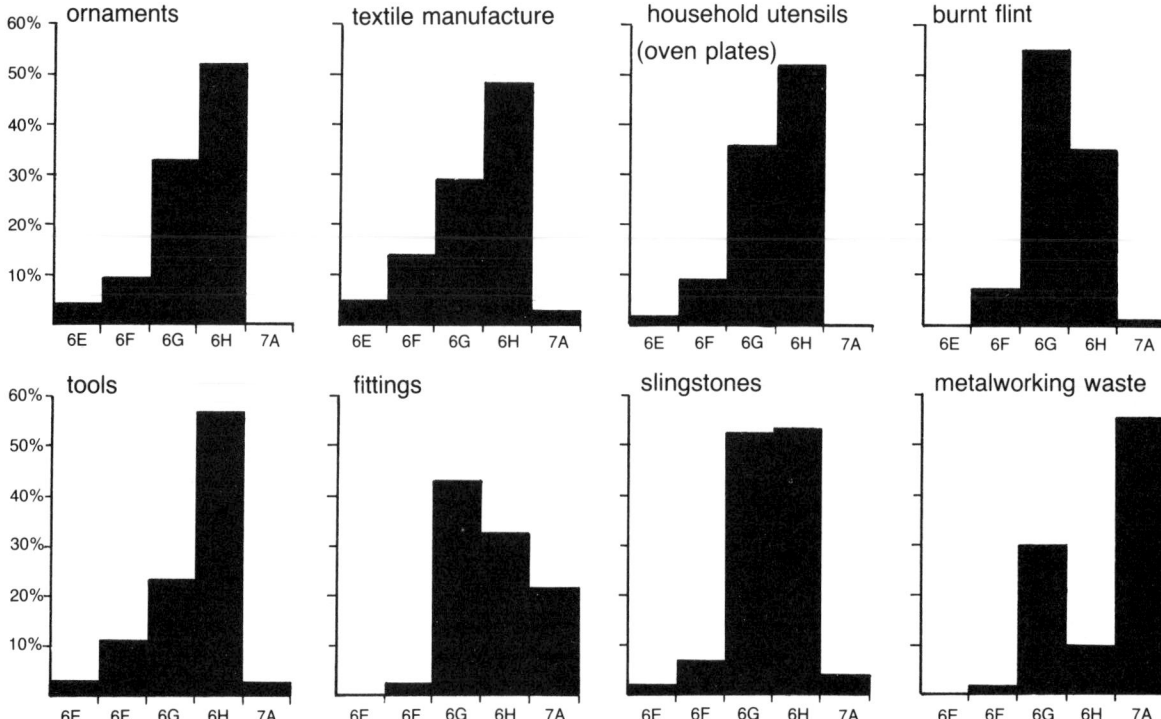

with noticeable differences in the nature of the material culture available to the inhabitants.

The most important distinction is in the volume of material goods the inhabitants had at their disposal. The overwhelming bulk of the finds assemblage from the recent excavations was found to belong to the last phase of occupation and there was a steady increase in the quantities of finds from most categories throughout the four phases identified (88). This is particularly clear for the items which seem to derive from the specialist production centres. Pottery produced from Poole Harbour dominated the final two phases and imported whetstones were only found in the same two phases; briquetage and shale (both probably coming from Purbeck) were almost exclusively concentrated in the last phase. The evidence from the production centres themselves also indicates a general rise in productivity in the later periods. Most of the shale and salt manufacturing sites in Purbeck are of Roman date and though they had Late Iron Age precursors Middle Iron Age production centres have not yet been identified and appear to have been very rare.

The growth in these commodities is a clear sign of a general increase in production in the late Middle Iron Age which is related to the

88 The chronological distribution of various categories of material found during the recent excavations. The most obvious trend is the concentration of objects in the final phase in the main trench (6H) and the lack of objects in the first two phases of this trench (6E and 6F). Evidence for metalworking is, however, largely concentrated in the trench in the eastern entrance (7A) and phase 3 in the main trench (6G) and this activity might also effect the distribution of fittings and burnt flint.

appearance of a number of distinct tribal territories. The most obvious manifestation of the development of these territories is the regional distribution of pottery types. The pottery produced at Poole Harbour and used throughout Dorset and areas of Somerset is of a style different from the pottery used in Devon and north Somerset or Hampshire and Wiltshire. The Dorset style was characterized by large jars with distinctive countersunk handles and where decoration occurred it consists of dimples and bosses or wide channelled lines. To the east the most distinctive vessels are straight-sided flat-bottomed vessels (known as saucepan pots because of their shape) which have fine complex grooved decoration often concentrated in bands under the rim. To the west there is a range of very fine bowls decorated by complex curvilinear designs incised onto the surface. Other objects are less regionally diagnostic but there do appear to be some distinctions between the quantity and quality of brooches and decorative objects in some areas.

The increase in commodities arriving at Maiden Castle coincided with a major rationalization of the settlement inside the hillfort and an abandonment of any great interest in the defences and it is possible that these changes were connected. The abandonment of defence building would have released a considerable amount of surplus grain which had been stored in the hillfort to feed the seasonal influx of people constructing the ramparts. This grain could be redistributed and used as a commodity to develop specialized industries in areas that did not produce a sufficient agricultural surplus. The reorganization of the occupation in the hillfort can be viewed as part of the same process as it appears to be aimed at separating different activities within the agricultural settlement.

Political developments may also be discernible in this specialization during the Middle Iron Age. Maiden Castle and the hillforts at South Cadbury and Hod Hill appear to have extended their control beyond the immediate localities, and entered into a tribal confederation which deflected internal stress into conflict between competing tribal groups. This type of wider regional conflict would involve a very different type of warfare from that of the early stages of the Iron Age. The ability to control and deploy resources would be essential and it is likely that a semi-specialist class of warriors would be required for the extended campaigns against other tribes. This increased specialization was, however, a threat to the structure of Middle Iron Age Society; dramatic changes were to result and these were emphasized by the Roman invasion.

9

The end of the hillfort
50 BC to AD 450

Over much of southern England the hundred years around the turn of the millennium are marked by a dramatic change in the archaeological record. Many of the settlements that had been occupied for the previous 500 years moved to new locations and the material culture of the inhabitants changed completely. In Dorset these changes were not as pronounced as they were further east but the same basic patterns can now be identified: a movement from the hillfort into small undefended homesteads; the development of formal cemeteries; an increase in craft specialization (particularly in the ceramic industry) and the development of coinage.

It has been suggested that this transformation resulted from increasing contact with the Roman Empire, for it was at the beginning of this period that the Romans came into direct contact with southern England. The coast from Brittany to the Rhine was captured and incorporated into the empire between 58 and 51 BC, and in 55 and 54 BC Julius Caesar actually crossed the Channel for a brief campaign in south-east England. There followed a period of relative stability when a number of tribes in south-east England established trading relationships with Rome and extended their power in the region. Internal power struggles within these tribes were probably a contributory factor in the Roman invasion in AD 43.

The principal focus of this chapter will be the developments in the Late Iron Age occupation of Maiden Castle and the surrounding area but the Roman occupation of the hilltop and the character of the Roman town of Dorchester will also be discussed.

The end of the hillfort
The main feature of the Late Iron Age occupa-
tion of Maiden Castle was the abandonment of the street system and internal organization that was such a striking feature of the hillfort around 100 BC. This was clear in trench IV where the line of houses of the third phase was replaced by occupation of a more random type, consisting of a spread of pits, post-holes and hearths, from at least one house. The abandonment of this area before the Roman conquest confirms evidence from other more limited excavations that the western half of the hillfort was largely deserted in the first century and that occupation was concentrated in the eastern half (the area of the Early Iron Age fort).

The area excavated by Wheeler in the centre of the orignal fort provides clear evidence for these general observations. The principal Late Iron Age feature in this area was a house built across a road which had originally traversed the interior of the hillfort (**89**). The position of this house in the centre of the hilltop and astride a major road may indicate that it was the residence of an important individual or that it had some special significance. Whichever interpretation is correct its position is distinctively different from anything present in earlier phases of occupation. The house itself was similar to previous circular houses. It had a stone outer wall, 8–9.5 m (27–31 ft) in diameter, and structural posts were indicated by an internal ring of post-holes. Unfortunately most of the interior was removed by later Roman occupation so it was not possible to identify any special function it may have had by archaeological methods.

There was very little evidence for occupation contemporary with this house in the rest of the area examined by Wheeler. There were, however, very large quantities of Late Iron Age

ceramics and other finds recorded from this trench in the centre of the hillfort which must indicate occupation. The activities occurring in this area may have been represented by very slight archaeological traces which, unlike the large storage pits and gullies belonging to the earlier occupation, could have been missed by the excavation techniques used in the thirties.

The most obvious change in the occupation of the hillfort occurred at the eastern entrance. There is clear evidence that many of the outwork ditches were infilled and that settlement spread out of the entrance between the banks and surviving ditches of the outworks. In the area between the original gateway and the inner earthwork of the outer defences Wheeler's excavations revealed at least five houses and associated grain storage pits, an important industrial area (largely concerned with iron working) and an extensive cemetery

89 *The Late Iron Age house excavated by Wheeler in the centre of the original hillfort. This house sits across an earlier road which would have been an important right of way in the Middle Iron Age hillfort. (The Society of Antiquaries.)*

(90) which stretched across most of the flat land in the earthworks that surround the eastern entrance.

Most of these houses had been badly damaged by later activity and the only remaining trace was the ring of post-holes that would have formed the roof support. One house, however, was better preserved as it was built over the inner ditch that had been deliberately filled in. The house was about 5 m (16 ft) in diameter and was surrounded by a ramshackle stone wall. The recent excavation of trench VI identified a clay hearth just slightly off centre. The main

117

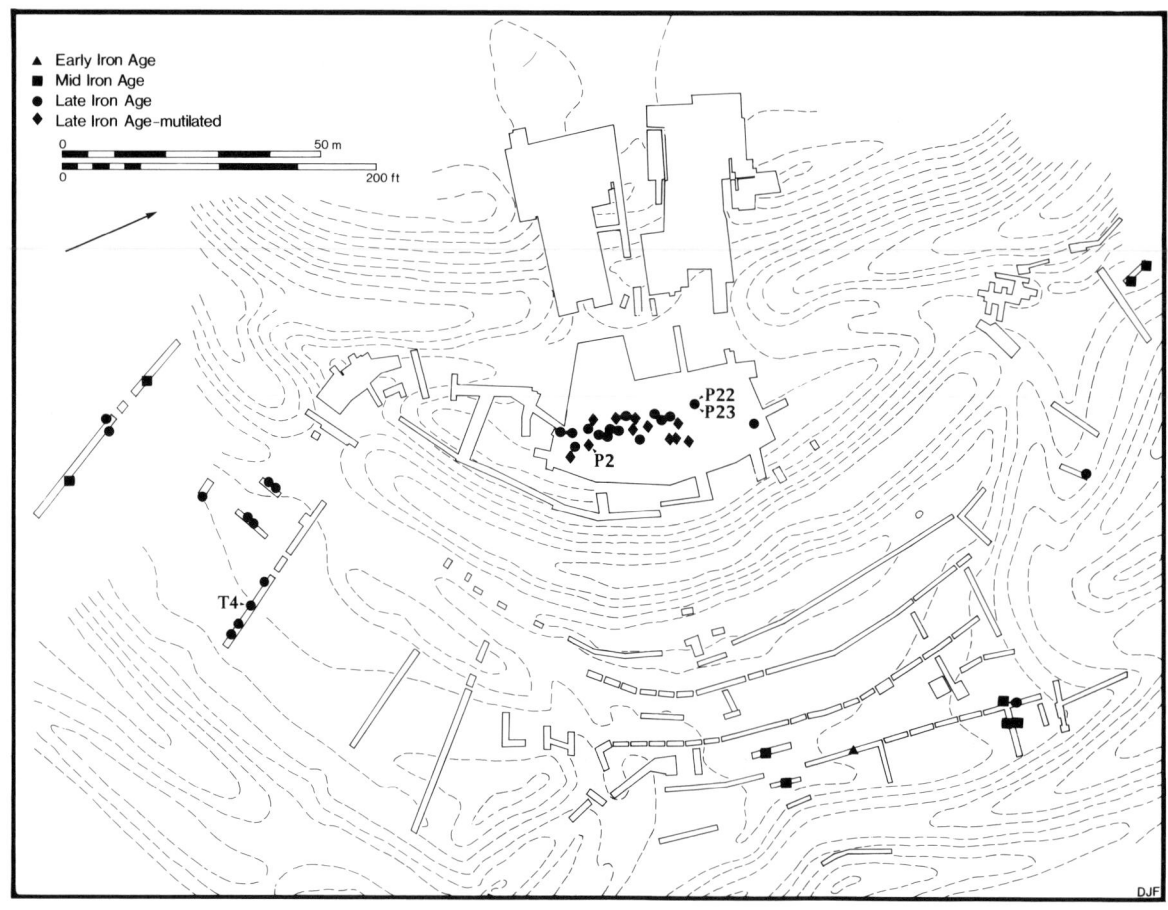

Early Iron Age
Mid Iron Age
Late Iron Age
Late Iron Age-mutilated

0   50 m
0   200 ft

90 *The distribution of burials in Wheeler's excavations in the eastern entrance.*

structural posts appear to have been placed on the ground surface, since no internal post-holes were identified. This house and the one in the centre of the fort were similar to houses in the Middle Iron Age settlement and indicate a level of basic continuity in domestic buildings.

The iron working, in contrast, is quite different from anything that has been found in the earlier occupation of the hillfort. Over 62 kgs (136 lbs) of iron slag was found covering an area of only 30 sq. ms (323 sq. ft) (**91**). It is estimated that about 200 kg (441 lbs) of iron could have been produced at this workshop which was solely concerned with secondary forging and welding. This is one of the most important artefact production centres discovered in southern England. The quantity of ore required for this workshop was too large to be derived from local sources and must have come from trade with specialist iron production areas. These are

known to have existed at this time in the Weald, Wales and the south-west. The workshop was set up on the site of the abandoned hut in trench VI and three separate layers were identified during the excavations. This could therefore be interpreted as the workshop of an itinerant smith who visited the site at intermittent intervals, but it is equally possible that the smith was permanently based at the site but only carried out his trade when demand required it or supply enabled it.

The discovery of a cemetery also indicates a radical change from earlier Iron Age practice. Burial in the Middle Iron Age has not been discussed in previous chapters because there is

91 *The Late Iron Age iron smithing area in the eastern entrance to the hillfort.*

very little evidence for it. There are a few instances of individual burials found at the base of grain storage pits excavated by Wheeler (**92**) but the most common mode of burial was a form of excarnation (exposure) as parts of bodies and isolated bones have been found scattered across the settlement mixed with occupation debris.

This contrasts quite dramatically with the formal cemeteries which are common in south Dorset in the Late Iron Age, one of which was found in the entrance at Maiden Castle. In these the position of the body and its orientation were carefully prescribed and almost universally adhered to (**93**). Individuals were placed in a shallow grave in a crouched position on their right side with their head pointing to the east, though young males of between 20 to 30 years old were often placed in a supine position oriented towards the south-east. Placed in the grave was a restricted range of objects which appear to be largely aimed at providing food for the deceased. The most common grave goods were pots (**94**), probably used as containers, followed by joints of meat (mainly sheep but cattle were present in male graves and pig in female graves), but in many burials there were other objects which indicated the individual's status – beads, weapons, brooches and rings. This burial tradition continued for at least a hundred years after the Roman invasion and indicates some continuity across this period in the region.

Over 52 burials were discovered in the eastern entrance and as only a small area was examined it is likely that there were at least double this number in the original cemetery. One small part of the cemetery is worth describing in more detail. The 'war cemetery' lay behind the inner bank of the entrance outworks and it can be distinguished from the rest of the graves because of the discovery of a large number of individuals within it who met a violent death. The most famous example is of a young man

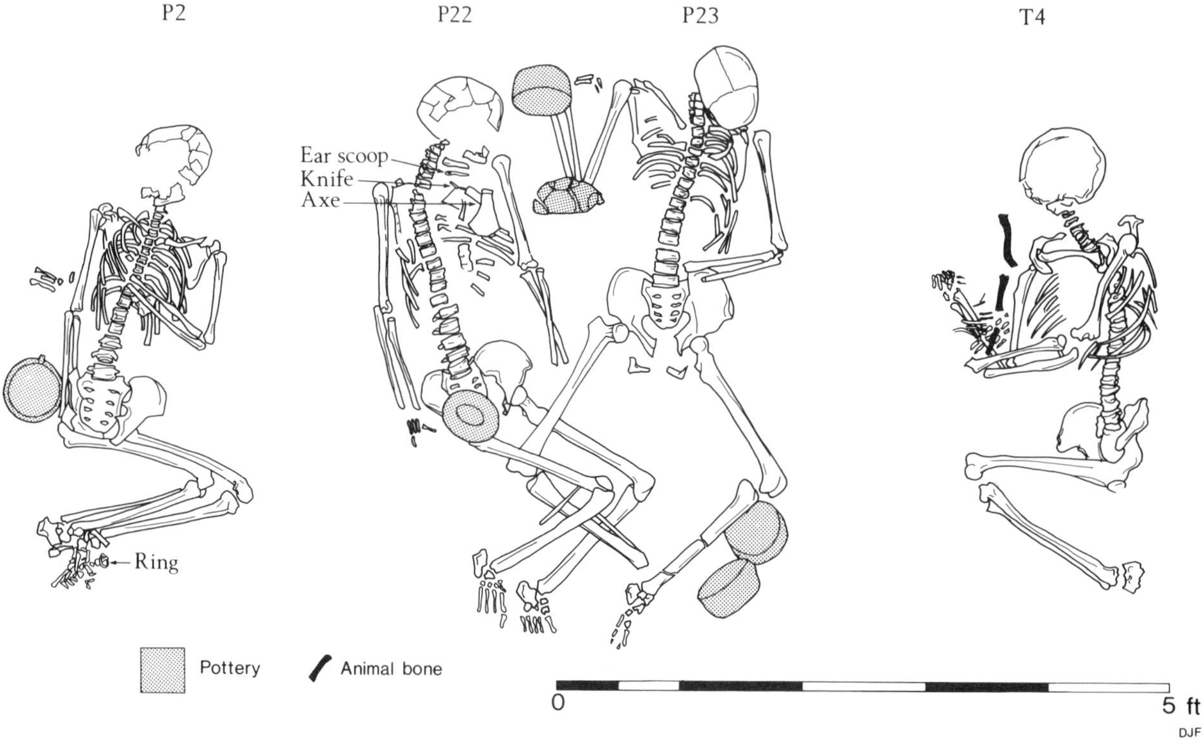

P2 P22 P23 T4

Ear scoop
Knife
Axe

Ring

Pottery Animal bone

0 5 ft

DJF

120

92 *(above left) A human burial placed in an abandoned grain storage pit in the Middle Iron Age. Very few burials are found during this period and the dead appear to have been disposed of by exposure. (The Society of Antiquaries.)*

93 *(left) Representative plans of the burials in the Durotrigian cemetery at Maiden Castle. P2 and T4 are characteristic adult male burials. T4 was accompanied by a leg and side of lamb, P2 had a tankard and was wearing a toe ring. P22 and 23 are two adult males. They were accompanied by five vessels and P22 was accompanied by an iron axe head, a knife and a bronze Roman ear scoop.*

94 *(above) The 'war cemetery' burials P24 and 25. These are two adult males accompanied by two bowls and an ox skull. (The Society of Antiquaries.)*

with a Roman spearhead embedded in his backbone. The most common injuries, however, were cut marks indicating that the deceased's head had been hacked by swords (**95**); one skull bore the clear impression of a spear which had pierced it. The discovery of these burials caused quite a stir and the evidence was used by Wheeler to present a vivid narrative of the Roman attack on Maiden Castle which will be discussed later (p. 124–5).

The change in the status of Maiden Castle indicated by the abandonment of the street system and the occupation and burials in the eastern approaches was echoed by a number of changes that now occurred in the landscape around Maiden Castle. The principal amongst these was an increase in the number and size of the surrounding settlements (**96**). Excavations have now revealed important settlements in front of the hillfort at Poundbury, at Allington

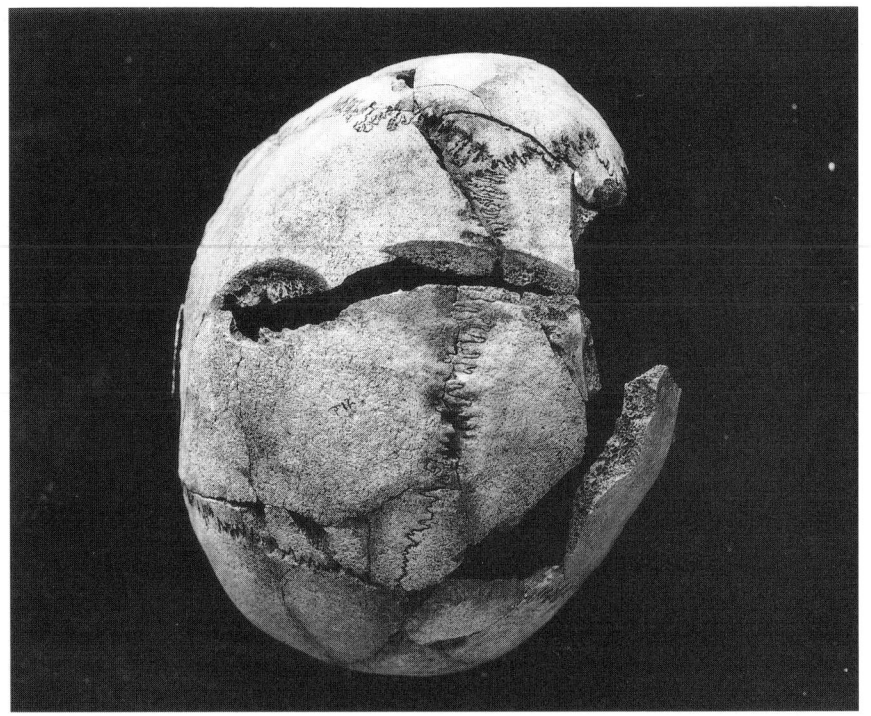

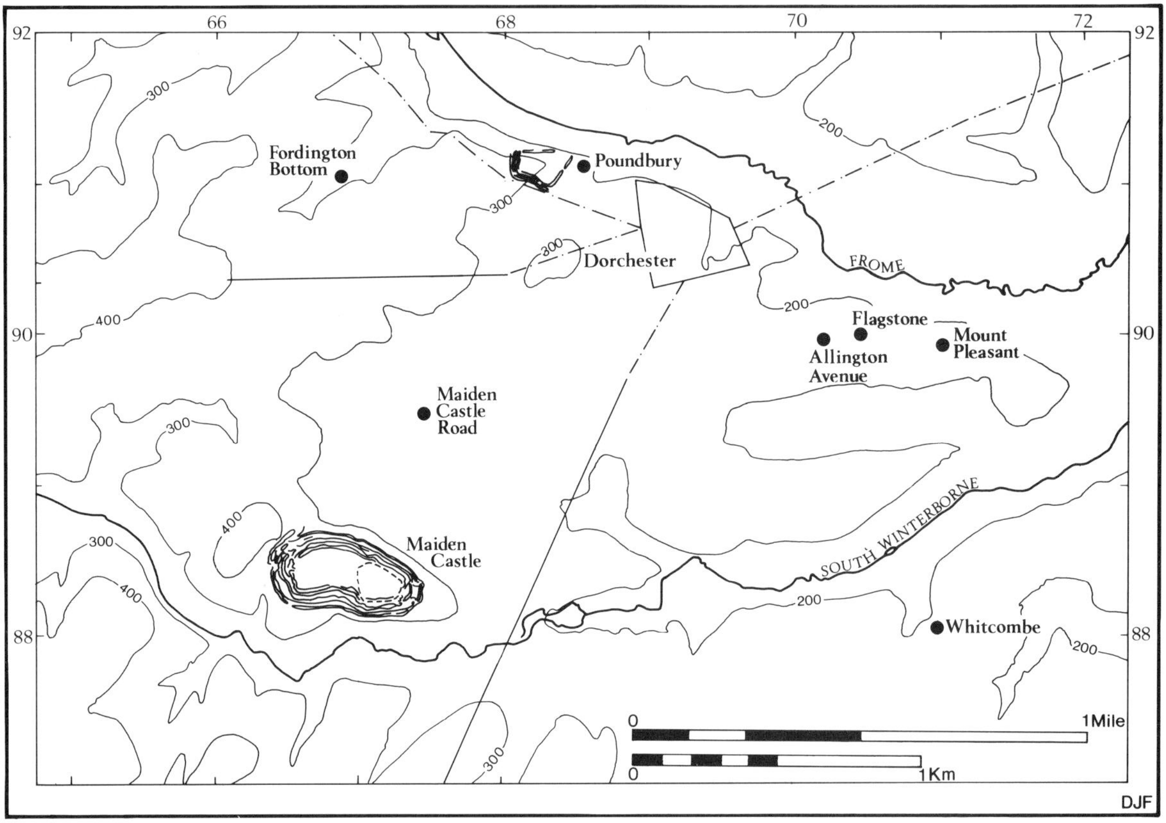
66
68
70
72
92
90
88
300
400
200
Fordington Bottom
Poundbury
Dorchester
FROME
Flagstone
Allington Avenue
Mount Pleasant
Maiden Castle Road
Maiden Castle
SOUTH WINTERBORNE
Whitcombe
0
1Mile
1Km
DJF

Avenue on the east side of Dorchester, at Whitcombe, further to the east, and at Fordington Bottom on the Dorchester bypass to the west of the town. A site known only from crop marks immediately in front of Maiden Castle probably also began life in the Late Iron Age. Excavations at these sites have not been extensive and few have been fully published but they have revealed that an important feature of the settlements was the development of an elaborate series of ditched enclosures which probably defined the arable land belonging to the inhabitants.

Field systems were unknown in the Middle Iron Age, when hillforts were important, so their development in the Late Iron Age may be taken to indicate a breakdown of the communal ownership which the previously undifferentiated settlements seem to suggest. The partition of the landscape could be an attempt by individuals to claim ownership of land which had formerly been a communal resource. The increasing importance of individual power is also visible in the adoption of new burial rites. A formal burial in a cemetery allowed individuals to express their status by the placing of more important and prestigious objects in the graves, and by marking their place of burial.

The new emphasis on individual status was also enhanced by the increasing availability of a variety of goods produced by specialist industries. The development of an iron working industry at Maiden Castle has already been noted; the exploitation of shale, salt and various important stone resources and the production of ceramics had begun to be restricted to particular groups at the end of the Middle Iron Age. It is only in the Late Iron Age, however, that these specializations acquired the characteristics of important industries which were crucial to the economic structure of the region. Settlements throughout Dorset became

95 *The skull of skeleton P12 showing several sword blows which must have caused immediate death. (The Society of Antiquaries.)*

96 *The Late Iron Age settlements and their distribution in relation to the hillforts at Poundbury and Maiden Castle and Roman roads and the town.*

increasingly dependent on the ceramic industries of Poole Harbour for the production of their cooking pots and storage jars. These industries produced a much wider range of vessels in this period, and some of these were clearly produced for restricted and specific groups. The sites of Hengistbury Head, Cleavel Point and Maiden Castle have specific types of pot which are rarely found elsewhere (**97**). At Hengistbury Head these were necked jars with an unusual type of decoration, at Cleavel Point there were large quantities of shallow bowls or dishes, which were probably copies of continental imports, and at Maiden Castle the 'war cemetery' bowls were found in unusually large numbers. Vessels such as the handled tankards found at Maiden Castle and Gussage All Saints could also have been restricted to a specific market or distribution. Shale bracelets, bronze rings and brooches, and glass beads were becoming much more common in this period and could have been used to indicate an individual's status: only those of reasonable wealth and high status would have the ability to acquire such traded goods.

It is possible that the development of these industries was the reason for the breakdown of the communal system prevailing in the hillfort in the Middle Iron Age. Although the industries may originally have developed in part to provide a form of communal identity for those who lived in Dorset, they may eventually have become a powerful force in themselves. Once developed, the control of resources, production processes and exchange networks would be a source of power with the potential to challenge the economic superiority of the hillfort elite which was based on the control of agricultural resources.

This seems a more likely explanation for the changes that distinguish the Late Iron Age than to attribute them all to the influence of the Roman Empire. There was never any direct influence in the years before the Roman invasion in AD 43 in the south-west and all the historical evidence indicates that south-east England was the area which had the strongest and most direct contacts across the Channel even before the campaigns of Caesar. There was a scatter of ceramic imports, however, along the south coast which were thought to indicate a period around the middle of the first century BC when contact with Rome (channelled through Breton middlemen) was sufficiently frequent to

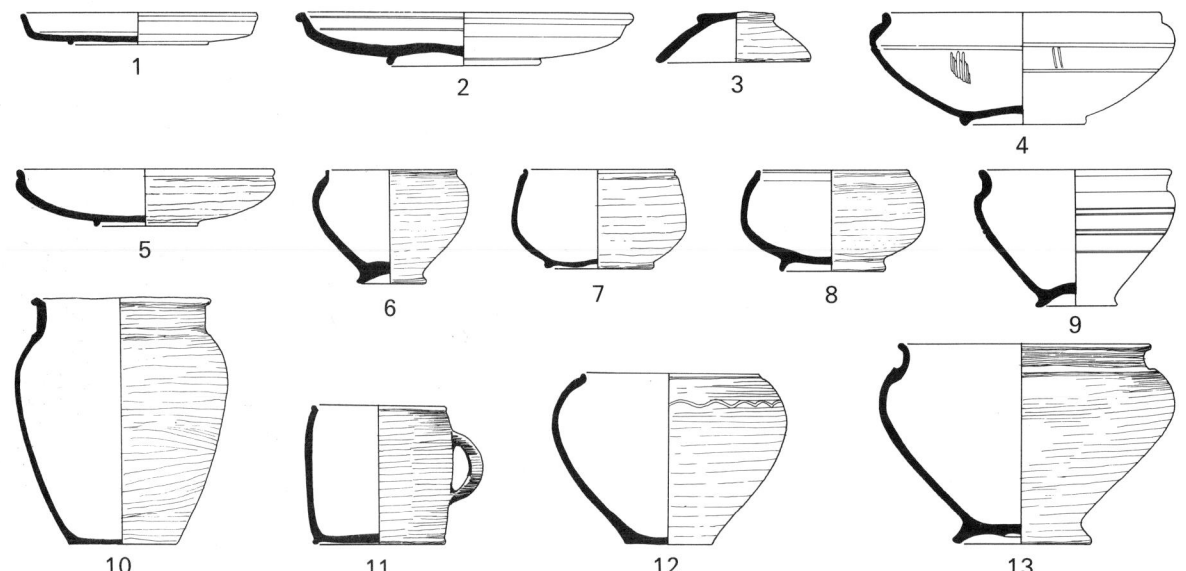

suggest that luxury goods were being supplied to the highest social classes in Iron Age Britain. Recent excavations have shown, however, that these imports were concentrated almost exclusively at a few isolated industrial settlements on the coast which had a very specialized function. The number of vessels penetrating into the tribal heartlands was negligible; for example, only 14 small sherds of Roman amphorae were found at Maiden Castle which was still a very important settlement in the Late Iron Age. It is unlikely therefore that trade with Rome was ever important enough to cause a major transformation in the lives of the inhabitants of Dorset.

The Roman invasion

The invasion of AD 43 was the first time the inhabitants of Maiden Castle had experienced change in their lives as a direct result of Roman activity but even then the effects were not as dramatic or as sudden as might have been expected. A vivid portrayal of the sequence of events at Maiden Castle was written by Wheeler; this has gained such fame that it is worth examining in detail.

First, the regiment of artillery which usually accompanied a legion was ordered into action and put down a barrage of ballista arrows. The arrows have been found about the site, and buried amongst the outworks was a man with an arrowhead still embedded in one of his vertebrae (to be seen in the Dorchester

97 *Late Iron Age ceramics of the Durotrigian style. 1 and 2 are from Cleavel Point, 4 and 9 are from Hengistbury Head. The rest are from Maiden Castle. The former vessels appear to be particularly characteristic of these sites and 8 and 11 are found as grave goods accompanying burials at Maiden Castle.*

Museum). Following the barrage, the Roman infantry advanced up the slope, cutting its way from rampart to rampart until it reached the innermost bay, where some circular huts had recently been built. These were set alight, and under the rising clouds of smoke the gates were stormed and the position carried. But resistance had been obstinate and the fury of the legionaries was aroused. For a space, confusion and massacre dominated the scene. Men and women, young and old, were savagely cut down before the troops were called to heel. A systematic slighting of the defences followed, whereafter the legion was withdrawn, doubtless taking hostages with it, and the dazed inhabitants were left to bury their dead amongst the ashes of their huts beside the gates. The task was carried out anxiously and without order but, even so, from few graves were omitted those tributes of food and drink which were the proper prerequisites of the dead. With their cups and food-vessels and trinkets, the bones, often two or more skeletons huddled into a single grave and many of the skulls deeply scored with sword cuts, made a sad and dramatic showing – the earliest British war-cemetery known to us.

This dramatic interpretation contains a number of assumptions which cannot be supported by an examination of the data Wheeler assembled. The story is largely based on the 'war cemetery' burials, but it does not account for the fact that the burials were placed within an established cemetery and that only 14 out of the 52 burials in this part of the cemetery show evidence of violent death. It is quite possible, therefore, that the burials were brought from elsewhere to this cemetery and do not indicate death in the immediate vicinity of the graves. All of the bodies were carefully placed, in the orientation and with the offerings they would expect to have had in normal conditions. The supine position in which some of the bodies were buried may be a tradition used to distinguish an age-class or the status of the deceased and is too consistent to indicate casual disposal. The number and quality of the objects in the graves is exceptional and would indicate that some trouble had been spent gathering together material which would reflect the dead men's status. Two individuals were accompanied by legs of lamb and these animals would have had to be slaughtered. Furthermore at least four individuals had wounds which had partially healed (there was bone regrowth) which would indicate that they were buried some time after they had been injured, although the injury could still have been the ultimate cause of their death.

The evidence for the attack on the hillfort is also open to question. The burning of the houses in the entrance is based on the presence of a thick layer of charcoal in this area; however, this almost certainly derived from the iron working. Many of the 'arrows found about the site' probably belong to the Late Iron Age occupation. The principal evidence for a 'slighting' of the defences consisted of a collapsed stone-lined entrance way into the fort. This was sealed by a layer containing early Roman pottery and overlies a layer containing late pre-Roman coins so it must have occurred around the time of the Roman invasion.

Viewed objectively, therefore, the vivid description of the sack and slighting of the hillfort, followed by the hasty burial of the dead is not altogether consistent with the evidence on the ground. This is not to claim that the Roman invasion was a peaceful occupation: individuals – presumably on both sides – doubtless met a violent end in the first century AD as a result of battles connected with the Roman invasion. Indeed there were many occasions when the subjugated inhabitants of southern England defied the empire in the early years of the Roman occupation.

The Roman occupation
The situation following the Roman invasion is unclear. There is evidence that the hillfort was occupied for at least several decades as the eastern entrance to the fort was refurbished during this period and large quantities of Roman finds of first-century date have been recovered from the entrance and in the centre of the hillfort. These included a range of brooches and pins but the principal evidence for the date of the occupation was derived from the assemblage of samian, the fine Roman tableware imported from southern Gaul. This largely dates to the reigns of the emperors Claudius and Nero though there are a few sherds of Hadrianic and Antonine date. The earlier (and larger) assemblage was mixed in with Late Iron Age occupation material and Wheeler argued that it indicated a continuity of domestic occupation for some 20 to 30 years after the invasion. The later group, which is chronologically separate, may have been the result of a short visit, perhaps by squatters.

The high quality and large quantities of samian found on the site, coupled with the belief that there must have been a Roman military presence somewhere in the vicinity of Dorchester, has led to the suggestion that Maiden Castle was occupied by the Roman army and not retained as a settlement. A Roman fort could be expected in this area for a number of reasons: there is no known fort near this densely settled, agriculturally rich area; the Roman road from London to Exeter crossed the River Frome at this point and meets a road from the harbour at Radipole (Weymouth) (**98**). It has been argued that any Roman fort that existed hereabouts lay under the Roman town since that is where the roads cross and it would be normal for a town to develop from an existing fort. Prolonged and extensive excavations have failed, however, to identify any trace of this fort and most of the likely areas have now been examined.

Reuse of native fortifications has been identi-

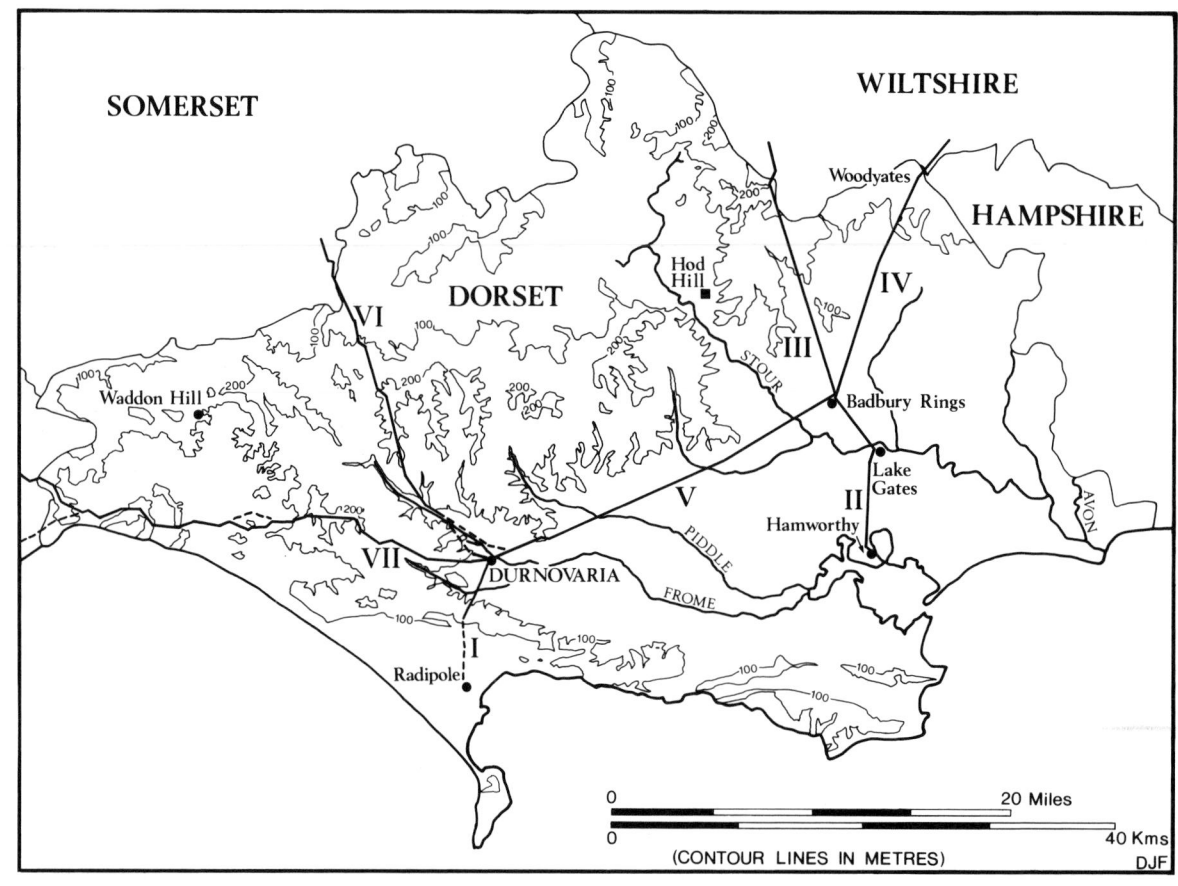

98 *The network of Roman roads in Dorset showing the Roman forts and major settlements (after Putnam 1984).*

fied as a feature of Vespasian's campaigns in south-west England. A Roman fort in the corner of the hillfort at Hod Hill (**99**) has been known for many years but recent excavations have now revealed Roman military occupation of the hillforts of Hembury in Devon and South Cadbury in Somerset, and finds from Ham Hill in Somerset suggest that it also was occupied. These forts are directly comparable to Maiden Castle in size and status and so it would be surprising if Maiden Castle was not also occupied by Roman troops.

The recent excavations at Maiden Castle provided some evidence to suggest that Maiden Castle was at least temporarily occupied by the Roman army. The remains of a rectangular building similar to those identified as of Roman type and found at South Cadbury and Hembury was found on top of the Early Iron Age rampart in the middle of the fort. This question will only be conclusively settled, however, by more extensive excavations in both Maiden Castle and Dorchester.

By the end of the first century AD, Maiden Castle had been abandoned. By around AD 70, Dorchester (or *Durnovaria* to give it its Roman name) was set up as the regional capital (*civitas peregrina*) of the Durotriges who retained a tribal identity as a regional unit in the Roman province. At least eight tribes achieved their administrative independence at this time and it appears to mark the consolidation of Roman control in southern England and a return to expansion in the north. The town appears to have been an average-sized provincial town. Information about its development and layout is limited, since the town regained its status as an urban centre in the Middle Ages and is completely built over today. The location and plan of the major administrative centre, the

99 *An aerial view of the Middle Iron Age hillfort of Hod Hill. In the foreground is the later Roman fort. (Crown copyright/MOD.)*

forum and basilica, is unknown though it is suspected to have been close to the church of St Peter in the centre of the town. Recent excavations have, however, revealed new and significant information, and exposed, amongst other buildings, the municipal baths. Many important features, including the defences, the aque-

duct and the amphitheatre are still visible in part today.

The amphitheatre, Maumbury Rings, was constructed in the first century AD and lay on the east side of the main road immediately south of the town walls. Its shape and size were partly constrained by its construction over a Neolithic henge but with its oval bank and its overall length of 100 m (330 ft), it was similar to many other British amphitheatres.

The aqueduct is exceptional, being the longest and best preserved in the British Isles. It was an open channel extending for up to 19 km (12 miles) along the south side of the Frome Valley and entered the town at the west gate. This is the highest point in the town so it could have supplied water to every area within it. An estimated 59 million litres (13 million gallons) of water could be supplied every day and this would be used for municipal outlets such as the baths, toilets, sewers and fountains. Domestic supplies would be largely met by private wells and excavations have shown these are widely distributed across the town.

The defences were probably built at the end of the second century ad when a period of imperial instability and the departure of the governor, Clodius Albinus, with a large part of the army, may have created a climate of fear. The Dorchester defences are the largest known for a town in the British Isles and comprise a massive inner bank originally 15 m (50 ft) wide with three ditches and a large but low outer bank. In some areas the bank overlies part of the town grid which appears to have been set out on a rather optimistic scale. Around the beginning of the fourth century a stone wall was added to

the front of the earthen bank. This possibly indicates the increasing wealth of the town during this period rather than any threat to which the inhabitants might have been exposed. All these municipal buildings and the general facilities provided for the inhabitants of the town, and presumably the surrounding countryside, emphasize the difference between these Roman towns and the hillforts of the Iron Age.

The extensive excavation of large areas of the town in recent years has provided a better idea of what the settlement sequence was. In the early years most of the buildings were made of wood and the occupation was restricted. In the third century, however, stone buildings (**100**) became more common and the area occupied increased to fill completely the area defined by

100 *The Roman town house in the north-west corner of Durnovaria.*

101 *The Late Roman temple and ancillary buildings on Maiden Castle.*

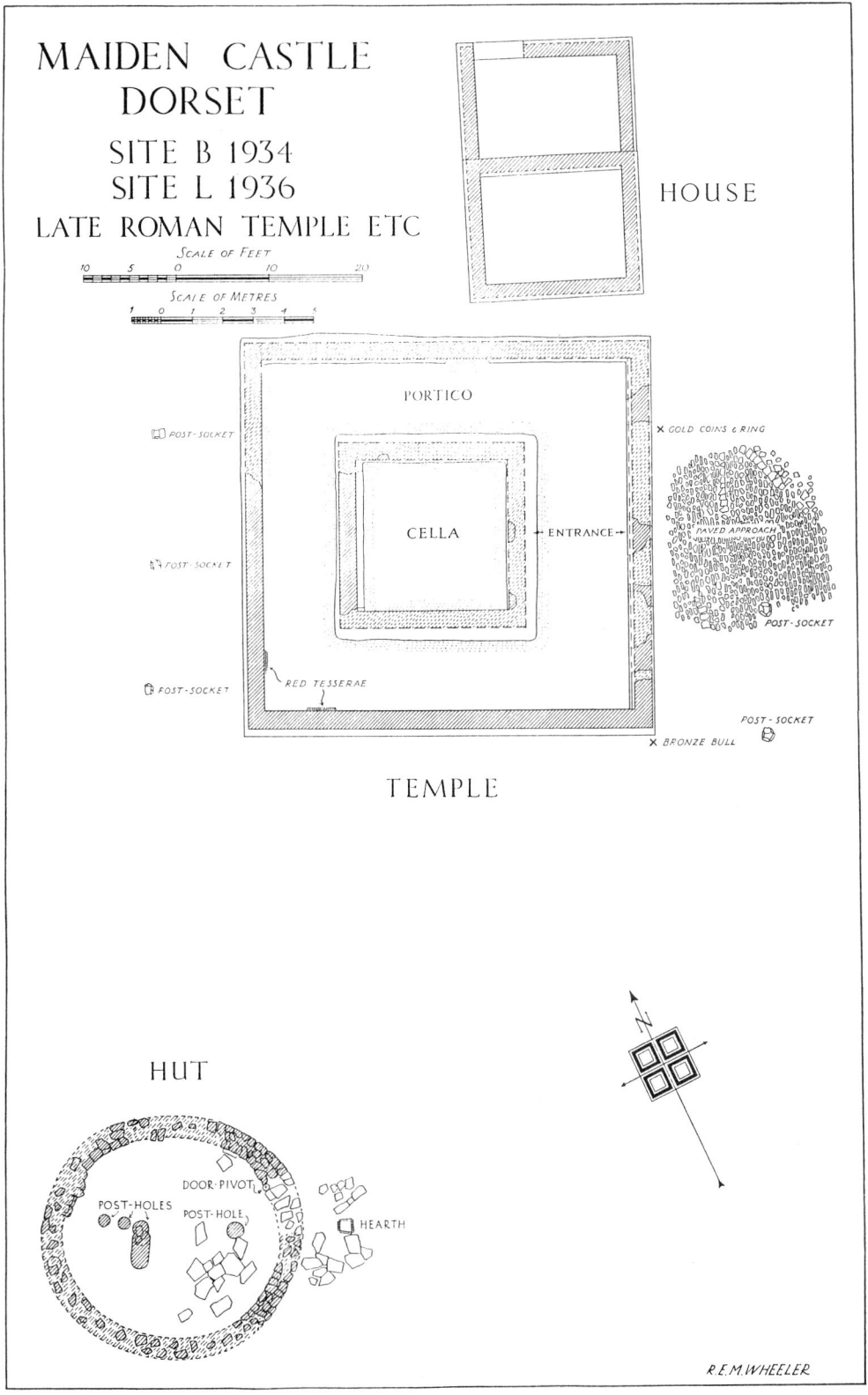

MAIDEN CASTLE
DORSET
SITE B 1934
SITE L 1936
LATE ROMAN TEMPLE ETC

HOUSE

Scale of Feet
10   5   0   10   20

Scale of Metres
1   0   1   2   3   4   5

PORTICO

POST-SOCKET

POST-SOCKET

POST-SOCKET

CELLA

ENTRANCE

RED TESSERAE

× GOLD COINS & RING

PAVED APPROACH

POST-SOCKET

POST-SOCKET

× BRONZE BULL

TEMPLE

HUT

POST-HOLES

DOOR-PIVOT

POST-HOLE

HEARTH

N

R.E.M.WHEELER

the towns walls. Elaborate mosaic floors and painted wall plaster are frequent discoveries in the town and suggest that in the third century the inhabitants were wealthy. It is likely that a specialist school of mosaic craftsmen was based in the town to serve the inhabitants and the occupants of the rich villas that are found throughout the region of the Durotriges at this time.

Contemporary with the construction of increasingly elaborate buildings in Dorchester was the construction of a temple on Maiden Castle (**101**). Its construction can be fairly accurately dated to after AD 367 by a hoard of coins sealed under the plain mosaic floor. Temples like this are found throughout the western empire and many examples have been discovered in southern England. They are known as Romano-Celtic temples because they are believed to represent a fusion of celtic and classical religions that is restricted to this area.

The basic feature of the temple was a central room, the cella, roughly 6 m (20 ft) square, surrounded by a passage, or ambulatory, roughly 3 m (10 ft) wide. The entrance was in the middle of the west wall. Most Romano-Celtic temples have these basic features though they can be round or octagonal and sometimes extra rooms were added. The temple was probably dedicated to a god whose statue stood in the cella to which only priests had access. Visitors to the site could enter the ambulatory and view the statue and the priest from this area. They brought with them many small offerings which they hoped would encourage the gods to intervene on their behalf. Offerings were buried around the site and excavation of these temples often results in the recovery of large quantities of artefacts, coins and votive tablets.

Immediately to the north of the temple was a rectangular two-roomed building, 7.9 m (26 ft) by 5.5 m (18 ft), and to the south-west was a circular building built on top of the Late Iron Age house. The rectangular building may have been the priest's house but the quantity and quality of the finds in the circular building indicate that this was a shrine. The eastern entrance to the hillfort was also refurbished at this time. The southern portal was blocked by a wall and a distinguished masonry gateway was placed in the entrance through the northern portal. Just inside this entrance was the base of pedestal which may have been another shrine.

There are a number of possible reasons why

this temple was sited at Maiden Castle. There seems little doubt that celtic rituals were often carried out in a natural setting. Also the historical aura of the great earthworks may have been used to give a greater credibility to what was in essence a new religion. By the latter part of the fourth century, Christianity may well have become the religion of the middle class elite that controlled the towns; worship of the old pagan gods was doubtless excluded from the towns. Temples of this form are only found outside towns – often in Iron Age settlements. There is evidence for Christianity in Dorchester at this date and the large cemeteries outside the town at Poundbury indicate that by now the bulk of the inhabitants might have been Christians.

Post-Roman occupation

There is some evidence to suggest that the temple continued to form a focus of attention after the formal end of Roman control in Britain. It has been suggested by Rahtz that the circular building mentioned above was a shrine which replaced the temple as Roman influence became less and less important. There are four graves to the west of the temple, whose east–west alignment may indicate Christian influence and certainly suggests a late-Roman or post-Roman date. To the south-east there was a Saxon burial accompanied by a scramasax (short sword) and knife. Directly south of the temple was the burial of a man who had been brutally hacked to pieces. This was originally thought to belong to the Neolithic period, but radiocarbon dating has shown that is more likely to belong to the post-Roman or Saxon period.

There is very little evidence to indicate what happened on Maiden Castle after the gradual decline of the temple. The absence of any late Saxon or Medieval settlement on the hilltop suggests that throughout this period it was important only as pasture for the sheep from communities in the South Winterbourne and Dorchester/Fordington areas. References in the Anglo-Saxon Chronicle indicate that Dorchester was an important administrative centre in the late-Saxon period and it is likely that the inhabitants of the town controlled the grazing rights.

The only substantial occupation after the Roman period occurred in the sixteenth and probably seventeenth centuries when a large barn was built in the eastern entrance, over the site of the 'war cemetery'. This may be associated with a phase of cultivation on the hilltop recorded in the seventeenth century by Speed, and ridge and furrow cultivation was identified in the recent survey of the interior.

By the eighteenth century, however, Maiden Castle had reverted to pasture and when Wheeler excavated it in the 1930s it had probably been open pasture for over two hundred years.

Appendix

Visiting Maiden Castle

Maiden Castle is one of the most spectacular prehistoric monuments in the British Isles and anyone with an interest in archaeology would be rewarded by a visit. Even the casual and untutored visitor feels somewhat in awe of the massive defences which surround the hilltop. The site is readily accessible as it lies immediately south of Dorchester, the county town of Dorset. The town has two train stations; Dorchester South, which is on the main line from London Waterloo to Weymouth (with trains every hour during the day) and Dorchester West, which is on a branch line from Weymouth to Bristol (with a much more infrequent service). The hillfort is well signposted and it would take just over 30 minutes to walk there from the centre of town. Display boards in the car park give a brief outline of the history of the monument and within the fort other display boards highlight the more important features.

For the visitor with plenty of time the most pleasant approach to any visit is to wander wherever there appears to be fewest visitors. This gives some sense of the atmosphere of one of the few areas of unaltered and easily accessible chalk downland in southern England. For those with a more limited amount of time available (and an hour is about the minimum necessary) I can recommend the following route.

After entering through the south-west gate head south along the crest of the inner rampart. Just barely visible on the high ground to the left is a small round barrow, the only definite example inside the hillfort. Directly in front is a spectacular view of the South Dorset Ridgeway, and many of the barrows that are so well preserved on this high ground are visible on the skyline. The southern defences of the hillfort are particularly impressive as they are well spaced out on the relatively gentle slopes leading to the valley of the South Winterborne. Half way along the south side of the fort the abandoned western rampart of the Early Iron Age hillfort is clearly visible as a terrace cutting across the interior of the hillfort and the later ramparts make a distinct kink at this point. Continuing along the southern ramparts one eventually comes to the eastern entrance which was extensively excavated by Sir Mortimer Wheeler between 1935 and 1937. The famous war cemetery lies in the large open space between the gateways through the rampart and the first hornwork. The cemetery extends further out, however, and would appear to cover all the flat ground within the entrance. The view from the ramparts at this point is quite spectacular and on a clear day it is possible to see the Isle of Wight. From the entrance cut back across the interior to the Roman temple which lies on the northern slopes looking towards the Roman town. Immediately south of the temple is the eastern end of the Bank Barrow, which is just visible as a bank running east to west. A path follows the line of the southern ditch of this barrow back to the western entrance. The barrow is most clearly visible immediately to the west of the remains of the Early Iron Age rampart (next to a post-medieval dew pond). It is likely that this indicates a primary long barrow just outside the causewayed enclosure ditch, which directly underlies the Early Iron Age rampart.

Visiting Dorchester

Any visit to Maiden Castle should include a thorough exploration of Dorchester as this small market town has a long and interesting history. The most important building for any visitor interested in the archaeology of the area is the County Museum. This is situated in the centre of the town immediately adjacent to St Peter's, the principal church. The museum has an excellent archaeological display which uses the material recovered from Maiden Castle to explain the prehistoric and Roman occupation of Dorset. Other galleries provide interesting displays on the natural history, geology and recent history of the area and are well worth examination.

The principal archaeological importance of the town is its Roman origins but very little of this can be seen today. The defences, which were the largest in Roman Britain, have been almost completely dismantled, though their circuit is marked by a series of tree-lined walks established in the nineteenth century. These are well worth perambulating as they provide access to most of the town's open space. The only preserved section of the Roman wall lies immediately south of the western gate (which is now the 'top o'town' roundabout). The only Roman building on view lies within the north-west corner of the defences, behind County Hall (see **100**). This is an elaborate stone building of the third century AD which was discovered during rescue excavations that preceded the construction of County Hall, between 1937 and 1939.

South of the town, on the road to Maiden Castle, is the Roman amphitheatre of Maumbury Rings (see **44**). This was in fact formed by the Romans out of a Neolithic henge and is one of the few visible reminders of what an important early prehistoric centre the land around Dorchester was. The only other record occurs in the rather incongruous setting of the basement car park in the Waitrose supermarket. Marked out on the floor of this are the positions of the great posts which formed the west side of a massive timber enclosure (see **45**). A mural in front of the supermarket lifts gives some impression of what this enclosure might have looked like during its construction.

To the north-west on the outskirts of the present town is the small Early Iron Age hillfort of Poundbury (see **57**). This is situated on a bluff overlooking the River Frome and encloses a well-preserved Bronze Age round barrow. The houses that lay in its south-east corner have been obliterated by cultivation and the

entrance has been destroyed by an industrial estate. Running along the southern edge of the Frome Valley at this point (and actually cutting through the outer defences of the hillfort) is the Roman aqueduct. This is the best preserved aqueduct in the British Isles and extends for up to 19 km (12 miles) along the valley side.

Archaeology in Dorset

Many of the other Dorset sites mentioned in the text are worth visiting and though not on display as public monuments are traversed by rights of way which allow easy access. It is not possible to give a complete list of the sites worth visiting in this book but most of these are marked on the Ordnance Survey 1:50,000 scale maps; 193, 194, 195 and 184. For greater details of the public rights of way, necessary for a walking holiday, the 1:25,000 maps are more useful and the special outdoor leisure map for the Isle of Purbeck is very good value.

A suggested tour of Dorset sites

A trip from Dorchester which will take a day by car will enable the visitor to encounter all the most important types of monuments present in Dorset and mentioned in the text.

Start the trip by heading west out of Dorchester towards Bridport. At the roundabout marking the end of the Dorchester ring road turn south on the Martinstown road. Once through Martinstown there is a left turn, signposted for Hardy's monument and Portesham. This road takes you up on to the South Dorset Ridgeway. Access to the best preserved barrows at Bronkham Hill (see **47**) is by a well-signposted path on the left just before the summit. It is possible to park here or in the large car park at Hardy's monument. The path leads along the crest of the Ridgeway and there are extensive views to the south and north.

If you continue south-east along this road you come to a crossroads, with the main road from Abbotsbury/Portesham to Winterborne Abbas/Dorchester. Cross this on the road to Gorwell and pull up in the parking place on the left-hand side. A path leads north-west from here into the Valley of Stones (see **9**). This is one of the strange Wessex valley bottoms which are covered with large sarsen boulders. It is also, however, the centre of one of the best preserved and most extensive celtic field systems in Dorset. This will only be clearly visible, however, in the strong low light of winter.

Continue on the road to Gorwell and just before your descent to the coastal plain there is a turning to the right. This takes you to a large field which is the location of the local model airplane enthusiasts flight meetings. (It is decorated with 'Beware low flying aircraft' signs.) Follow the right of way along the south side of the field to the chambered tomb, the Grey Mare and Her Colts (which lies slightly to the south of the main track, behind a hedge (see **17**)) and then to the stone circle of Tennants Hill. Both these monuments are characteristic of the prehistoric settlement of Devon and Cornwall and are amongst the most easterly outliers of these types.

Continue on this road until it joins the coast road to Bridport. Then head west through the picturesque town of Abbotsbury, with its important Medieval remains. About 1.6 km (1 mile) out of town the road rises up from the coast and just before it begins to flatten out take a turn to the right. Within 91 m (100 yds) there is a parking place on the left and a path leads from this west to the hillfort of Abbotsbury Castle. This is a very well-preserved Early Iron Age hillfort. The eastern half of the interior has never been ploughed and the remains of about eight stone-walled round houses survive in a cluster to the north-east of a well-preserved round barrow. These are only clearly visible when the vegetation is low.

From Abbotsbury Castle it is a rather long drive to the next interesting monument, Eggardon Hill. Take the coast road to Swyre then turn north through Chilcombe to Askerswell and from here head north through Spyway on the road to Toller Porcorum. As you climb to the top of the chalk massif on this road you will see the hillfort of Eggardon Hill on the left. Access is by a path just before the crossroads at the summit. Again this hillfort is fortunate to retain a large area of the interior that has never been ploughed. This is covered in depressions which are the traces of infilled grain storage pits. The southern defences of the fort were almost completely destroyed by a massive land slide which could well have been caused by the digging of the ditches of the fort.

From Eggardon head south and join the main road (A35) from Dorchester to Bridport. Continue east along this road until you pass a turning to Long Bredy on the right. Immediately after this there is a parking area on the right and a path leading up the hill to the bank barrow of Long Bredy. This bank barrow runs north-south across the ridge and marks the western end of the Bronze Age cemetery which covers the South Dorset Ridgeway.

Continue east back to Dorchester for just over 3.2 km (2 miles) and on your right-hand side, just after a small wood, you will pass the last site on the tour, the Nine Stones, a very picturesque stone circle. Safe parking is available a little bit further on by a barn on the left hand side.

Further reading

1 An introduction to the monument
R. Bradley (1984), *The social foundations of prehistoric Britain: themes and variations in the archaeology of power*, Longman, London.
J.M. Coles and Coles, B.J. (1986), *Sweet Track to Glastonbury: The Somerset Levels in Prehistory*, Thames and Hudson, London.
T. Darvill (1987), *Prehistoric Britain*, Batsford, London.
Royal Commission on Ancient and Historical Monuments, *Dorset* Volumes 1 to 5.
N.M. Sharples (forthcoming), *Maiden Castle: Excavations and Field Survey 1985–86*.
R.E.M. Wheeler (1943), 'Maiden Castle', *Report of the Research Committee of the Society of Antiquaries XII*, Oxford.

2 The environment and agricultural settlement of Dorset
J.G. Evans (1975), *The Environment of Early Man in the British Isles*, Paul Elek, London.
P. Mellars and Rheinhardt, S.C. (1978), 'Patterns of Mesolithic land use in Southern England: a geological perspective', in Mellars, P. (ed.), *The Early Post Glacial Settlement of Northern Europe*, Duckworth, London.
M. Shackley (1981), *Environmental Archaeology*, G. Allen & Unwin, London.
I.G. Simmons and Tooley, M.J. (1981), *The Environment in British Prehistory*, Duckworth, London.
R.W. Smith (1984), 'The ecology of Neolithic farming systems as exemplified by the Avebury region of Wiltshire', *Proceedings of the Prehistoric Society* 50, 99–120.
L.E. Taverner (1937), 'Land Classification in Dorset', *Institute of British Geographers No 6*.
L.E. Taverner (1955), 'Dorset Farming 1900–1950', *Proceedings of the Dorset Natural History and Archaeological Society* 75.
J. Thomas (1989), 'Neolithic explanations revisited: The Mesolithic-Neolithic transition in Britain and South Scandanavia', *Proceedings of the Prehistoric Society* 54.

3 The Causewayed Camp
H.M. Bamford (1985), 'Briar Hill: Excavations 1974–78', *Northampton Development Corporation Archaeological Monograph 3*, Northampton.
R. Bradley and Startin, W. (1981), 'Some notes on work organisation and society in prehistoric Wessex', in C. Ruggles and Whittle, A.W.R. (eds), *Astronomy and Society in Britain during the Period 4000–1500 BC*, British Archaeological Reports 88, 289–96.
E.C. Curwen (1934), 'Excavations in Whitehawk Neolithic camp, Brighton 1932–33', *Antiquaries Journal* 14, 99–133.
M. Douglas (1966), *Purity and Danger: an Analysis of Concepts of Pollution and Taboo*, Routledge and Kegan Paul, London.
C. Evans (1989), 'Acts of enclosure: a consideration of concentrically organised causewayed enclosures', in J. Barrett and Kinnes, I.A. (eds.), *The Archaeology of Context*.
R. Palmer (1976), 'Interrupted ditch enclosures in Britain: the use of aerial photographs for comparative studies', *Proceedings of the Prehistoric Society* 47, 161–86.
S. Piggott (1952), 'The Neolithic camp on Whitesheet Hill, Kilmington', *Wiltshire Archaeological Magazine* 56, 404–10.
I.F. Smith (1965), *Windmill Hill and Avebury: Excavations by Alexander Kieller 1925–39*, Clarendon Press, Oxford.

4 Activity at the Causewayed Camp

J.C. Barrett and Kinnes, I.A. (1989), *The Archaeology of Context in the Neolithic and Bronze Age: Recent Trends*, Department of Archaeology and Prehistory University of Sheffield, Sheffield.

R. Bradley and Gardiner, J. (1984), 'Neolithic Studies: a review of some current research', *British Archaeological Reports* 133, Oxford.

P.L. Drewett (1977), 'The excavation of a Neolithic Causewayed enclosure on Offham Hill, East Sussex 1976', *Proceedings of the Prehistoric Society* 43, 201–41.

A. Legge (1981), 'Aspects of cattle husbandry', in R. Mercer (ed.), *Farming Practice in British Prehistory*, 169–81, Edinburgh University Press, Edinburgh.

R.J. Mercer (1980), *Hambledon Hill – a Neolithic Landscape*, Edinburgh University Press, Edinburgh.

R.J. Mercer (1986), 'The Neolithic in Cornwall', *Cornish Archaeology* 25, 35–80.

S. Piggott (1954), *Neolithic Cultures of the British Isles*, Cambridge University Press, Cambridge.

H. Quennell (1987), 'Cornish Gabbroic pottery: the development of a hypothesis', *Cornish Archaeology* 26, 7–12.

I.F. Smith (1966), 'Windmill Hill and its implications', *Palaeohistoria* 12, 469–81.

I.F. Smith (1971), 'Causewayed enclosures', in D.D.A. Simpson (ed.), *Economy and Settlement in Neolithic and Early Bronze Age Britain and Europe*, 89–112, Leicester University Press, Leicester.

5 South Dorset 3500 to 700 BC

R.J.C. Atkinson (1956), Stonehenge, Hamish Hamilton, London.

J.C. Barrett and Bradley, R. (1980), 'Settlement and Society in the Later Bronze Age', *British Archaeological Reports* 83, Oxford.

R. Bradley (1975), 'Maumbury Rings Dorchester: the excavations of 1903–1913', *Archaeologia* 105, 1–98.

D.V. Clarke, Cowie, T. and Foxon, A. (1985), *Symbols of Power*, HMSO, Edinburgh.

L.V. Grinsell (1959), *Dorset Barrows*, Dorset Natural History and Archaeological Society, Dorchester.

C. Malone (1989), *Avebury*, Batsford, London.

S.M. Pearce (1980), 'The Bronze Age Metalwork of South Western Britain', *British Archaeological Reports* 120, Oxford.

P. Rahtz and ApSimon, A.M. (1962), 'Excavations at Shearplace Hill, Sydling St Nicholas, Dorset, England', *Proceedings of the Prehistoric Society* 28.

I.J. Thorpe (1984), 'Ritual Power and Ideology: a reconstruction of earlier Neolithic rituals in Wessex', in R. Bradley and Gardiner, J. (eds.), *Neolithic Studies*.

G.J. Wainwright (1979), 'Mount Pleasant: Excavations 1970–71', *Report of the Research Committee of the Society of Antiquaries* XXXVII, London.

G.J. Wainwright and Longworth, I.H. (1971), 'Durrington Walls: excavations 1966–68', *Report of the Research Committee of the Society of Antiquaries* XXIX, London.

D.A. White (1982), 'The Bronze Age cremation cemeteries at Simons Ground, Dorset', *Dorset Natural History and Archaeological Society Monograph* 3, Dorchester.

P.J. Woodward (forthcoming), 'The Landscape Survey', in N.M. Sharples, *Maiden Castle: Excavations and Field Survey 1985–86*.

6 The first hillfort

B.W. Cunliffe (1978), *Iron Age Communities in Britain* (2nd edition), Routledge & Kegan Paul, London.

B.W. Cunliffe and Phillipson, D.W. (1968), 'Excavations at Eldons Seat, Encombe, Dorset', *Proceedings of the Prehistoric Society* 34, 191–237.

P.S. Gelling (1977), 'Excavations at Pilsdon Pen 1964–71', *Proceedings of the Prehistoric Society* 43, 263–86.

C.J.S. Green, (1987) 'Excavations at Poundbury Vol 1: The settlements', *Dorset Natural History and Archaeological Society Monograph* 7, Dorchester.

M. Whitley (1943), 'Excavations at Chalbury Camp, Dorset 1939', *Antiquaries Journal* 23, 98–121.

P.J. Woodward (1987) 'The excavations of an Iron Age and Romano-British Settlement at Rope Lake Hole, Corfe Castle, Dorset', in N. Sunter and Woodward, P.J. (eds.), 'Romano British Industries in Purbeck', *Dorset Natural History and Archaeological Society Monograph* 8, Dorchester.

7 The developed hillfort

L.A. Alcock (1972), *'By South Cadbury is that Camelot . . .' The excavations at Cadbury Castle 1967–70*, Thames and Hudson, London.

J.M. Coles (1987), *Meare Village East: The excavations of A. Bulleid and H. St George Grey 1932–1956*, Somerset Levels Papers No 13, Hertford.

B.W. Cunliffe (1983), *Danebury: anatomy of an Iron Age hillfort*, Batsford, London.

B.W. Cunliffe (1984), *Danebury Vol. 1 and 2: The Excavations 1969–78*, Council for British Archaeological Research Report 52, London.

B.W. Cunliffe (1984), 'Iron Age Wessex: Continuity and Change in B.W. Cunliffe and Miles, D. (eds.), *Aspects of the Iron Age in central southern Britain*, Oxford University Committee for Archaeology Monograph 2, Oxford.

H. Gent (1983), 'Centralised Storage in Later Prehistoric Britain', *Proceedings of the Prehistoric Society* 49.

G. Guilbert (1981), 'Double ring roundhouses, probable and possible examples in prehistoric Britain', *Proceedings of the Prehistoric Society* 47.

P.J. Reynolds (1979), *Iron Age Farm: The Butser Experiment*, British Museum, London.

S.C. Stanford (1974), *Croft Ambrey*, Leominster, Hereford.

G.J. Wainwright (1979), *Gussage All Saints: An Iron Age settlement in Dorset*, HMSO, London.

8 Social relationships and economic activity, 450–50 BC

J.B. Calkin (1953), 'Kimmeridge Coal Money: The Romano British Shale Armlet Industry', *Dorset Natural History and Archaeology Society* 75, 45–71.

J. Collis (1984), *Oppida: Earliest towns north of the Alps*, Sheffield.

R.A.H. Farrer (1975), 'Prehistoric and Roman saltworks in Dorset', in K.W. de Brisay and Evans, K.A. (eds.), *Salt: The Study of an Ancient Industry*, Colchester Archaeological Group.

A. Grant (1984), 'The Animal Bones' in B.W. Cunliffe, *Danebury Vol 2: The Excavations 1969–78*.

A. Grant (1984), 'Animal Husbandry in Wessex and the Thames valley' in B.W. Cunliffe and Miles, D. (eds.), *Aspects of the Iron Age in Central Southern Britain*.

M. Jones (1984), 'Regional patterns in crop production', in B.W. Cunliffe and Miles, D. (eds.), *Aspects of the Iron Age in Central Southern Britain*.

M. Jones (1985), 'Archaeobotany beyond subsistance reconstruction', in G. Barker and Gamble, C. (eds.), *Beyond Domestication: Subsistence Archaeology and Social Complexity in Prehistoric Europe*, Academic Press, London.

J.P. Northover (1984), 'Iron Age bronze metallurgy in central southern England', in B.W. Cunliffe and Miles, D. (eds.), *Aspects of the Iron Age in Central Southern Britain*.

C.J. Salter and Ehrenrich, R. (1984), 'Iron Age iron metallurgy in central southern Britain' in B.W. Cunliffe and Miles, D. (eds.), *Aspects of the Iron Age in Central Southern Britain*.

9 The end of the hillfort: Maiden Castle 50 BC to AD 450

B.W. Cunliffe (1987), *Hengistbury Head Vol 1: The prehistoric and Roman settlement, 3500 BC – AD 500*, Oxford University Committee for Archaeology Monograph 13, Oxford.

S. MacCready and Thompson, F.H. (eds.), (1984), *Cross-Channel trade between Gaul and Britain in the pre-Roman Iron Age*, Society of Antiquaries Occasional Paper 4, London.

W.G. Putnam (1984), *Roman Dorset*, Dovecote Press.

P. Rahtz and Watts, L. (1979), 'The end of Roman temples in the west of Britain', in P.J. Casey (ed.), 'The end of Roman Britain', *British Archaeological Reports* 71, Oxford.

I. Richmond (1968), *Hod Hill Vol. II: Excavations carried out between 1951 and 1958 for the Trustees of the British Museum*, British Museum, London.

M. Todd (1984), 'Excavations at Hembury (Devon) 1980–83: A summary report', *Antiquaries Journal* 64, 251–68.

J. Wacher (1974), *The Towns of Roman Britain*, Batsford, London.

R.P. Whimster (1981), 'Burial Practices in Iron Age Britain', *British Archaeological Reports* 90, Oxford.

P.J. Woodward (1987), 'The Excavation of a Late Iron Age settlement and Romano-British Industrial site at Ower, Dorset', in N. Sunter and Woodward, P.J. (eds.), *Romano-British Industries in Purbeck*, Dorset Natural History and Archaeological Society Monograph 8, Dorchester.

Glossary

amphora Large ceramic container designed by the Romans to ship wine, olive oil, fish paste and other liquids around the Roman empire. They had very distinctive shapes and fabrics and so, if a large enough piece survives, can be accurately dated and sourced to the production centre. Amphorae were one of the earliest Roman goods to find their way into Britain and their presence is an important indication of the network of contacts open to Late Iron Age societies.

ard A primitive type of plough without a mould board to turn the earth. It can be pulled by animal or person and often has a metal-tipped share.

barrow These are earthen mounds normally assumed to mark burials. Long barrows are rectangular, trapezoidal or oval mounds with flanking ditches which date to the Early Neolithic period. Round barrows are circular mounds, normally completely surrounded by a ditch, which date to the Late Neolithic and Bronze Age, though a few Early Neolithic examples are known. Bank barrows are particularly long 'long barrows' which are found in Dorset and which date to the final stages of the Early Neolithic. Most barrows cover burials but some do not and it seems that long barrows in particular had a specific additional function, perhaps as territorial markers, quite separate from the burials with which they are normally associated.

Beakers A distinctive type of high quality pottery which was in use between about 2400 and 1800 BC. Most of the finest Beakers were deposited with burials but later examples are also found in domestic contexts. Similar pots are found throughout western Europe and there is little doubt that the first Beakers were introduced to Britain from the Continent. After they were introduced, however, British Beakers developed in a manner unique to these islands.

briquetage Ceramic containers, often very poorly fired, which are used to dry and transport salt. The salt was created by evaporating seawater and would be placed in the containers as a sludge which dried out as they were being transported.

Bronze Age The period of time between about 2100 and 700 BC when bronze became an important resource. Initially the use of the metal was restricted to the production of prestige goods – particularly knives and ornaments – but by the end of the period it had completely replaced flint as the raw material for basic tools.

causewayed camps A form of enclosure characteristic of the Early Neolithic period. The ditches were created by excavating a series of elongated pits which were not joined together leaving 'causeways', hence the name. (These are also referred to as 'segmented ditches'.) There can be anything from one to five concentric ditches and the enclosures are scattered throughout southern England and the Midlands. Isolated enclosures of a similar form and date are known from Ulster and Scotland.

chambered tomb Burial monuments which largely date to the Early Neolithic in the British Isles. They are characterized by chambers which are constructed from large (megalithic) stones which are normally covered by mounds of earth or smaller stones. The chambers are accessible either because they are situated at the edge of the mound or because there is a passage which links the chamber to the outside.

These tombs are found all along the western seaboard of Europe in the Neolithic.

Celtic field Small rectangular fields found throughout the chalk lands of Wessex. They are defined by positive and negative 'lynchets' caused by soil creep over years of ard cultivation. For many years they were assumed to be of Iron Age date but work in the 1970s has shown that they are in some cases earlier than large linear earthworks dated to the beginning of the first millennium BC. A date in the second millennium for most of those systems is now generally accepted.

crop mark Many of the archaeological monuments in southern England have been superficially destroyed by centuries of continuous cultivation. Any features, such as ditches or pits, cut into the subsoil will, however, survive and these can affect the growth of the overlying vegetation. The depth of disturbed and nutrient-rich soil encourages growth and causes crops to ripen earlier than those on thin soils. This differential growth creates crop marks which can in particularly dry summers reveal detailed plans of ancient settlements.

cursus A type of monument which consists of two parallel ditches and/or banks. Though the ditch and bank can be quite insubstantial the monuments can be very long. They were created at the end of the Early Neolithic (or beginning of the Late Neolithic) and are found scattered across southern England and as far north as Yorkshire.

Durotriges The tribe identified by the Romans as living in the area of England roughly equivalent to Dorset at the time of the conquest. The adjacent tribes were: the Atrebates to the east; the Dumnonii to the west; and the Dubonni to the north-west. It is unclear exactly how ancient these tribes were but the first century BC is the most likely date for the origin of the societies the Romans knew. A distinctive type of pottery is found in the Dorset area from the third century BC up until the Roman period: this may indicate permanence of settlement by one distinctive folk from that date.

Gabbroic Ware The Lizard peninsula in Cornwall is the source of a clay which is used for the production of high quality ceramics throughout prehistory. The clay contains inclusions of gabbro which give the pots thermal properties which are very valuable given the production methods used in prehistory. This gabbro is easily identifiable by analysis of small sherds and it is clear that pots from this area were exchanged throughout south-west Britain.

Grooved Ware Distinctive flat-based, tub- or barrel-shaped vessels dating to the Late Neolithic period. These vessels are characterized by decoration which in England and southern Scotland was formed by grooving the surface with elaborate patterns. In northern Scotland cordons and other ornamentation was more common.

henge Roughly circular enclosures defined, in general, by a single ditch and an exterior bank. They were constructed between 2500 and 1800 BC and are generally assumed to have had a special, possibly religious, function. They vary considerably in size and are often associated with circles of stones or posts.

hillfort Enclosures originally defined by large banks and ditches which are presumed to serve some sort of defensive function. They are a characteristic feature of the Iron Age in Wessex, though defended enclosures are known in other periods, and are more often than not found on hills. In recent years it has become fashionable to question the defensive nature of the banks and ditches but though it is true that the very complex 'defences' of some hillforts are far too elaborate to have been all that effective for defence the original reason for their construction is likely to have been related to warfare.

Iron Age The period of time between about 700 BC and the Roman conquest when the inhabitants of the British Isles begin to produce and use iron. Initially the amount of iron in circulation was small and the quality was poor but by the end of the period specialist iron production centres existed and the craftsmanship was of the highest quality.

Mesolithic The period of time between the end of the last glaciation and the introduction of agriculture. The archaeological evidence of this period is very poor and normally consists solely of scatters of flint tools and debris. These scatters, however, contain distinctive flint tools known as microliths which are only found in this period.

microlith A type of flint implement which is characteristic of the Mesolithic period. A microlith is made from a small parallel sided flint flake which is shaped by snapping the flake and blunting an edge by very fine retouch. An apparent preference for distinctive shapes and sizes of microlith has been used to define cultures and chronological divisions, perhaps of doubtful significance within the Mesolithic.

multivallate defences Fortifications consisting of repeated lines of ditch and bank.

Neolithic The period of time between about 4200 and 2100 BC before the introduction of bronze technology and after the introduction of agriculture. The period is divided into an Early Neolithic period, characterized by monuments such as long barrows and causewayed camps, and tools, such as leaf-shaped arrowheads, and a Late Neolithic period, characterized by monuments, such as henges and round barrows, and tools, such as transverse and oblique arrowheads.

rampart The defences of a hillfort are created by digging a ditch and mounding up the earth from the ditch into a bank, known as a rampart. These ramparts can be simple dumps of soil or they can be given structure by internal and external revetments either of stone or wood.

shale A soft, easily carved stone which because of its high oil content can be polished to create a lustrous black surface. These qualities make it a valued material for the production of decorative objects, particularly bracelets. The principal source is Kimmeridge Bay in Purbeck and it was intensively quarried during the Late Iron Age and Roman periods.

Wessex An area of central southern England which can be defined in a number of different ways. Essentially it harks back to the Saxon kingdom of Wessex and it has no administrative significance today. For the purpose of this book it loosely refers to the area covered by the counties of Dorset, Wiltshire, Berkshire and Hampshire but it can also include parts of Oxfordshire and West Sussex.

Index

INDEX